Quick Guide

W9-CFQ-170 NGS

WRITE SOURCE

A BOOK FOR WRITING, THINKING, AND LEARNING

Written and Compiled by

**Dave Kemper, Patrick Sebranek,
and Verne Meyer**

Illustrated by

Chris Krenzke

WRITE SOURCE®

GREAT SOURCE EDUCATION GROUP

a division of Houghton Mifflin Company
Wilmington, Massachusetts

Reviewers

Theresa Clymer
Renton School District
Renton, Washington

Kay Dooley
Naperville S D #203
Naperville, Illinois

Paula Findley
White Hall, Arkansas

Mary M. Fischer
Arlington Public Schools
Arlington, Massachusetts

Elma G. Jones
Wallingford-Swarthmore
  School District
Swarthmore, Pennsylvania

Pickett Pat Lema
Pattonville School District
St. Louis, Missouri

Mary Osborne
Pinellas County
  School District
Largo, Florida

Pamela J. Strain
Rosemead School District
Rosemead, California

Technology Connection for *Write Source*

Visit our Web site for additional student models, writing prompts, updates for citing sources, multimedia reports, information about submitting your writing, and more.

The Write Source Web site . . . www.thewritesource.com

Printed in the United States of America

International Standard Book Number: 0-669-51807-7 (hardcover)
International Standard Book Number: 978-0-669-51807-8 (hardcover)

3 4 5 6 7 8 9 10 -RRDC- 11 10 09 08 07

International Standard Book Number: 0-669-51811-5 (softcover)
International Standard Book Number: 978-0-669-51811-5 (softcover)

3 4 5 6 7 8 9 10 -RRDC- 11 10 09 08 07

Using the *Write Source* Book

Your *Write Source* book is loaded with information to help you learn about writing. One section that will be especially helpful is the "Proofreader's Guide" at the back of the book. This section covers all of the rules for language and grammar.

The book also includes four main units covering the types of writing that you may have to complete on district or state writing tests. At the end of each unit, there are samples and tips for writing in science, social studies, and math.

The *Write Source* book will help you with other learning skills, too—study-reading, test taking, note taking, and speaking. This makes the *Write Source* book a valuable writing and learning guide in all of your classes.

Your Write Source guide . . .

With practice, you will be able to find information in this book quickly using the guides explained below.

The **TABLE OF CONTENTS** (starting on the next page) lists the six major sections in the book and the chapters found in each section.

The **INDEX** (starting on page 607) lists the topics covered in the book in alphabetical order. Use the index when you are interested in a specific topic.

The **COLOR CODING** used for "The Basic Elements of Writing," "A Writer's Resource," and the "Proofreader's Guide" make these important sections easy to find.

The **SPECIAL PAGE REFERENCES** in the book tell you where to turn for additional information about a specific topic.

The Writing Process

The Forms of Writing

PARAGRAPH WRITING

DESCRIPTIVE WRITING

NARRATIVE WRITING

EXPOSITORY WRITING

PERSUASIVE WRITING

RESPONSE TO LITERATURE

PERMISSION SLIP

RESEARCH WRITING

Speaking and Writing to Learn

SPEAKING TO LEARN

WRITING TO LEARN

The Basic Elements of Writing

WORKING WITH WORDS

A Writer's Resource

Proofreader's Guide

Why Write?

You may think of writing simply as an assignment. But there are many other ways to look at writing.

Writing can . . .

- **exercise your brain.** Essays and learning logs can give you a deeper understanding of the things you are learning in school.

- **guide your life.** Personal journals can help you sort out your thoughts and feelings about the things that happen around you.

- **connect you with friends.** Letters and e-mail messages help you communicate with people you care about.

- **rocket you through time and space.** Poems, stories, and plays can carry you away to any places that you can dream of.

Remember . . .

To be a writer, all you have to do is write. Some people seem to be born writers. Others become successful writers thanks to practice and determination. Spend a little time writing every day, and you're on your way to becoming a terrific writer.

Using the Writing Process

Understanding the
Writing Process

Olympic athletes train for years. They exercise, lift weights, eat special foods, and practice their sports. The training process helps everyday athletes become world-class competitors.

Writers follow a process, too. They read a lot, keep a personal journal, and follow the steps in the writing process. If you "train" in the same way, you can become a world-class writer!

Mini Index

- **Becoming a Writer**
- **The Steps in the Writing Process**
- **The Process in Action**
- **Working with the Traits**

Becoming a Writer

The following tips can help you become a good writer.

Keep Reading!

One of the best ways to learn about writing is to read.

> "I love reading, so naturally I like to write."
>
> —Beverly Cleary

Make Writing Fun.

At home, write in a journal about anything and everything. Try writing poems, stories, or even a TV script. Find a pen pal!

> "I keep the stories enjoyable for my readers by keeping them enjoyable for me."
>
> —Gordon Korman

Play with Words.

English overflows with dazzling words. Enjoy them!

> "All was a-shake and a-shiver—glints and gleams and sparkles, rustle and swirl, chatter and bubble."
>
> —from *Wind in the Willows* by Kenneth Grahame

Write about a quotation. Write nonstop for 3 to 5 minutes about one of the quotations on this page. Tell what it means to you.

The Steps in the Writing Process

Some writers try to do everything all at once. However, it's much better to work on your writing one step at a time.

The Steps in the Writing Process

 Prewrite At the beginning of the process, the writer chooses a topic, gathers details about it, and makes a plan to organize the details.

 Write Creating the first draft is the exciting step of getting all the ideas on paper.

 Revise After reviewing the first draft, the writer can add new details, delete ideas that don't belong, and change parts that aren't clear.

 Edit Next, the writer looks over the revised writing for mistakes in capitalization, punctuation, spelling, and grammar.

 Publish In the end, the writer shares the final copy with a parent, some classmates, or the world!

 Think about writing. Look at the steps above. What part is the hardest for you to do? What part is the easiest? Why?

The Process in Action

Using the writing process is like following a recipe. The next two pages will tell you what to do during each step of the process.

tip The graphic below shows how writing can move forward *and* backward. Collecting more details after writing a first draft is an example of moving backward.

Prewriting

Selecting a Topic

- Think about your assignment: What do you want your writing to do? Who is your audience? What form of writing are you using?
- Choose a topic that really interests you.

Gathering Details

- Search for interesting details about your topic and take notes.
- Find a focus for your writing—what you want to emphasize about your topic.
- Organize your details.

Writing

Developing the First Draft

- Write freely to get your ideas on paper (or on your computer screen).
- Use your prewriting notes as you write.
- Include a beginning, a middle, and an ending.

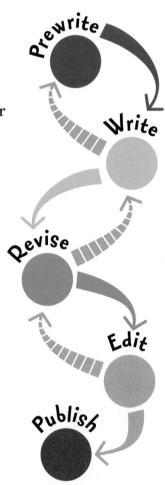

Revising Improving Your Writing

- Read your writing out loud. Then read it silently.
- Ask a classmate, family member, or teacher to read your work.
- Use these questions to guide your changes:
  1. Does the beginning grab the reader's attention?
  2. Do the details in the middle support my focus?
  3. Does the ending say something important about the topic?
  4. Do I sound interested in the topic?
  5. Do I use specific nouns and verbs?
  6. Are my sentences and ideas connected?
- Improve your writing by adding, cutting, moving, or rewriting parts.

Editing Checking for Conventions

The Writing Process
Writing is a step-by-step process.

- Correct errors in capitalization, punctuation, spelling, and grammar.
- Ask another person to help you check your writing for errors.
- Write a neat final copy and proofread it.

Publishing Sharing Your Writing

- Share your finished writing.
- Put your best pieces of writing in a portfolio.

Study the process. Pick one step in the writing process. Write down at least two reasons why the step is important.

Working with the Traits

Writers have to answer many questions about the traits of writing.

What main ideas should I write about?

How should I organize my details?

How can I make my writing voice stronger?

What are the best words to use?

Are my sentences easy to read?

Have I checked for errors?

The writing process helps writers focus on each question at the proper time. For example, **ideas** are important in the beginning of a writing project, while **word choice** becomes more important later on.

The Writing Process in Review

Use the process. Colin wrote an essay about dolphins. On your own paper, match Colin's activities with the correct step of the writing process.

____ 1. Fix a spelling mistake—"dollphin."

____ 2. Research dolphins at the library.

____ 3. Add drawings to the final draft.

____ 4. Ask Josh to read the finished essay.

____ 5. Create a first draft.

A. Prewriting

B. Writing

C. Revising

D. Editing

E. Publishing

One Writer's Process

Producing a piece of pottery involves several steps. The potter must prepare the clay, shape the pot, fire it in a kiln, and glaze it. Each step affects the quality of the final piece.

Writing also involves several steps. The steps in the writing process include *prewriting, writing, revising, editing,* and *publishing.* This chapter shows how Fumi used the writing process to create an essay about an activity she enjoys—making pottery!

Mini Index

- Previewing the Goals
- Prewriting
- Writing
- Revising
- Editing
- Assessing the Final Copy
- Reflecting on Your Writing

Previewing the Goals

For a class assignment, Fumi needed to write a how-to essay about an activity she enjoyed. Before she started writing, she studied the goals for the assignment.

Your goal is to . . .

Ideas
Select a favorite activity you know how to do and can explain to others.

Organization
Make sure your essay is easy to follow from beginning to ending.

Voice
Let your reader know that you are interested in the topic.

Word Choice
Use specific nouns and verbs.

Sentence Fluency
Write sentences that flow smoothly and clearly.

Conventions
Follow the rules for punctuation, capitalization, spelling, and grammar.

Answer the following questions about Fumi's assignment.

1 What type of topic should Fumi select?

2 How will she know if her work is well organized?

3 How should her writing voice sound in the essay?

Prewriting Selecting a Topic

Fumi was given the following assignment: *Write an expository essay that explains how to do an activity you enjoy.* To think of topics, Fumi created a list.

List

Activities I Enjoy

playing soccer	making sushi
painting	camping
making pottery	swimming

Fumi decided to write about making pottery. She knew the process had clear steps that she could explain.

Gathering and Organizing Details

Now that she had a topic, Fumi needed to gather and organize details about her topic. She used a time line to list the main steps in the process of making pottery.

Time Line

Making Pottery

First	Prepare the clay.
Next	Shape the pot.
Then	Bake the pot in a kiln.
Then	Glaze the pot.
Last	Bake the pot in the kiln again.

Writing **Completing Your First Draft**

When Fumi wrote her first draft, she tried to get all of her thoughts down on paper. She used her time line (page 11) as a basic guide. (There are some errors in Fumi's first draft.)

The beginning paragraph includes a focus statement (underlined).

Fumi writes about the steps in middle paragraphs.

Transitions help to show time order and connect details.

Did you ever think pinching is fun? I did when I learned how to make a pinch pot. <u>There are four steps to making a pinch pot.</u>

Start by preparing the clay. Bubbles can make the clay explode when it's heated in the kiln. SLAM the clay on the table a couple of times. This is the lowdest part of the proces! If there's a whole group making pinch pots, it's one huge slamma-ramma! Next, shape the pinch pot. Roll out a ball of clay. Push you're thumb into the center. Keep pinching and turning the clay. When your pinch pot looks right, flatten the bottom on a table.

Get an adult to put your pinch pot in a kiln. A kiln is an oven that fires the clay. The clay hardens in the kiln. After firing, the pot comes out pale white. It is ready for glazing.

Glaze is a wierd paint. It looks gray when you put it on your pot. Have the adult put the pinch pot in the kiln again. The glaze will come out smooth like glass. A completely new color!

I love seeing a finished pot. It's almost as good as making it. When I'm done, all I want to do is start pinching again!

Unfamiliar terms are defined.

Fumi tells why she enjoys the activity.

Practice

Review the goals for ideas, organization, and voice on page 10. Does Fumi reach those goals in her first draft? Explain.

Revising **Improving Your Writing**

After Fumi reviewed her first draft, she made the following changes.

An idea is made clearer.

Did you ever think pinching is fun? I did
when I learned how to make ^(a small bowl called) a pinch pot. There

are four steps to making a pinch pot.

An explanation is added.

Start by preparing the clay. Bubbles can

make the clay explode when it's heated in the

kiln. ^(To get rid of bubbles,) SLAM the clay on the table a couple of

An unneeded detail is removed.

times. This is the lowdest part of the proces!

~~If there's a whole group making pinch pots, it's~~

~~one huge slamma-ramma.~~ ⁋ Next, shape the pinch

A new paragraph is started for the second step.

pot. Roll out a ball of clay. Push you're thumb

into the center. Keep pinching and turning the

An important detail is added.

clay, ^(to form the sides of the bowl) When your pinch pot looks right, flatten the

bottom on a table.

Practice

Review Fumi's changes. Which change seems most important to you?
Explain your choice.

Revising **Using a Peer Response**

Fumi asked a classmate to comment on her essay. Then she made more changes to improve her work.

What are
the four
steps?

What does
it mean to
prepare the
clay?

Why flatten
the bottom
on the
table?

Did you ever think pinching is fun? I did when

I learned how to make a small bowl called a pinch
        preparing, shaping, firing, and glazing.
pot. There are four steps to making a pinch pot.
        this means getting rid of bubbles.
Start by preparing the clay. Bubbles can

make the clay explode when it's heated in the

kiln. To get rid of bubbles, SLAM the clay on the

table a couple of times. This is the lowdest part of

the proces!

Next, shape the pinch pot. Roll out a ball of

clay. Push you're thumb into the center. Keep

pinching and turning the clay to form the sides of

the bowl. When your pinch pot looks right, flatten
        Then your pot will sit level.
the bottom on a table.

Practice

Answer the following questions: How did peer responding help Fumi?
What do you think is the most helpful comment above? Why?

Editing Checking for Conventions

Before writing a final copy, Fumi checked her essay for punctuation, capitalization, spelling, and grammar errors. (See the inside back cover of this book for a list of editing and proofreading marks.)

A verb tense is corrected.

Punctuation errors are corrected.

Capitalization errors are corrected.

Misspellings and a misused word are fixed.

> was
> Did you ever think pinching is fun? I did when
>
> I learned how to make a small bowl called a pinch
>
> pot. There are four steps to making a pinch pot,
>
> preparing, shaping, firing, and glazing.
>
> Start by preparing the clay. this means
>
> getting rid of bubbles. Bubbles can make the clay
>
> explode when it's heated in the kiln. To get rid of
>
> bubbles, SLAM the clay on the table a couple of
>
> loudest   process
> times. This is the lowdest part of the proces.
>
> Next, shape the pinch pot. Roll out a ball
>
> your
> of clay. Push you're thumb into the center.
>
> Keep pinching and turning the clay to form the

Practice

Review Fumi's editing. Do you make some of the same types of errors? How do you use editing marks in your writing?

Fumi's Final Copy

Fumi felt proud of her final essay. It clearly described each step in the process of making pottery.

Fumi Akimoto

Pinching for Fun

Did you ever think pinching was fun? I did when I learned how to make a small bowl called a pinch pot. There are four steps to making a pinch pot: preparing, shaping, firing, and glazing.

Start by preparing the clay. This means getting rid of bubbles. Bubbles can make the clay explode when it's heated in the kiln. To get rid of bubbles, slam the clay on the table a couple of times. This is the loudest part of the process!

Next, shape the pinch pot. Roll out a ball of clay. Push your thumb into the center. Keep pinching and turning the clay to form the sides of the bowl. When your pinch pot looks right, flatten the bottom on a table. Then your pot will sit level.

Afterward, get an adult to put your pinch pot in a kiln. A kiln is an oven that fires, or bakes, the clay. The clay hardens in the kiln. After firing, the pot comes out pale white. It is ready for glazing.

Glazing is the last step. Glaze is a weird paint that looks gray when you paint it onto your pot. To set the glaze, have the adult put the pinch pot in the kiln for one more firing. The glaze will come out smooth like glass. It will be a completely new color!

It's exciting to look at the finished pot. It's almost as much fun as making the pot. In fact, when I'm done, all I want to do is start pinching again!

Assessing the Final Copy

The teacher used the rubric on pages 176–177 to assess Fumi's final copy. A six is the very best score a writer can receive for each trait. The teacher also included helpful comments under each trait.

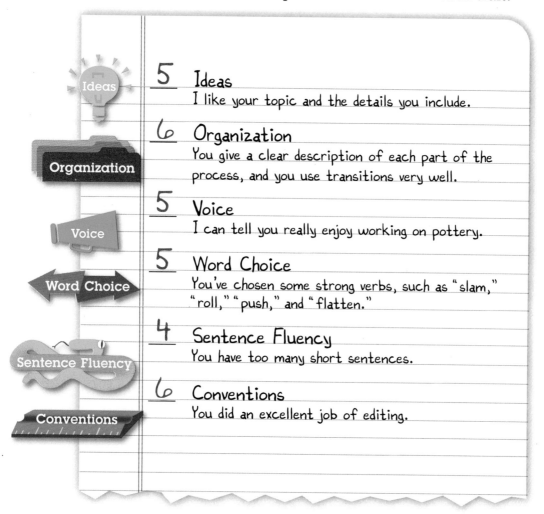

5 Ideas
I like your topic and the details you include.

6 Organization
You give a clear description of each part of the process, and you use transitions very well.

5 Voice
I can tell you really enjoy working on pottery.

5 Word Choice
You've chosen some strong verbs, such as "slam," "roll," "push," and "flatten."

4 Sentence Fluency
You have too many short sentences.

6 Conventions
You did an excellent job of editing.

Discuss the assessment. Do you agree with Fumi's teacher? Why or why not? What parts of the essay do you like? Would you have written any part in a different way?

Reflecting on Your Writing

Once the process was finished, Fumi filled out a reflection sheet. This helped her think about how she would do her next writing assignment.

> Thinking about your writing helps you find ways to improve as a writer.

Fumi Akimoto

My Expository Essay

1. **The best part of my essay is . . .**
   how I describe each step of making pottery.

2. **The part that still needs work is . . .**
   the lengths of my sentences.

3. **The main thing I learned about writing an expository essay is . . .**
   you have to use specific terms. Words like "fire," "kiln," and "glaze" are important for the reader to understand.

4. **The next time I write an expository essay, I would like to . . .**
   explain how to make sushi.

5. **Here is one question I still have about expository writing.**
   What other kinds of expository essays are there?

Understanding the
Traits of Writing

Picture a friend of yours. How tall is your friend? What does he or she like to wear? What makes your friend laugh? You can describe people by sharing both physical and personality traits about them.

Now think about an essay or a story you have written. What is the main **idea**? How is your writing **organized**? Does the writing have **voice**? You can describe your work by talking about the traits of writing. This chapter will show you how.

Mini Index

- **Introducing the Traits**
- **Understanding the Traits**

Introducing the Traits

Writing has six main traits, or qualities. Knowing about these traits will help you become a better writer.

 Ideas The best writing focuses on a specific topic and includes specific ideas and details to support that topic.

Organization Good writing has a clear beginning, middle, and ending. It is easy to follow.

Voice The best writing has an appealing voice. Voice is the special way a writer shares ideas and feelings.

 **Word Choice** Good writing uses specific nouns (*zebra, plum, canoe*), strong verbs (*squish, pounce, ooze*), and colorful adjectives (*soggy, crooked, delicate*).

 **Sentence Fluency** Strong writing flows smoothly. Sentences begin in different ways and have different lengths.

 **Conventions** Good writing has correct punctuation, capitalization, spelling, and grammar.

 tip Don't forget **presentation!** The final copy of the writing should look neat and follow guidelines for margins, spacing, and design. (See pages 44–46.)

Understanding Ideas

Good writing starts with quality ideas. Author Jane Yolen gives this advice: "Think of an idea or topic that is so strong within you that it's going to come out passionately as you write about it."

How can I select a topic that fits my purpose?

Make sure that you understand the purpose of the assignment before you select a topic. The lists below will help you select the best topics for different kinds of assignments.

- **For Descriptive Writing**

  Purpose: To show what a topic looks like, sounds like, and so on

  Reminder: Choose people, places, or things that you know well.

  Example Topic: Describing your favorite aunt or uncle

- **For Narrative Writing**

  Purpose: To share an experience

  Reminder: Choose experiences that you clearly remember.

  Example Topic: Telling about a bicycle adventure or accident

- **For Expository Writing**

  Purpose: To share information, to explain

  Reminder: Select topics that truly interest you.

  Example Topic: Sharing information about tarantulas or iguanas

- **For Persuasive Writing**

  Purpose: To convince someone to agree with you

  Reminder: Select topics that you have strong feelings about.

  Example Topic: Persuading someone to read a book or see a movie

Practice

On your own paper, list two possible writing topics for each type of writing listed above.

What details should I gather about a topic?

The details you collect will depend on your writing assignment.

■ **For Descriptive Writing**

1 List everything that you remember.

2 Observe your topic, if possible, to gather even more details.

3 Complete a sensory chart. (See page **71** for an example.)

■ **For Narrative Writing**

1 Write down what you remember about the experience.

2 Ask other people what they remember.

3 Complete a 5 W's chart. (See page **93** for an example.)

■ **For Expository Writing**

1 List what you already know and questions that you have.

2 Research your topic. (See pages **342–345**.)

3 Complete a cluster or web if you are sharing information. (See page **456** for an example.) Complete a time line if you are explaining steps. (See page **457** for an example.)

■ **For Persuasive Writing**

1 Write down your thoughts and feelings (an opinion) about the topic.

2 Research the facts about your topic.

3 Complete a table diagram. (See page **205** for an example.)

Practice

Gather details for one of the descriptive or narrative topics that you listed for page 23.

Understanding Organization

Writer Joan Lowery Nixon understands the importance of organization right from the beginning: "Work extra hard on the beginning of your story, so it snares readers instantly."

Why is the beginning important?

The beginning gets the reader's attention and gives the focus.

Beginning Paragraph

Interesting opening	My backyard has an enormous oak tree. A family of squirrels lives in the tree. To them, the tree is a home, a playground, and a grocery store! An oak tree has everything a squirrel needs.
Focus (underlined)	

What should I include in the middle?

The middle part of your writing should include specific details that support your focus. Here are some ways to do this.

Explain: Share information about your topic.

Define: Tell what important terms mean.

Describe: Give sensory details.

Compare: Show how two things are alike.

Middle Paragraph

Shared information	All year, the squirrels spend their time in our oak tree. In the fall, squirrels collect the tree's acorns and bury them. They also build leaf nests in the tree's top branches. During the winter, these nests are cozy sleeping places. Once spring comes, the squirrels hop along the ground and dig up their acorns.

Why is the ending important?

The ending is the last part of your writing. An ending works well when it does one or more of these things:

- reminds the reader about your topic.
- reviews the important points.
- stresses one main point.
- answers any last questions.
- gives the reader something to think about.

Ending Paragraph

Something to think about

The oak tree helps the squirrels in many ways. Squirrels help the oak tree, too. They love to bury acorns, but sometimes they forget where they buried them. Some of the acorns grow into new oak trees! I wonder what forgetful squirrel planted the tree in my backyard. I'd like to thank him.

End strong! Give yourself plenty of time to create a powerful finish to your writing.

Practice

Write a new ending to the squirrel essay, using one of the other techniques mentioned above.

Understanding Voice

Writing that has "voice" sounds as exciting as a real conversation. As writer Peter Elbow says, "Writing with *real voice* has the power to make you pay attention."

Why is voice so important?

Voice is what makes you want to read every book that your favorite author wrote.

WRITING THAT LACKS VOICE

I saw a deer on a path. It came close to me. It was neat.

WRITING THAT HAS VOICE

Crash! A huge buck came leaping out of the woods. Instantly, he stopped just a few feet away from me. My heart felt like it would pop out of my chest. Then, before I knew it, the deer disappeared back into the woods.

How can I write with voice?

You can practice **freewriting**. It is one of the best ways to discover your writing voice. Read these steps before you freewrite.

1 Think about something that recently happened to you.

2 Write nonstop about this experience for 3 to 5 minutes.

3 After you finish, read your writing out loud. Does it sound as if you were talking to a friend?

4 Practice freewriting every day, and you'll begin to unlock your personal writing voice.

Practice

Write for 3 to 5 minutes nonstop on the following topic: *a time I remember.* Afterward, underline two or three ideas that sound like the real you.

Understanding Word Choice

Working with words is fun. As author Paul Fleischman says, "We grew up knowing that words felt good in the ears and on the tongue, that they were as much fun to play with as toys."

How can I choose the best words?

Look for words that add meaning and feeling to your writing.

Choose Specific Nouns

General nouns like *building, rock,* and *insect* give the reader a general picture. Specific nouns like *post office, granite,* and *ladybug* give a clearer, more detailed picture.

Use Strong Action Verbs

Specific action verbs add energy to your writing. A statement like "The cat *pounced* on the string" is much more interesting than "The cat *stepped* on the string."

Select Effective Modifiers

The right **adjectives** paint clear word pictures. "Roscoe is a *playful* dalmatian" says much more than "Roscoe is a dalmatian."

The right **adverbs** make action more specific. The sentence "Todd looked *nervously* around the classroom" is clearer than "Todd looked around the classroom."

Practice

Read over the last story you wrote. Replace at least one noun and one verb with more specific words. Also add an adjective or an adverb to make an idea clearer.

Understanding Sentence Fluency

Smooth-reading sentences help the reader follow your ideas. As writer Russ Freedman says, "You want the reader to feel swept along, as if on a kind of trip, from sentence to sentence."

How can I make my sentences flow smoothly?

Vary Your Sentence Lengths. If your sentences are all the same length, your writing will sound choppy. (See pages 445–447.)

TOO MANY SENTENCES ABOUT THE SAME LENGTH

My neighbor Betty is my friend. She is old enough to be my grandmother. Sometimes we just chat. She tells me stories about when she was a girl. She remembers a lot.

VARIED SENTENCE LENGTHS

My neighbor Betty is my friend, yet she's old enough to be my grandmother. Sometimes we just chat, and she tells me stories about when she was a girl. She remembers a lot.

SHORT, CHOPPY SENTENCES

Betty loves hats. She wears wooly hats. She also has floppy hats and sun hats. She has plastic rain hats. She also collects baseball caps. My favorite hat is her blue hat. It is straw.

COMBINED SENTENCES

Betty loves hats. She wears wooly hats, floppy hats, sun hats, plastic rain hats, and even baseball caps. My favorite one is her blue straw hat.

Practice

Review a paragraph or story you have written. Try to improve one or two sentences to make your writing easier to read. Use the information above as a guide.

Understanding Conventions

Conventions cover the rules of punctuation, capitalization, spelling, and grammar. When you follow these rules, your writing will be clear and easy to understand.

How can I make sure my writing follows the rules?

A conventions checklist like the one below will guide you as you edit and proofread your writing. When you are not sure about a rule, check the "Proofreader's Guide." (See pages 478–605.)

Conventions

PUNCTUATION

_____ **1.** Do I use correct end punctuation after every sentence?

_____ **2.** Do I use commas in compound sentences?

_____ **3.** Do I use apostrophes correctly to show possession *(the dog's bed)*?

CAPITALIZATION

_____ **4.** Do I start every sentence with a capital letter?

_____ **5.** Do I capitalize the names of people and places?

SPELLING

_____ **6.** Have I checked my spelling?

GRAMMAR

_____ **7.** Do my subjects and verbs agree *(she walks,* not *she walk)*?

_____ **8.** Do I use the right words *(to, too, two)*?

Always have at least one other person check your writing for conventions. Ask a classmate, a teacher, or a family member for help.

Using a Rubric

During checkups, doctors listen to your breathing, check your pulse, look in your ears, tap your knees, and take a blood sample to be tested in the lab. Checking these things tells a doctor about your general health.

As a writer, you can use a rubric to check the "health" of your stories and essays. A **rubric** is a chart that lists the traits or characteristics for a specific form of writing. Once you learn to use a rubric, you'll understand the importance of traits like effective ideas, word choice, and sentences in your writing.

Mini Index

- Understanding Rubrics
- Reading a Rubric
- Assessing with a Rubric
- Reviewing an Assessment
- Assessing a Narrative

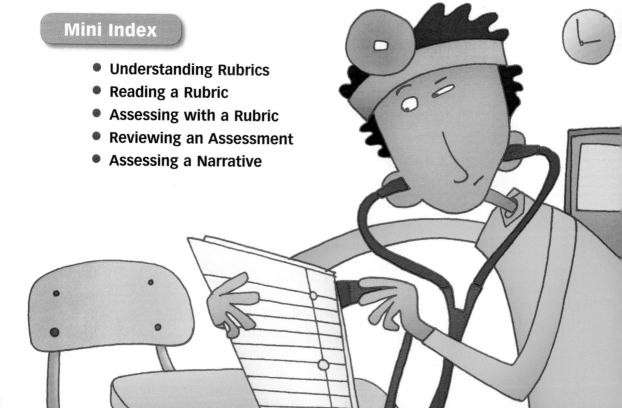

Understanding Rubrics

Teachers often use rubrics to rate writing. The rubrics in this book use a 6-point scale.

6 Amazing	5 Strong	4 Good	3 Okay	2 Poor	1 Incomplete

tip The rubrics are arranged according to the main traits of writing—*ideas, organization, voice, word choice, sentence fluency,* and *conventions.*

Rating Guide

This guide will help you understand the rating scale.

A **6** means that the writing is truly **amazing**.
It far exceeds the main requirements for a trait.

A **5** means that the writing is very **strong**.
It meets the main requirements for a trait.

A **4** means that the writing is **good**.
It meets most of the requirements for a trait.

A **3** means that the writing is **okay**.
It needs work to meet the main requirements for a trait.

A **2** means that the writing is **poor**.
It needs a lot of work.

A **1** means that the writing is **incomplete**.
It is not yet ready to assess for a trait.

Reading a Rubric

For the rubrics in this book, each trait has its own color bar (green for *ideas,* pink for *organization,* and so on). Descriptions for each rating help you evaluate the quality of a certain trait.

Rubric for Narrative Writing

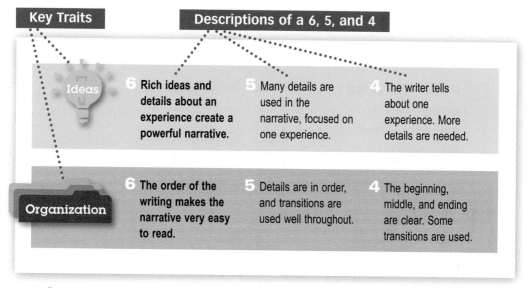

Key Traits

Descriptions of a 6, 5, and 4

Ideas

6 Rich ideas and details about an experience create a powerful narrative.

5 Many details are used in the narrative, focused on one experience.

4 The writer tells about one experience. More details are needed.

Organization

6 The order of the writing makes the narrative very easy to read.

5 Details are in order, and transitions are used well throughout.

4 The beginning, middle, and ending are clear. Some transitions are used.

A Closer Look

When you read a rubric to judge a trait, follow these steps:

1 First read the 5 descriptions. (A 5 is very strong writing that meets the main requirements for that trait.)

2 Decide if your writing should get a 5 for that specific trait.

3 If not, read 6, 4, 3, and 2 until you find the rating that best fits your paper.

4 If you are still revising and your rating is 4 or lower, make the necessary changes to improve the rating for that trait.

Review the complete narrative rubric. Look at the rubric on pages 120–121. For which traits will it be hard for you to achieve a 5 or 6 rating? For which will it be easy? Explain.

Assessing with a Rubric

Follow the steps below when you use a rubric like the one on page 35 to assess a piece of writing.

1 Make an assessment sheet. Create a sheet like the one on this page.

2 Read the final copy. Get an overall feeling for the writing before you evaluate it.

3 Assess the writing. Find the rating on the rubric that best fits each trait in the writing. Write that number on your assessment sheet.

ASSESSMENT SHEET   Title: _____

____ IDEAS
        1.
        2.

____ ORGANIZATION
        1.
        2.

____ VOICE
        1.
        2.

____ WORD CHOICE
        1.
        2.

____ SENTENCE FLUENCY
        1.
        2.

____ CONVENTIONS
        1.
        2.

        Evaluator: _____

4 Make comments under each trait.
(Your teacher may or may not ask you to do so.)

Make an assessment sheet. Make an assessment sheet like the one above. Then evaluate one of your personal narratives using the rubric on pages 120–121. For each trait, write something you did well and something you'd like to do better. (See the sample on page 37.)

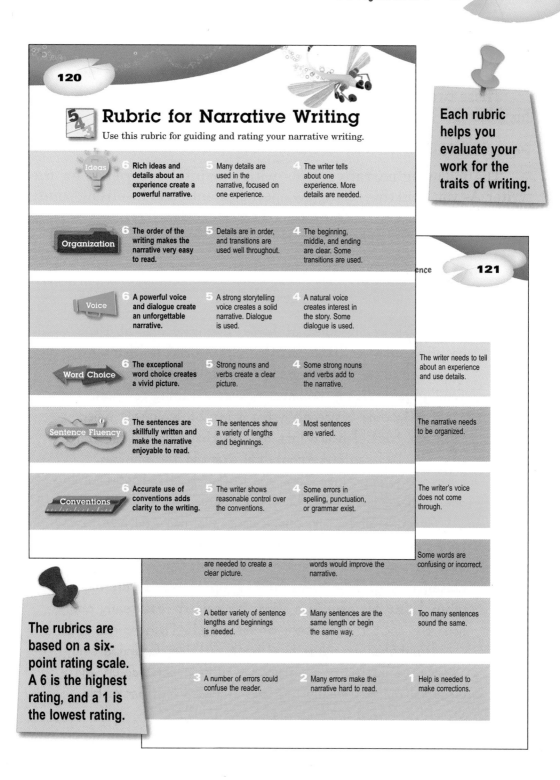

120

5 Rubric for Narrative Writing

Use this rubric for guiding and rating your narrative writing.

Ideas

6 Rich ideas and details about an experience create a powerful narrative.

5 Many details are used in the narrative, focused on one experience.

4 The writer tells about one experience. More details are needed.

Organization

6 The order of the writing makes the narrative very easy to read.

5 Details are in order, and transitions are used well throughout.

4 The beginning, middle, and ending are clear. Some transitions are used.

Voice

6 A powerful voice and dialogue create an unforgettable narrative.

5 A strong storytelling voice creates a solid narrative. Dialogue is used.

4 A natural voice creates interest in the story. Some dialogue is used.

Word Choice

6 The exceptional word choice creates a vivid picture.

5 Strong nouns and verbs create a clear picture.

4 Some strong nouns and verbs add to the narrative.

Sentence Fluency

6 The sentences are skillfully written and make the narrative enjoyable to read.

5 The sentences show a variety of lengths and beginnings.

4 Most sentences are varied.

Conventions

6 Accurate use of conventions adds clarity to the writing.

5 The writer shows reasonable control over the conventions.

4 Some errors in spelling, punctuation, or grammar exist.

ence   121

The writer needs to tell about an experience and use details.

The narrative needs to be organized.

The writer's voice does not come through.

Some words are confusing or incorrect.

are needed to create a clear picture.

words would improve the narrative.

3 A better variety of sentence lengths and beginnings is needed.

2 Many sentences are the same length or begin the same way.

1 Too many sentences sound the same.

3 A number of errors could confuse the reader.

2 Many errors make the narrative hard to read.

1 Help is needed to make corrections.

Each rubric helps you evaluate your work for the traits of writing.

The rubrics are based on a six-point rating scale. A 6 is the highest rating, and a 1 is the lowest rating.

Reviewing an Assessment

These two pages show how one student used a rubric to evaluate his writing.

Personal Narrative

The following narrative deals with a painful experience for the writer. As you read this essay, pay special attention to its strong points and weak points.

Left Behind

It was really quiet at home. Everyone was at the hospital with my little brother José. José had hurt his wrist while playing baseball with our cousins. My dad's family was visiting, because it was a family reunion.

I had come inside to get a drink of lemonade when José got hurt. I heard lots of shouting. Mom was really worried. Dad ran out front. He started the minivan. Everyone jumped into cars and headed to the hospital. No one realized that I had been left behind.

After a while, the phone rang. My dad said he'd be home soon. The dog herd the cars before I did. He started barking and jumping. Before long the house was full of noisey family. José came running up to me. I felt worried when I saw his arm in a sling. He said it was really cool how the doctor took care of his wrist. Then he ran out.

I watched everyone head back outside. Grandpa said, "Sorry we rushed off without you." He bent down and wrapped me in a really big hug. I hugged him back. He stood up, "Now let's go play some ball, eh?"

Sample Self-Assessment

The student who wrote "Left Behind" used the rubric on pages 120–121 to evaluate his narrative. Beneath each trait, he named one strength (1) and one weakness (2) in his writing.

ASSESSMENT SHEET   Title: <u>Left Behind</u>

__4__   IDEAS
1. My background details are clear.
2. I need more details about what I did while I was alone.

__4__   ORGANIZATION
1. The beginning names my topic.
2. I could have used more transitions.

__4__   VOICE
1. I sound interested.
2. I should have shared more of my feelings.

__5__   WORD CHOICE
1. My words are clear.
2. I could have used more feeling words.

__4__   SENTENCE FLUENCY
1. The sentences are easy to read.
2. I have too many short, choppy sentences in the second paragraph.

__4__   CONVENTIONS
1. I used correct punctuation.
2. I need to double-check my spelling.

Evaluator: <u>Pablo Sanchez</u>

Review the self-assessment. Read through the assessment sheet. Then list one strength and one weakness (for any trait) that the writer may have missed.

Assessing a Narrative

Read the personal narrative below and pay attention to the strengths and weaknesses in the writing. Then follow the directions at the bottom of the page.

Rainy Day

I stared out the window. "Why does it have to rain today?" I asked my dad. We were supposed to go camping. Rotten rain.

"Guess we'll have to camp right here in the living room," Dad said. I turned around. He was unrolling the sleeping bags. He put them in front of the fireplace. Then he pulled out the little camping table. He set that in the corner. It wasn't the same as camping outside, but it still looked fun.

Later we were sitting by a roaring fire. Dad ran outside in the rain for some more wood. We roasted hot dogs and marshmallows. I drank hot cider that Mom had put in a thermos. We turned out all of the lights. Dad read a book by the firelight. I was starting to like camping indoors.

Later that night I curled up in my sleeping bag. I watched the hot coals glowing in the fireplace. I listened to the rain outside. I whispered in the dark, "Dad? Can we go camping again next weekend?"

Use a narrative rubric. Assess the narrative you have just read using the rubric on pages 120–121 as a guide. Before you get started, create an assessment sheet like the one on page 34.

Peer Responding

Have you ever made chili and asked someone to try it? The person's response will tell you if the chili is as good as you hoped it would be. Having people "try" your writing is helpful, too.

Your classmates can read your writing and tell you what works well and what could work even better. This chapter explains the process of sharing writing in peer-response conferences.

Mini Index

- Peer-Responding Guidelines
- Making Helpful Responses
- Peer Response Sheet

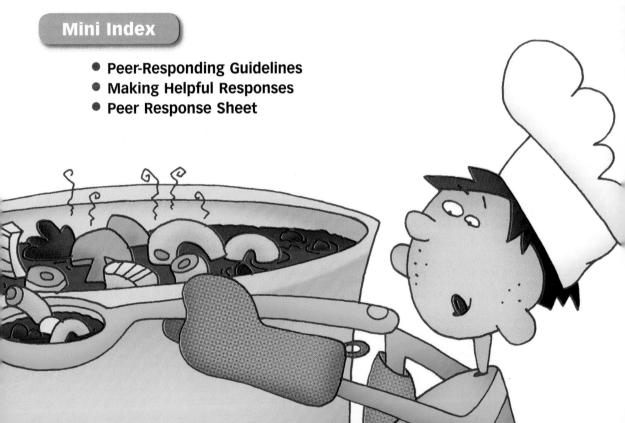

Peer-Responding Guidelines

Peer responding takes teamwork. The writer has one job, and the responder has a different job.

The Writer's Job

As the writer, you need to present a piece of your writing. Try to have a copy for each responder. Then follow these guidelines:

- **Introduce your writing,** but don't say too much.
- **Read your work aloud,** or let the responders read it silently.
- **Ask for comments.** Listen carefully.
- **Write down** the suggestions to help you remember them.
- **Ask for advice** about any specific trouble spots.

The Responder's Job

As a responder, be kind, respectful, and helpful. Follow these guidelines:

- **Listen (or read) carefully.** Take some notes.
- **Mention what you like** about the writing. Be specific. *(Sample responses: I like the way you explain new words. Your characters seem so real.)*
- **Ask questions** if you are unsure about something or have an idea about what could be improved.

tip Get to the point. "Nice job!" sounds encouraging, but it won't help the writer discover ways to make the paper better.

Making Helpful Responses

The best responders ask questions that will help the writer discover ways to improve the writing.

Ask Specific Questions

Avoid asking questions that can be answered yes or no. Instead, ask questions that really help the writer think about the writing.

- How did you get interested in this topic?
- Which detail is your favorite?
- What one idea do you want the reader to remember?

Ask Positive Questions

Negative questions don't help the writer very much.

NEGATIVE QUESTIONS:	POSITIVE QUESTIONS:
✗ Why didn't you tell more about your lighthouse?	✔ How big is the lighthouse light?
✗ Why are your verbs so dull?	✔ What exciting verbs could you use?
✗ Where's your ending?	✔ What new idea could you include in your ending?

Practice

As a class, discuss the types of comments that are most helpful to writers during peer-responding sessions. Make a chart of helpful comments to post in the classroom.

Peer Response Sheet

A sheet like the one below can guide your peer response. Tasha filled in this sheet for Tristan's expository essay about lighthouses.

Peer Response Sheet

Writer: Tristan Jones   Responder: Tasha Kirk

Title: "The Lighthouse, A Ship's Best Friend"

What I liked about your writing:

* I like how you began the essay with a line about lighthouses from a sailor song.

* I didn't know lighthouses are so important.

* I like the quotation from the lighthouse keeper.

Questions I have . . .

* How many lighthouses in the United States still have keepers?

* What kind of fuel did old-time lighthouses use?

Practice

Now it's your turn! Exchange a piece of writing with a classmate. Read the writing and then fill out a response sheet like the one above.

Publishing and Portfolios

Once you complete a writing assignment, it's time to publish it! Dress up your work to make it look its very best. You can also put it in a portfolio, something like a photo album for writing. Each essay or story in your portfolio shows something important about your writing. This chapter will explain publishing and different kinds of portfolios.

Mini Index

- **Designing Your Writing**
- **Types of Portfolios**
- **Parts of a Portfolio**
- **Portfolio Reflections**

Designing Your Writing

A computer can help you make your paper look great. The following guidelines tell you how to design the final look of your paper.

Typography—the style or appearance of letters

- Use a simple font for most of your paper.
- Use a bold font for headings.
- Keep the title and headings short.

Spacing and Margins—the white space on a page

- Leave one-inch margins on all four sides.
- Double-space your writing.
- Indent the first line of every paragraph.
- Don't leave a heading or the first line of a paragraph at the bottom of a page. Put it at the top of a new page instead.

Graphics—lists, pictures, and charts

- Use lists to highlight important points.
- Include a picture or chart if it will make an idea clearer. Add a label if necessary.

Practice

Look through this book to find a page that looks good to you. Discuss the page with your classmates and point out at least three design details that you like.

Great-Looking Design in Action

Aaron Olson

Seeing the Windy City

The font is easy to read.

Do you enjoy dolphins, stars, dinosaurs, or sports? Then Chicago has something for you! This amazing city is located in the northeastern part of Illinois, along Lake Michigan.

Sharks, Stars, and Dinosaurs

Chicago, often called the Windy City, has many great attractions.

- **Shedd Aquarium:** The entrance has a gigantic circular tank filled with fish, sea turtles, and stingrays. Other underwater viewing areas let visitors watch otters, penguins, and dolphins.
- **Adler Planetarium and Astronomy Museum:** The planetarium has a constellation show that makes visitors feel like they are sitting under a night sky. The guide tells what ancient cultures thought about the stars.

A list helps organize the essay.

- **Field Museum of Natural History:** This place has the biggest T. rex skeleton ever found. With exhibits about dinosaurs, animals, gemstones, and even Native American traditions, this museum is an adventure!

Batter Up!

Chicago is famous for its baseball teams. The Chicago Cubs play at Wrigley Field, one of the most historic baseball parks. It was built in 1914. The White Sox play at U.S. Cellular Field, one of the most high-tech baseball parks! FUNdamentals is a baseball-skills area in the park for kids.

Map Out an Adventure

For people who would like to spend time in the Windy City, there are four ways to reach Chicago.

1. Ride into the city on a train.
2. Drive into Chicago on one of the freeways.
3. Fly into O'Hare or Midway Airport.
4. Sail into Chicago on Lake Michigan or on the Chicago River.

Thousands of people visit Chicago every year. They enjoy parks, concerts, festivals, shops, and food. Don't just dream about it. Plan a visit to the Windy City soon!

White space makes the page look better.

A numbered list makes the essay easy to read.

Types of Portfolios

A portfolio is a group of writing samples collected for a special purpose. Here are four basic types.

Showcase Portfolio

A showcase portfolio features samples of your very best writing. Teachers use these portfolios to evaluate your work. (See page 48.)

Personal Portfolio

A personal portfolio holds writing that is important to you, your friends, and your family. It is a great place to keep ideas, poems, letters, journal pages, and other finished writing.

Growth Portfolio

A growth portfolio shows how your writing has improved over time. You can see your growth as a writer throughout the year as you compare different essays and stories.

Electronic Portfolio

An electronic portfolio is posted on a Web site or saved on a disk or hard drive. It includes writing, graphics, and sometimes even sounds and animation. Electronic portfolios let you share your work with many people.

Practice

Pick a type of portfolio that appeals to you. Think of two or three pieces of writing you would like to include in a portfolio of this type. Explain why you chose each piece.

Parts of a Portfolio

You may be asked to keep a showcase portfolio. It should include the following parts.

- A **table of contents** lists the writing samples you have included in your portfolio.

- An **introduction** (either a paragraph, a short essay, or a letter) tells how you created the portfolio and what it means to you.

- The **writing samples** show off your best writing. Your teacher may want to see each step for some pieces (planning, research notes, drafts, revising, editing, final draft).

- **Reflection sheets** or **checklists** show what you have learned during each project.

- A **creative cover** uses drawings, special lettering, and perhaps a poem to express your unique personality.

GATHERING TIPS

- **Save all of your work.** Keep prewriting notes, first drafts, and revisions. Make sure everything is dated.
- **Store your writing in a pocket folder.** It's easier to create a portfolio if your work is organized in one place.
- **Be proud of your work.** You want your portfolio to show your best writing skills.

Practice

Plan a unique cover for a showcase portfolio. Include your name, a title, and drawings or graphic elements.

Sample Portfolio Reflections

For each essay or story in your portfolio, write a reflection. See the samples below.

Student Reflections

After writing my essay "Pinching for Fun," I realized how much more I have to learn about pottery. During my research, I read about all sorts of ways to decorate pottery, like soda and salt glazes. I can't wait to ask my grandpa about these things.

—Fumi Akimoto

I wrote "Seeing the Windy City" because I had a great time in Chicago with my family. I didn't know what to write about, so I looked through our photo album. I took notes as I flipped through the pages. My notes were about different places, so that's what I wrote about. When I read it, I feel like I am back in Chicago.

—Aaron Olson

Professional Reflections

Thurber did not write the way a surgeon operates; he wrote the way a child skips rope, the way a mouse waltzes.

—E. B. White

In beginning to write *The Giver*, I created—as I always do, in every book—a world that existed only in my imagination—the world of "only us, only now."

—Lois Lowry

Paragraph Writing

Writing Paragraphs

A paragraph is a group of sentences that tell about one topic. The first sentence usually identifies the topic or main idea. The other sentences give details and facts about it.

Here are the four main reasons to write a paragraph.

1. **Describe** a person, place, or thing.
2. **Tell a story** about an event or an experience.
3. **Explain** or give information about a topic.
4. **Share** your opinion about something.

Mini Index

- **The Parts of a Paragraph**
- **Writing Strong Topic Sentences**
- **Using Details**
- **Organizing Your Paragraph**
- **Writing Guidelines**
- **Test Prep for Paragraphs**

The Parts of a Paragraph

A paragraph has three main parts. (1) It begins with a **topic sentence** that states the main idea. (2) The **body** contains sentences that share details about the main idea. (3) The **closing sentence** sums up the paragraph's message.

Topic sentence

Body

Closing sentence

The Mystery of King Tut

Scientists are still trying to solve the mystery of what happened to King Tut. He became an Egyptian king when he was only eight years old, and he died when he was just a teenager. For years, scientists have wondered how he died. Recently, they looked at King Tut's mummy using a special X-ray called a CT scan. Scientists took more than 1,700 pictures of the mummy's bones and organs. They hoped that these special pictures would show what happened to the young king. The X-rays showed that King Tut had a broken leg, but there were no clues about how he might have died. Now, the mystery of what happened to the king may never be solved.

Respond to the reading. (1) What is the main idea of this paragraph? (2) Which details do you feel are most important? (3) What does the title tell you about the paragraph?

A Closer Look at the Parts

The Topic Sentence

The **topic sentence** tells the reader what the paragraph is about. A good topic sentence (1) names the topic and (2) shares an important idea or feeling about it.

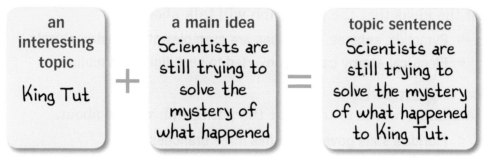

an interesting topic		a main idea		topic sentence
King Tut	**+**	Scientists are still trying to solve the mystery of what happened	**=**	Scientists are still trying to solve the mystery of what happened to King Tut.

The Body

The **body** sentences share details about the topic.

- **Use specific details.** Details are highlighted (in blue) below:

    He became an Egyptian king when he was only eight years old, **and he** died when he was just a teenager. **For years, scientists have** wondered how **he died. Recently, they looked at King Tut's mummy using a** special X-ray called a CT scan. **Scientists took more than** 1,700 pictures **of the mummy's** bones and organs.

- **Organize the sentences.** Put your sentences in the best possible order *(time order, order of location, order of importance,* or *logical order).* (See pages 56–57.) Transition words are highlighted (in blue) below:

    For years, **scientists have wondered how he died.** Recently, **they looked at King Tut's mummy using a special X-ray called a CT scan.**

The Closing Sentence

The **closing sentence** sums up the paragraph's message.

Now, the mystery of what happened to the king may never be solved.

Writing Strong Topic Sentences

A good paragraph begins with a strong topic sentence. Here are some ideas that might help you write a strong topic sentence. (For more strategies, see page 460.)

Make a List:

List the ideas that the paragraph will talk about.

- Pyramids, spheres, **and** cubes **are examples of geometric objects.**
- **Electrical energy can be converted to** heat, light, **and** motion.

Use a Number:

Use number words to tell what the paragraph will be about.

- **Florida's state government has** three **branches.**
- **There are** several **ways to solve the problem of poor eating habits.**

Use Word Pairs:

Use pairs of conjunctions to connect ideas.

- Both **a safe bicycle** and **a careful rider are necessary to avoid accidents.**

Word Pairs

either . . . or
not only . . . but also
whether . . . or
both . . . and

Practice

Reread the information above. Then write three topic sentences, using each of the ideas listed.

Using Details

The sentences in the body (middle) of a paragraph include different kinds of specific details about the topic—facts, reasons, and explanations. Examples are often added to make the ideas clear.

Facts add information.

Topic sentence: Yesterday, our class had a special visitor.

Facts: His name is Charles Hoover. He was born in 1925, and he is 81 years old.

Reasons answer the question *why?*

Reason: He came to explain what life was like here in Montgomery, Alabama, more than 75 years ago.

Examples: He told us about old-time cars, Negro baseball leagues, and games he played as a boy.

Explanations show something.

Reason: He could tell us a lot about the history of our state.

Explanation: That's what we have been studying this month.

Example: Mr. Hoover was part of the Selma-to-Montgomery civil rights march in 1965.

 Match the colors for facts, reasons, examples, and explanations to see how details are arranged in the paragraph below.

Yesterday, our class had a special visitor. His name is Charles Hoover. He was born in 1925, and he is 81 years old. He came to explain what life was like here in Montgomery, Alabama, more than 75 years ago. He talked about old-time cars, Negro baseball leagues, and games he played as a boy. He could tell us a lot about the history of our state. That's what we have been studying this month. Mr. Hoover was part of the Selma-to-Montgomery civil rights march in 1965.

Organizing Your Paragraph

The sentences in a paragraph should be put in order so that the reader can easily follow the ideas. Here are four ways to organize paragraphs.

Time Order . . .

Time order gives details in the order in which they happened. Transition words like *first, next,* and *then* are used.

First, read the directions for the recipe carefully. Next, gather all the ingredients. Then get a large bowl and the measuring spoons and cup you'll need. Finally, begin mixing the best trail mix you'll ever eat.

■ Time order works well with narrative and expository paragraphs.

Order of Location . . .

Order of location describes a topic from top to bottom, left to right, near to far, or in some other order. Transition words and phrases like *on top of, next to,* and *underneath* are used.

In the picture, a team of oxen stands in front of a tall prairie schooner wagon. Above the wagon, the white cover looks like a giant sail. The wagon box below the canvas is made of thick, gray wood. Four big wheels are attached to the bottom of the box at the corners.

■ Order of location works well for descriptive paragraphs.

Order of Importance . . .

Order of importance tells the most important detail first or last. Transition words and phrases like *first of all, also,* and *most importantly* are used.

> **Every family should have a fire-escape plan.** For one reason, a plan makes sure that everyone knows where to go in case there is a fire. In addition, practicing the plan will make you less afraid if there is a real fire. Most importantly, an escape plan can save your life.

■ Order of importance works well with persuasive and expository paragraphs.

Logical Order . . .

Logical order means that you organize details in a way that makes the best sense. Transition words like *in fact, for example,* and *also* are used.

> **Trees are a very important form of plant life.** Trees add beauty to the landscape and give shelter to wildlife. Because of their deep root system, trees also prevent soil erosion and help store water. In addition, some types of trees supply lumber for building houses and furniture. Other trees provide food and medicines . . .

■ Use a logical order in expository paragraphs.

Practice

Find a paragraph in one of your school texts that uses one of the organizational patterns shown on these two pages.

Writing Guidelines

Prewriting Selecting a Topic

The instructions below and on the next page can be used to write a paragraph. Your teacher may give you a general subject, and you will need to select a specific topic to write about. (See page 455.)

1 **Choose a topic that interests you.**

2 **Make sure that your topic is the right size.**

Too big: My whole school year
Too small: A few minutes early this morning
Just right: My first week in fourth grade

3 **Collect your details.**

For descriptive paragraphs,	*collect*	sights, sounds, smells, and tastes.
For narrative or story paragraphs,	*answer*	who? what? when? where? and why?
For expository (factual) paragraphs,	*gather*	important facts and examples.
For persuasive paragraphs,	*list*	reasons that explain your opinions.

4 **Use graphic organizers.**

Choose a cluster, time line, sensory chart, 5-W's chart, or story map to help you organize your details. (See pages 456–457.)

5 **Write a topic sentence.**

Once you have gathered your details, try writing a topic sentence that states the main idea of your paragraph. Then, think about the best way to organize your details.

Writing Creating Your First Draft

When you write your first draft, your goal is to get all of your ideas on paper. Begin with your topic sentence. Then add supporting details (facts, reasons, examples, and explanations) in the body sentences. End with a closing sentence that sums up the message of your paragraph.

Revising Improving Your Paragraph

Ask yourself the following questions. Then make changes to your paragraph.

1 Is my topic sentence clear?
2 Have I included all of the important details in the best order?
3 Do I sound interested in my topic?
4 Do I use specific nouns and action verbs?
5 Do I use a variety of sentence lengths?
6 Do my sentences read smoothly?

Editing Checking for Conventions

Carefully check your revised paragraph for punctuation, capitalization, spelling, and grammar errors.

1 Do I use correct punctuation and capitalization?
2 Do I use the right words (too, to, two)?
3 Do I spell words correctly? Have I used my spell-checker?

Practice

Plan and write a paragraph about something in the news. Review the sample paragraph on page 52 and the guidelines on pages 58–59.

Test Prep for Paragraphs

On a writing test, you may be asked to write a paragraph summarizing a reading selection. Use the tips below.

WRITING TIPS

Before you write . . .

- **Read the selection twice.** Read it once for the general meaning. Read it again to understand all the details.
- **Plan your paragraph.** Write a topic sentence that sums up the main idea of the selection. Decide which details to use in the middle of the paragraph.
- **Use your time wisely.** Spend a few minutes planning what you will write.

During your writing . . .

- **Keep it short**. A summary paragraph for a short reading selection should be about six to eight sentences long.
- **Use your own words.** Include words from the selection only when you are sharing basic facts.

After you write . . .

- **Reread your summary paragraph.** Change any ideas that are unclear or incorrect.

Practice

Find an informational section in a science or history text. (Your teacher may assign one.) Write a short summary of the reading. Follow the tips above and look at the sample summary on the next page before you begin.

Original Reading Selection

Still Celebrating Earth Day

Earth Day is celebrated on April 22. It is a special day when people take care of the earth and sponsor environmental cleanups. On this day, people all around the world find special ways to improve the earth where they live. Some walk or bike to work instead of driving their cars. Many people plant flowers and trees.

The first Earth Day was held on April 22, 1970. A senator from Wisconsin named Gaylord Nelson created it. He worried that the world was becoming polluted. On that day, he asked everyone to do something to make our earth a better place for all.

Today, people all over the world know that the earth needs help. There is still much to be done. Some people argue that it is not enough to have one special day to remember the earth. They think that every day should be Earth Day.

Sample Summary

Topic sentence

Body

Closing sentence

Earth Day Anniversary

Earth Day is a special day when people help the earth to be a better place. Some people walk to work instead of drive. Others have cleanup projects and plant trees. The first Earth Day was April 22, 1970. Senator Gaylord Nelson from Wisconsin created it. He wanted the earth to be a better place for everyone. People still celebrate Earth Day on April 22. Some of them believe that Earth Day should be every day.

Descriptive Writing

Descriptive Writing

Descriptive Paragraph

What is your favorite place? The school gym or your bedroom at home? A busy street or a quiet backyard? The local zoo or a giant shopping mall?

In this chapter, you'll learn how to use sensory details to describe a favorite place. Your goal is to use sights, sounds, smells, and other senses to take your classmates on a tour of that special spot.

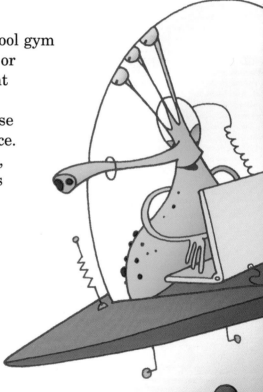

Writing Guidelines

Subject: A favorite place

Form: Descriptive paragraph

Purpose: To describe a place you know well

Audience: Classmates

Descriptive Paragraph

Your descriptive paragraph will use sensory details to create a clear picture of a place. The **topic sentence** should name your favorite place, and the **body sentences** should include specific details. The **closing sentence** ends the description. In the following paragraph, Joe describes his backyard and its bird feeders.

Topic sentence

Body

Closing sentence

Backyard Buffet

Our backyard is a restaurant for birds. The lilac bush by the kitchen window has tangerine halves stuck on it. Orange and black orioles love to eat the fruit and drink the sweet juice. Next to the lilacs, a crabapple tree holds a narrow cloth bag. Goldfinches hang on the bag and pluck thistle seeds out of tiny holes. On the other side of the tree, a green metal bird feeder stands on a pole. A squirrel leaps onto it, but it slams shut! The squirrel chatters and scolds because he can't get at the sunflower seeds. Below the squirrel, cardinals and blue jays find the seeds that have fallen on the ground. If I were a bird, our backyard buffet would be my favorite place to visit.

Respond to the reading. On your own paper, answer the questions below.

- **Ideas** (1) What details help the reader see the backyard buffet?

- **Organization** (2) What transition words and phrases help you picture the location of each detail?

- **Voice & Word Choice** (3) What specific words make the writer's voice sound excited about the topic?

Prewriting Selecting a Topic

Think about a few of your favorite places. Freewriting can help you choose a place to write about. Here is some of Joe's freewriting.

Freewriting

What places do I know? Bob's bike shop is cool, but I guess I don't know it that well. What about the mall? That's too big. Is there a small place that I know? I've got a very small backyard. It's just a bunch of bird feeders. Birds and squirrels that come there are fun to watch. . . .

Select a topic. Freewrite for 3 to 5 minutes to find a place you know well enough to describe in a paragraph.

Gathering Details

A strong description contains sensory details. They help the reader experience the place. Joe used a sensory chart to gather his details.

Sensory Chart

See	Hear	Smell	Taste	Touch
purple lilacs cardinals blue jays goldfinches	scolding chattering slam	lilacs tangerines	tangerines sunflower seeds sweet juice	smooth metal

Make a sensory chart. Write *See, Hear, Smell, Taste,* and *Touch* on the top. List details about your topic for each sense.

Writing Creating Your First Draft

In your first draft, you want to get your ideas on paper. Your topic sentence should introduce the place. Write body sentences that include sensory details. Use transition words and phrases to connect the details. End with a closing sentence that shares a final thought.

Write your first draft. Be sure to include sensory details to help the reader experience your place.

Revising Improving Your Paragraph

When you revise your paragraph, you make changes to improve your work. You may add, rearrange, and cut details.

Improve your paragraph. Use the following questions.
1. Does my topic sentence tell which place I will describe?
2. Do I use transition words and phrases?
3. Do I sound like I know the place I am describing?
4. Have I used sensory words to describe the place?
5. Have I used complete sentences that flow smoothly?

Editing Checking for Conventions

After you have revised your paragraph, check the punctuation, capitalization, spelling, and grammar. Correct any errors you find.

Check for conventions. The questions below will help.
1. Are my punctuation and capitalization correct?
2. Have I spelled words correctly?
3. Have I used the right words (*too, to, two*)?

Descriptive Writing
Describing a Place

Everyone has a favorite room. Maybe you like the art room at school because of its sunrise mural and the mobiles that dangle from the ceiling. Maybe you like your uncle's workshop because of the smell of sawdust, the buzz of the saws, the tap-tap-tap of the hammers, and the sight of the beautiful things he makes out of wood.

Whatever room is your favorite, a descriptive essay can let you explore it. This chapter will help you write your descriptive essay. When you are finished, your reader can "take the tour" of your favorite room!

Writing Guidelines

Subject: A favorite room
Form: Descriptive essay
Purpose: To describe a place
Audience: Classmates

Descriptive Essay

In the following essay, Jack describes his favorite room. The side notes will help you understand the different parts of his essay.

Little Cabin in the Woods

You might think that staying in a one-room log cabin would be rough. I did, too, until I went to a summer camp on Norton's Lake. At first, the little cabin seemed kind of unfinished, but now it is one of my favorite places!

The cabin is one big room. The walls are real logs that someone notched and put together without nails. The edges of the logs have rough ax marks on them, but the wood floor feels smooth from camper's feet. Because of all that wood, the cabin smells of pine. Only the dusty stone fireplace isn't made of wood, but it smells like wood ashes!

The cabin has old furniture in it. Metal bunk beds stand along the walls near the fireplace. They have musty mattresses on plywood boards. On the wall across from the fireplace, there's a window and a white rusty sink. A pump sticks out the top, and it's fun to pump it to get water. The cabin has no bathroom, but there's an outhouse down the hill!

The third middle paragraph focuses on one special part.

The best part about the cabin is the fold-up table. It's next to the sink, and it lifts up to attach to the wall. Whenever the table's down, campers pull up the split-log benches and play board games. When the table is up, campers sit on the benches for cabin meetings or for evening storytelling times.

ENDING

The writer tells why the room is special to him.

The counselors call the cabin "rustic." At first, I thought that word meant "junky." Now I know it means everything you really need and nothing you don't need. Whenever I smell wood smoke or pine trees, it always makes me want to be back in the cabin in the woods.

Respond to the reading. Answer the following questions about the essay.

- **Ideas** (1) What details help you see, hear, feel, or smell things in the cabin?

- **Organization** (2) What words and phrases tell you where each part of the cabin is?

- **Voice & Word Choice** (3) What words show how the writer feels about the cabin?

Prewriting Selecting a Topic

A topic list can help you select a favorite room to describe in your essay.

Topic List

Everyday Rooms	Fun Rooms
bedroom	train depot
school auditorium	ice-cream shop
Grandma's living room *	

Make a topic list. Use the sample above as a guide. Put a star (*) next to the room you want to write about.

Drawing the Room

You can draw a floor plan to show a top-down view of your room.

Floor Plan

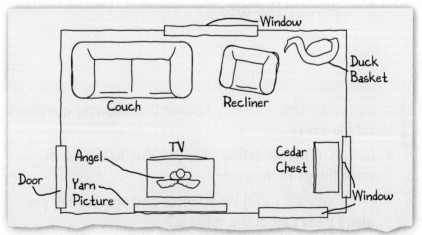

Draw a floor plan. Create a picture of your room seen from above. Label the parts of your picture.

Making a Sensory Chart

Once you draw your floor plan, you need to gather sensory details about the room. A sensory chart like the one below can help you.

Sensory Chart

See	Hear	Smell	Feel	Taste
windows couch basket	jazz CD meowing	pinecones, oranges cinnamon sticks scented apples	yarn picture knitting	

Create a sensory chart. Make a sensory chart like the one above to gather details about the room you will describe.

Creating an Organized List

Look at your floor plan and make a list like the one below to help you organize your details.

Directions   **Organized List**

Name your place.   Grandma's living room

Describe the room overall.   1. little room, wide windows, sunshine

Describe details by order of location.   2. couch, recliner, duck-shaped basket, TV, angel

Describe a special feature.   3. cedar chest where the puzzles are and where the cat sits

Create an organized list. Follow the directions above to write your own organized list.

Writing **Starting Your Essay**

Your beginning paragraph should get the reader's attention and introduce the room you will describe. Here are two ways to begin your description.

| Beginning |
| Middle |
| Ending |

Beginning Paragraph

■ **Ask the reader a question.**

> What's the coziest place you know of? The coziest place I know is my grandma's house. I go there for holidays and during the summer. The best room in the house is Gram's living room.

■ **Begin with a surprising fact.**

> My grandma was born in the house where she lives. No wonder she loves it so much. I just visit her, but I love it, too. My favorite place in her house is the living room.

Write your beginning paragraph. You can use one of the ideas above to get started, or use one of your own. If your first version doesn't work well, try another one.

Focus on the Traits

Voice Your own special way of expressing yourself is called your *writing voice*. The words you choose, the details you include, and the ways you connect those details all help to shape your writing voice.

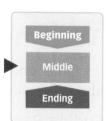

Developing the Middle Part

The middle paragraphs share the details you included in your organized list. The side notes below tell what goes in each paragraph.

| Beginning |
| Middle |
| Ending |

Middle Paragraphs

First, the writer gives an overall description of the room.

The living room is small, but it has big windows on three sides. Grandma calls this room her jewel box because it glows with sunlight. The windows are as tall as doors. Sun catchers hang in the windows and make rainbows on the yellow walls and the green carpet.

Then she tells about details by order of location.

The furniture is old but comfortable. Grandma has a big couch with a flowery cover on it. I sit there, but Grandma likes her recliner next to the couch. By the recliner, she has a duck-shaped basket. It holds pinecones, dried oranges, cinnamon sticks, and scented wooden apples. Across the room, Grandma has her big, old TV with a blue glass angel on top. Above the TV hangs a yarn picture of frogs, cattails, and dragonflies.

Last, she describes her favorite part of the room.

The best part of the room is the cedar chest. It sits below the biggest window. The chest has puzzles in it, which is why I like it. Grandma's cat, Merlin, sits on the chest so he can watch the birds and squirrels at the feeder outside. Sometimes he also curls up in Grandma's knitting if she leaves it on top of the chest.

Create your middle paragraphs. Use your organized list (from page 71) to help you write each paragraph.

Writing Ending Your Essay

Your ending paragraph should tell how you feel about the place you are describing.

Beginning
Middle
► Ending

Ending Paragraph

The writer tells how she feels about the room.

> Grandma's living room might be small, but the sunlight makes it feel big. I like to sit on the couch and read or sit by the cedar chest and pet Merlin. In fact, I like being in Grandma's living room better than almost anywhere else.

Write

Create your ending. Tell the reader why this room is so special to you.

Revising and Editing

Revise

Improve your description. Use the questions below as a guide when you make changes to your essay.

- **Ideas** Do I include enough sensory details?
- **Organization** Do my beginning, middle, and ending parts work together?
- **Voice** Do I show the reader how much I like the room?
- **Word Choice** Do I use specific descriptive words?
- **Sentence Fluency** Do my sentences read smoothly?

Edit

Check your description. Use the checklist on page 30 as a guide to edit your work. Then prepare a neat final copy and have a classmate or parent help you proofread it.

Descriptive Writing
Across the Curriculum

"What did you do during vacation?" Friends and family naturally want to know about things you've seen and done. What does the world look like, sound like, and feel like to you? To help them understand, it's important to be able to describe things well.

Descriptive writing is often required for school assignments. In social studies, you may describe a historical place; in science, you may describe a plant or an animal. This chapter will help you write descriptions that capture the world around you.

Mini Index

- **Social Studies:** Describing a Historical Landmark
- **Science:** Describing a Plant
- **Assessment:** Writing for Assessment

1620

Social Studies:
Describing a Historical Landmark

Your teacher may ask you to write about a landmark from history. Notice how descriptive writing is used in the essay below.

The **beginning** names the landmark.

The **middle** describes the landmark and what makes it interesting.

The **ending** shares a final thought about the landmark.

Plymouth Rock

Everybody has heard of Plymouth Rock, and people may have a picture of it in their heads. Actually seeing it, though, is very surprising.

The rock is surrounded by a special monument. It looks like a rectangular Greek temple with tall, white stone columns and a roof to protect visitors. The top level inside is a balcony. From there, people can look down on the rock. Plymouth Rock rests on beach sand at the bottom level of the monument. The walls near the rock have fenced openings to let in the ocean tides. Twice a day the sea surrounds the rock, just like when the Pilgrims first landed. The whole place smells like salt water, and seagull calls echo through the air.

I thought that Plymouth Rock would be as big as a car, but it's only half the size of my bed. The rock used to be much larger. Long ago, people chipped pieces off for souvenirs. The rock is gray and smooth and has the date 1620 carved into it. That's the year the Pilgrims landed in Plymouth.

So, Plymouth Rock isn't what I thought it would be. However, it was awesome to see a place that marks the early beginnings of our country.

WRITING TIPS

Before you write . . .

- **Choose a historical landmark.**
  Select a place you have been to or studied in school.
- **Do your research.**
  Find information about the place and look at pictures. What makes the place important in history?
- **Take notes.**
  Focus on the physical details that make the place unique and interesting.

During your writing . . .

- **Organize your details.**
  Introduce your topic in the beginning, give details in the middle, and end with a final thought.
- **Show, don't tell.**
  Use descriptive details that help the reader "see" the place.
- **Sound excited.**
  Use specific words that show you know the place well.

After you've written a first draft . . .

- **Check for completeness.**
  Make sure to include enough details to give a clear picture of the place.
- **Check for correctness.**
  Proofread your essay for errors in punctuation, capitalization, spelling, and grammar.

Plan and write an essay.
Choose a historical landmark and write a detailed description of the place following these writing tips.

Science: Describing a Plant

Scientists called botanists study and describe the many types of plants in the world. Describing a particular plant helps you to understand it better.

The Texas State Flower

> The **beginning** introduces the plant and its scientific name.

The Texas bluebonnet is the state flower of Texas. Its scientific name is Lupinus texensis (loo-PIE-nus teck-SEN-sis). Bluebonnets grow beside many highways in the state. These flowers can survive in the dry soil of the Texas prairie.

From the ground, the bluebonnet's round, velvety stem grows 12 to 24 inches high. The leaves sprout along the stem in bunches, and each bunch fans out from a leaf stem. The leaves are thin and have round tips. They look like tiny green bunny ears!

> The **middle** describes the plant and its parts.

At the top of the plant is a stalk of small, sweet-smelling flowers. Each one is bright bluish purple with a white center. These tiny blossoms give the bluebonnet its name because each little flower looks like an old-fashioned bonnet.

> The **ending** includes a final thought about the topic.

So, when you're in Texas, and you see huge fields of blue flowers, you'll know what they are. They're Texas bluebonnets, the state flower.

flower

stem

leaf bunch

WRITING TIPS

Before you write . . .

- **Choose a topic that interests you.**
  Select a plant that you have studied or one you know from everyday life.
- **Research the plant.**
  Look up the scientific name and other details. Include a pronunciation guide for hard words.
- **List the main ideas you want to include.**
  Describe the plant and any of its special features.

During your writing . . .

- **Write a clear beginning, middle, and ending.**
  Introduce the plant in the beginning, describe it in the middle, and end with a summary or personal comment.
- **Organize your details.**
  Describe your plant from bottom to top or from top to bottom.
- **Use specific words.**
  Select words that give the reader a clear picture of the plant.

After you've written a first draft . . .

- **Check for completeness.**
  Add details to make your topic clearer.
- **Check for correctness.**
  Proofread your description for errors in punctuation, capitalization, spelling, and grammar.

Describe a plant. Use these tips to guide your writing.

Writing for Assessment

Some writing tests include a descriptive writing prompt. Read the following prompt and the student's response.

Descriptive Prompt

Think of a place you have visited. Write a paragraph that describes it using sensory details. Paint a vivid picture with your words.

The **topic sentence** (underlined) paints a vivid picture.	<u>The subway station is a doorway to an underground world.</u> Stairs lead down, down to the concrete platform. A strange, cool wind always seems to be blowing. Wide yellow lines warn people to stand away from the deep
Descriptive details fill the **body** sentences.	trenches where tracks disappear into blackness in both directions. The air smells like an oily, old garage. When the train light appears, the ground shakes as the subway cars roar into the station. As the wheels screech to
The **closing sentence** makes a personal comment about the subject.	a stop, all the opening and closing doors sound like a monster breathing. My stepdad and I often ride the subway, and it always seems like a science-fiction adventure to me.

Respond to the reading. Answer the following questions about the response paragraph.

- **Ideas** (1) What sensory details stand out? Name two.
- **Organization** (2) How did the writer organize the details in the body of the paragraph?
- **Voice & Word Choice** (3) What words show that the writer cares about the topic?

WRITING TIPS

Before you write . . .

- **Understand the prompt.**
  Be sure you understand what you need to describe.
- **Use your time wisely.**
  Take a few minutes to plan and make some notes.

During your writing . . .

- **Write an effective topic sentence.**
  Use words related to the prompt to introduce your subject and form a topic sentence.
- **Be selective.**
  Choose sensory details that describe your topic.
- **End in a meaningful way.**
  Close with a personal comment about the topic.

After you've written a first draft . . .

- **Check for completeness and correctness.**
  Make sure your ideas make sense and correct any errors.

Descriptive Prompt

■ Think of a place where you had fun. Write a paragraph that describes that place and tells why it's special to you.

 Plan and write a response. Respond to the "descriptive prompt" above. Finish your writing in the amount of time your teacher gives you. Afterward, underline something that you like and something that could be better in your response.

Narrative Writing

Narrative Writing

Narrative Paragraph

What makes you laugh? What funny experiences have you had with your family or friends? If you think about it, you probably have many humorous stories to tell. And sharing these stories can be a lot of fun.

Writing about personal experiences is a form of narrative writing. The best narrative writing makes an experience come alive for the reader. On the following pages you will learn to write a narrative paragraph about something funny that happened to you.

Writing Guidelines

Subject: A funny experience

Form: Narrative paragraph

Purpose: To entertain

Audience: Classmates

Narrative Paragraph

Funny things can happen almost anywhere. In this story, Jason shares a humorous memory about the first time he went bowling.

Topic sentence

Body

Closing sentence

Crash Landing

Now I'm a great bowler, but I remember the very first time I went bowling with my dad. I was only five years old. His fingers fit into the ball like he was putting on his old baseball glove. I saw Dad's mighty swing and watched the ball sail down the alley. Pow! All ten pins went flying. Then it was my turn. The ball was so heavy, but I held on. Taking a deep breath, I aimed for the pins. "Come on, strike," I said as I ran a few steps and swung the ball hard. It crashed down and started rolling very, very slowly. I kept saying, "Go, go." But it stopped dead. Everybody was pointing and laughing. Dad had to call the manager to push my ball into the gutter. It was one of the most embarrassing and funny moments of my life.

Respond to the reading. Answer the following questions on your own paper.

■ **Ideas** (1) What is the topic of this paragraph?

■ **Organization** (2) Does Jason organize the details by time order or by order of location?

■ **Word Choice** (3) What words and phrases create pictures in your mind? Name two.

Prewriting Selecting a Topic

The writer of "Crash Landing" used a web to help him remember some of his funny experiences.

Web

my sister playing a trick on me

falling off a chair

throwing a bowling ball *

at school

at home

in other places

Funny Experiences

Prewrite

Create a web like the one above. Include your own funny experiences at home, at school, and in other places. Put a star (✱) next to the experience you want to write about.

Gathering Details

Asking questions is a good way to gather and organize details. Jason used a chart to collect details for his paragraph.

Details Chart

How does the story start?	What events lead up to the funniest moment?	What is the funniest moment in the story?
I went bowling with my dad.	My dad got a strike. I didn't throw the ball hard enough.	The ball crashed, rolled slowly, and stopped. The manager had to come.

Prewrite

Collect details. Make a chart like the one above. Fill it in with details about your experience.

Writing Developing the First Draft

In your narrative paragraph, your topic sentence introduces your story. The body sentences contain details about what happened to you. The closing sentence sums up your experience.

Write your first draft. Write with a natural writing voice as if you were telling a friend about your funny experience.

Revising Improving Your Paragraph

Here are three helpful revising tips.

- **Show, don't tell.** Instead of writing "Dad got a strike," write "I saw Dad's mighty swing and watched the ball sail down the alley. Pow! All ten pins went flying."
- **Check your organization.** Tell the events in the order in which they happened.
- **Check words and sentences.** Use specific nouns *(baseball glove)* and action verbs *(crashed)*. Make your sentences flow.

Revise your paragraph. Use the tips above as you make changes to improve the first draft of your narrative paragraph.

Editing Checking for Conventions

After revising your first draft, you must correct any punctuation, capitalization, spelling, or grammar errors in your paragraph.

Edit and proofread your work. Use the following questions to check and correct your narrative paragraph.

1 Have I ended each sentence with a punctuation mark?

2 Are my capitalization and spelling correct?

Narrative Writing

Sharing an Experience

Everyone has had unforgettable experiences. Some of these memories may be happy or exciting. Others may be sad or even scary. You can write about these times in personal narratives. A **personal narrative** is a form of writing that sheds light on a true story from your life.

In this chapter, you will write a personal narrative about an unforgettable experience. Your goal is to make your story as fresh and vivid for your reader as it actually was for you.

Writing Guidelines

Subject:	An unforgettable experience
Form:	Personal narrative
Purpose:	To share a true story
Audience:	Classmates

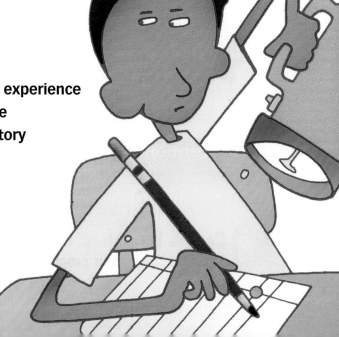

Understanding Your Goal

Your goal in this chapter is to write a personal narrative about an unforgettable experience. The traits listed in the chart below will help you meet that goal.

Your goal is to . . .

Ideas
Use specific details to show what happens. Make the reader want to know what happens next.

Organization
Grab the reader's interest in the beginning. Organize your ideas using time order. Bring your narrative together in the ending.

Voice
Use a strong storytelling voice. Show the personality of each person in your narrative.

Word Choice
Use specific nouns and verbs.

Sentence Fluency
Write sentences that flow smoothly from one to the next and keep the narrative moving.

Conventions
Be sure that the punctuation, capitalization, spelling, and grammar are correct.

 Get the big picture. Review the rubric on pages 120–121. It will help you check your progress as you write your narrative.

Personal Narrative

In this personal narrative, Shana shares an unforgettable memory of a scary storm.

The Green, Howling Day

One day, I was looking out my bedroom window when the sky began to turn a weird shade of green! Just then, I heard our city's emergency siren start wailing. That meant trouble.

Danika, my four-year-old sister, was in the hallway. She was crying, flapping her arms, and jumping up and down. That's what she does when she's scared. Mom came running upstairs to get us. She grabbed Danika and carried her down the steps. "Get to the basement!" she ordered.

By the time we reached the kitchen, the wind was howling like a wolf. I saw rain whizzing sideways past the window and trees bending over. It was like we were in the middle of the twister in The Wizard of Oz. As soon as we got to the basement steps, the sky turned as black as night. My sister screamed as the lights flickered and went out.

Suddenly the basement felt cold and damp. It smelled like laundry soap and bleach. Mom snapped on a flashlight and led us to a safe place. Then she tried to calm Danika. Finally, she turned on our portable radio. "A tornado is

MIDDLE
The middle includes strong details.

moving through this area," the weather reporter said. "Seek shelter immediately."

We huddled against the cold concrete blocks, far away from the windows. Mom sang lullabies for my little sister and squeezed us close. She tried to sound strong, but her voice was shaky. The wind rumbled and growled outside. It grew louder and louder until it sounded like a train roaring over our heads. Lightning flashes exploded and lit the room with a weird glow. Then everything was still.

ENDING
The closing tells how the experience ended.

We didn't know what we'd see when we went upstairs. What damage had the tornado done? Our house was fine, but tree branches and junk had blown all over the place. Danika crawled through the branches of the tree that had fallen across the driveway. Mom and Danika were afraid of the tornado, but I wasn't. Still, I was glad it was over and that we were all safe.

Respond to the reading.

- **Ideas** (1) What unforgettable experience does Shana share?

- **Organization** (2) How does Shana organize the events in her story?

- **Voice & Word Choice** (3) What words and phrases help you share in her experience? Name two.

Prewriting

First you need to choose an unforgettable experience to write about. Then you will gather details you remember.

Keys to Prewriting

1. **Think** of unforgettable experiences in your life.

2. **Choose** one experience to write about.

3. **Use** a time line to organize your story.

4. **Gather** sensory details to help the reader share your experience.

Prewriting **Selecting a Topic**

Tyrone found ideas for his personal narrative by making an "I remember when . . . " list like the one below.

List

I remember when . . .

I was a toad in our first-grade play.

my teacher retired, and I read her a poem.

my family went without TV for a whole weekend.

my guinea pig sneaked onto the school bus.

we had a snow day, and I built a snow fort.

I helped plant a memory tree in front of our school.

my wrist got broken when I fell off my bike.

> Some of your best stories come from your memories.

Brainstorm for topics. On your own paper, make an *I remember when . . .* list using the model above. Keep these things in mind:

1 Freewrite your list. Keep writing until you can't think of any more ideas.

2 Read your ideas and circle the one that you think will make the best story.

Sizing Up Your Topic Idea

A good story includes plenty of details. How much do you remember about your experience? Who was there? What happened? When, where, and why did it happen? What did people say? Making a 5 W's memory chart will help you remember.

> Do you remember enough interesting details about your experience?

5 W's Memory Chart

Who?	me, my brother, Dad, Mom
What?	My brother was upset. Dad built a campfire. Mom read a story. We ate pizza, played games, and carved pumpkins.
When?	Halloween time
Where?	the backyard, the kitchen table, our living room
Why?	no television for a whole weekend

Prewrite

Make a memory chart. Make a chart like the one above. Write down as much as you can about your experience.

Prewriting Putting Events in Order

Narratives are usually organized in chronological (time) order. Transition words and phrases (*first, second, after that, then, before long*) can help you put your events in order. See Tyrone's list below.

Transition Time Line

First . . .   my parents decided we wouldn't watch TV for a whole weekend.

Next . . .   we ate supper, and it got dark outside.

After that . . . we made a campfire in the backyard.

Then . . .   we went inside and carved pumpkins.

Before bed . . . we played a board game.

Finally . . .   my family decided to turn off the TV every Tuesday night and have fun together.

Prewrite

Create your time list. On your own paper, make a list like the one above. Use transitions to help you list important details in the order in which they happened.

Focus on the Traits

Organization A good story has an easy, natural order. Think of stories you've read or heard from your teacher, family, or friends. They often sound like someone is "telling" it just the way it happened.

Gathering Sensory Details

A good narrative includes sights, sounds, smells, tastes, and even details about how things feel. These kinds of details make the story real for the reader. Your choice of details gives the narrative your voice. You can gather sensory details in a chart like the one below.

Sensory Chart

Sights	Sounds	Smells	Tastes	Touch
sparks flying	doorbell ringing	wood burning	s'mores	warm jackets
glowing pumpkin faces	fire crackling	fresh air	pumpkin seeds	cool air
orange flames	Mom reading a story	pumpkin candles	pizza	gooey pumpkin seeds
starry sky				huddling together near the fire

Prewrite

Create a sensory chart. Think about your story. Then list sensory words and phrases that will help the reader share your memorable experience.

Prewriting Thinking About Dialogue

Dialogue makes an experience come alive for the reader. The chart below shows the three main things that dialogue can do.

		Without dialogue	With dialogue
1	Show something about a speaker's personality.	I was mad. How could I get along without TV?	"What?" I said. "No television! I don't think I can survive without it."
2	Add details.	I knew I'd miss Sunday afternoon football.	I looked at Dad and said, "What about Sunday afternoon football?"
3	Keep the action moving.	We went back in the house.	Once we got back in the house, Dad said, "I have a surprise."

Prewrite

Plan some dialogue. Think about what the people in your story said to each other. Make your dialogue sound real.

Focus on the Traits

Voice Your writing voice is like your fingerprint. It belongs to only you. When you write with your natural voice, your story will be interesting and believable.

Writing

Prewrite Write Revise Edit Publish

Now that you have collected and organized the details for your narrative, you are ready to write your first draft. Your goal is to put all your thoughts about your experience on paper.

Keys to Writing

1. Write a strong beginning paragraph.

2. Organize your story using time order.

3. Use the interesting details you have collected in the middle part.

4. Add sensory details and dialogue to hold your reader's attention.

5. Write an interesting ending.

Writing Getting the Big Picture

The chart below shows how the parts of a personal narrative fit together. (The examples are from the narrative on pages 99–102.) You're ready to write your essay once you have . . .

- gathered enough details to tell your story, and
- put the events of your story in time order.

Beginning

The **beginning** catches the reader's attention.

Opening Sentence

My parents decided we all watch too much television.

Middle

The **middle** part gives details about what happened during the experience.

- My brother was upset . . .
- Just then, the doorbell rang.
- We put on our warm jackets and headed to the backyard.
- Once we got back in the house, . . .

Ending

The **ending** shows how you feel, how you were changed, or what you learned from your experience.

Closing Sentences

Now we shut off the TV every Tuesday night, and we have family time. Now we all can't wait for Tuesday night.

Starting Your Personal Narrative

In the first paragraph, you should get the reader's attention and introduce your personal experience. Here are three ways to begin your paragraph.

- **Start by using dialogue.**

  "What?" I said. "No television! I don't think I can survive without it."

- **Begin with an interesting statement or fact.**

  My parents decided we all watch too much television. So they made a rule that no one would watch TV for one whole weekend.

- **Put yourself in the middle of the action.**

  When my parents said no one could watch television all weekend, I was so mad! I couldn't imagine Saturday without cartoons.

Beginning Paragraph

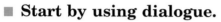

The writer begins with an interesting statement and includes dialogue.

My parents decided we all watch too much television. So they made a rule that no one would watch TV for one whole weekend. "What?" I said. "No television! I don't think I can survive without it."

You should write on every other line as you write your first draft.

Write

Write your beginning. Try at least two ways to begin your paragraph. Then choose the way you like best and finish your beginning paragraph.

Writing Developing the Middle Part

The middle part of your narrative shares your story. Choose details carefully to *show* the reader what happened.

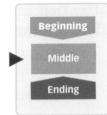

Beginning
Middle
Ending

- **Use sensory details** to help the reader share your experience.

- **Use dialogue** to reveal the personalities of the people in your story.

- **Share your feelings** so the reader will care about what happened to you.

Middle Paragraphs

Dialogue shows the speaker's personality.

My brother was upset because it was Halloween weekend, and he'd miss all the scary movies. I looked at Dad and said, "What about Sunday afternoon football?" Just then, the doorbell rang. It was the pizza guy delivering our supper. Instead of comparing who had the most pepperoni on a slice, we ate without saying much. Mom told us to finish up because it was getting dark outside. Who cared?

Transition words (blue) help connect the ideas.

After we ate, we grabbed our jackets and headed out to the backyard. Dad had built a roaring campfire. Then Mom brought out a dusty, old book. She began reading a scary ghost story out loud. I huddled closer to Dad and the fire. The fire crackled, and sparks shot up to the stars. Even when it got too cool to stay outside, I didn't want to go in.

Once we got back in the house, Dad said, "I have a surprise." Two huge pumpkins sat on newspapers on the kitchen table. We drew faces on them, pulled out all their gooey seeds, carved them, and lit them with candles. Meanwhile, Mom washed, salted, and roasted the pumpkin seeds. Then we ate them while we played a board game together.

Strong sensory details help the reader "see" and "feel" what happened.

Write freely, put your ideas on paper, and have fun!

Write your middle paragraphs. Before you begin, read through your memory chart, time list, and sensory chart from pages 93–95. Use your best details.

Writing **Ending Your Personal Narrative**

The last paragraph should bring your narrative to a close. Here are three possible ways to end your story.

Beginning
Middle
▶ Ending

■ **Tell how the experience made you feel.**

Going without television wasn't so bad after all.

■ **Explain how the experience changed you.**

Going without TV changed my family. Now we shut off the TV every Tuesday night.

■ **Share what you learned from the experience.**

I learned that it can really be fun to do things with my parents and my brother.

Ending Paragraph

The writer tells how the experience changed the whole family.	Going without TV changed my family. We had so much fun that whole weekend that we didn't even think about television. Now we shut off the TV every Tuesday night, and we have family time. Now we all can't wait for Tuesday night.

Write your ending. Try one of the three ways listed above to end your narrative. If you don't like how it sounds, try another of the ways or an idea of your own.

Revising

Revising your narrative is a very important step in the writing process. When you revise, you change and improve the ideas in your narrative.

Keys to Revising

1. **Read** your narrative to yourself.

2. **Read** your narrative to a classmate.

3. **Ask** your classmate to respond to your narrative.

4. **Mark** the parts that need to be changed.

5. **Revise** for the traits.

Revising for  Ideas

6 My details focus on one experience and make my narrative come alive.

5 My narrative tells about one experience. I use effective sensory details.

4 My narrative tells about one experience. More details would make it better.

When you revise for *ideas,* you make sure you have included important and interesting details that seem real. The rubric above will help you.

Does my narrative seem real?

Your narrative will seem real if your details help your reader clearly imagine the events in your story.

Practice

Read the following paragraph. Pay very close attention to the details (nouns). Then draw a picture showing as many of the details as you can. Trade drawings with a classmate and compare the details.

1   It rained and rained all night long. When I looked out my
2 bedroom window, I saw waves in the street. Parked cars looked
3 like boats along a dock. This would be a perfect day for an
4 adventure in our backyard. My brother and I put on our jackets
5 and boots. We saw that the sidewalk disappeared into the water
6 halfway to the garage. Then we hauled some boards from the pile
7 of lumber by the porch. We made a bridge to our climbing gym
8 that looked like a giant spider up to its knees in water.

Check your ideas. Read through your first draft or have a partner read it. Be sure your narrative includes enough interesting details to make your story seem real.

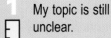
 3 | I need to focus on one experience. Some of my details don't relate to the topic.

 2 | I have more than one focus sometimes, and I need to add details about the topic.

1 | My topic is still unclear.

Have I included the important details?

If you have answered the 5 W's (*who, what, when, where,* and *why*), your narrative should have the important details it needs.

Practice

Read the paragraph below. Tell which of the 5 W's still need to be answered to make this paragraph clear.

1   I was in an important school event. When I went out there, I
2 looked straight ahead of me. I got scared. I was supposed to say
3 one sentence, but I couldn't. Someone whispered something to
4 me, and I knew what I had to do. I bravely stood up and said it.

 Review your details. Check to make sure you have included important details that answer the 5 W's.

Revising in Action

Below, the writer adds details to make the experience more real.

After we ate, we ⟨grabbed our jackets and⟩ headed out to the backyard. Dad had built a roaring campfire. Then Mom ⟨brought out a dusty old book.⟩ ~~came outside.~~ She began reading ⟨a scary ghost story⟩.

Revising for Organization

6 The way I order events makes my narrative enjoyable and easy to read.

5 My events are in time order. I have a strong beginning, middle, and ending.

4 My events are in time order. I have a beginning, a middle, and an ending.

When you revise for *organization,* you check that your narrative has a strong beginning, middle, and ending.

How do I know if my beginning works well?

Your beginning works well if it interests the reader and introduces the story. Have a partner read your beginning and answer these questions.

1. What grabs my interest?

2. What makes me want to keep reading?

3. What is this story about?

Review your beginning. Reread your beginning. Will it catch your reader's interest? If not, write a new beginning.

How do I check the middle?

The events in the middle of your story should be in time order.

Practice

Put these three sentences in time order.

1. We enjoyed lunch and rested our sore feet.
2. We hiked until noon.
3. We woke up, packed our backpacks, and hiked up the trail.

Check the middle part. Make sure the events of your story are organized in time order.

Some of my events are out of order. My beginning or ending is weak.

 I need to use time order. My beginning, middle, and ending all run together.

 My writing is confusing. I need to put my events in time order.

How do I know if my ending is strong?

You know your ending is strong if it . . .

- explains how you feel,
- tells how the experience changed you, or
- shares what you learned from the experience.

Check your ending. Did you end your narrative in one of the ways listed above? If not, try writing another ending.

Revising in Action

Below, the writer moves a sentence to put ideas in a clear order.

> Now we shut off the TV every Tuesday night, and we have family time. We had so much fun that whole weekend that we didn't even think about television.
>
> Going without TV changed my family. Now we all can't wait for Tuesday night.

Revising for Voice

6 My narrative voice and dialogue create an unforgettable memory for the reader.

5 I use a natural voice, and the dialogue works well.

4 My voice usually sounds natural, and I use some dialogue.

When you revise for *voice*, you want the reader to hear your excitement, your fear, your pain, your surprise. You want the reader to hear *you!* The rubric strip above can help you revise.

How can I improve my writer's voice?

You can improve your voice by saying things in a natural, real way. Writing in a natural voice will make your narratives fun to read.

Practice

Decide which of the first two passages sounds natural—almost like one of your classmates talking. Then rewrite the third passage so it sounds more like the real you.

1. The appearance of swans signals the arrival of spring. They are impossible to miss because of their large size and pure white color.

2. Spring must be here because I saw a flock of swans. They're so big and graceful and white. What a sight!

3. Coach Brown requires us to start practice promptly at 3:10. We begin practice with warm-up exercises. We run in place for a long period of time. Then we complete a series of challenging sit-ups and push-ups.

Revise your voice. Rewrite any sentences that don't sound natural—like the real you.

3 Sometimes my voice can be heard. I need to use more dialogue to tell my story.

2 My narrative voice needs to be heard. I need to use some dialogue.

1 My voice shows that I am not interested in my narrative.

Does the dialogue sound natural?

You can check your dialogue by making sure it matches each person's personality. Often, adults speak in a formal way. Others, such as your friends, speak in a casual way.

Practice

Tell if each sentence below has a *formal* or a *casual* voice.

1. Please read pages 2–9.
2. We'll miss the bus for sure.
3. He was totally awesome!
4. Your report is excellent.

Revise | **Check your dialogue.** Make sure the dialogue in your narrative matches each speaker's personality.

Revising in Action

In the sample paragraph below, the writer adds specific details and dialogue.

My brother was upset because ∧it was Halloween weekend and he'd miss all the ∧scary movies. I looked at Dad and ~~asked~~ said "What ∧about Sunday afternoon football∧?"

Revising for Word Choice

6 My original word choice creates a true-to-life picture for the reader.

5 I create a clear picture by using active verbs and words with the right feeling.

4 Most of my verbs are active, and most of my words have the feeling I want to express.

When you revise for *word choice,* check to see if you've used active verbs and words with the right feeling (connotation). The rubric strip above can guide you.

Have I used active verbs?

You have used an **active verb** if the subject of the sentence is doing the action:

Active Verb: The dog ate the hamburger.

You have used a **passive verb** if the subject is receiving the action:

Passive Verb: The hamburger was eaten by the dog.

The best way to replace a passive verb is to change the sentence so that the new subject is doing the action. Look at the verb and ask, "Who or what is doing the action?"

Practice

Rewrite each sentence, changing the passive verbs to active verbs.

■ I *was scared* by a cat's cry.
A cat's cry scared me.

1. The race *was won* by Mia.

2. The tree *was struck* by lightning.

Revise **Check your verbs.** Underline the verbs in your narrative. The subject should be doing the action in most of the sentences.

| 3 | I need to use more active verbs and words with the right feeling. | 2 | I need to replace many passive verbs with active verbs. | 1 | I am unsure about how to use words. |

Do my words have the right feeling (connotation)?

You can tell if your words have the right feeling by reading your narrative aloud. It should sound like you are experiencing the event again.

Practice

Read the following sentences. Then choose the word in parentheses that would give this mystery story the right feeling.

1. I *(went / crept)* toward the creepy, dark barn.
2. I carefully opened the *(squeaky / big)* wooden door.
3. Then I saw a pair of *(pretty / glaring)* eyes.

Revise

Check your words. How do you want the reader to feel? Use words that will make that feeling strong.

Revising in Action

In the sample below, the writer makes a passive verb active and adds words that give the right feeling.

> Mom told us
> ~~We were told by Mom~~ to finish up because it
>   Who cared?
> was getting dark outside.∧

Revising for Sentence Fluency

6 My sentences are skillfully written and keep the reader's interest from start to finish.

5 I use a variety of sentence lengths, and I vary my sentence beginnings.

4 I include a variety of sentence lengths, but I need to vary my sentence beginnings.

When you revise for *sentence fluency*, make sure you have varied your sentence beginnings and lengths. The rubric strip will guide you.

How can I vary my sentence beginnings?

You can vary your sentence beginnings by starting with an introductory word or phrase instead of the subject.

1. **Use an introductory word.**

First, Julius led us to the dinosaur exhibit.

Suddenly, we stood in front of a huge torosaurus skeleton.

2. **Begin with an introductory phrase.**

A little later, we entered an eerie cave.

Around another corner, a gigantic T. rex was fighting a triceratops!

Practice

Add an introductory word or phrase to each sentence below.

1. I nearly jumped out of my skin.
2. The dinosaurs looked real.
3. I felt as if I were back in the Cretaceous period.
4. Julius told us it was time to move on.
5. We backed away from the terrible T. rex.

Revise

Check your sentence beginnings. Make sure you have started some sentences with introductory words or phrases.

3 A few of my sentences need to be varied in length and in the way they begin.

2 I need to use different kinds of sentences and vary their beginnings.

1 Most of my sentences start the same way. I need to vary their beginnings.

How can I vary my sentence lengths?

You can vary your sentence lengths by expanding short, choppy sentences. Add details that answer *who, what, when, where,* or *why.* (See pages 445-448 for more information.)

SHORT SENTENCE

Julius took us.

EXPANDED SENTENCE

<u>Last Saturday,</u> Julius took us <u>to the public museum</u>
    When?   *Where?*

<u>to see the new dinosaur exhibit.</u>
              Why?

 Revise

Expand short, choppy sentences. Expand your short, choppy sentences by adding details that tell *who, what, when, where,* or *why*.

Revising in Action

In the example below, the writer varies a sentence beginning with an introductory phrase and expands another sentence.

On the way to the house,
∧Dad said, "I have a surprise." Two huge pumpkins
   on newspapers on the kitchen table.
sat/~~there~~ We drew faces on them, pulled out all . . .

Revising Using a Checklist

Check your revising. Number your paper from 1 to 10. Read each question and put a check mark after the number if the answer to a question is "yes." Otherwise, continue to work with that part of your essay.

Ideas

_____ **1.** Do I tell about one unforgettable experience?

_____ **2.** Do I include sensory details?

Organization

_____ **3.** Do my beginning, middle, and ending work well?

_____ **4.** Have I reordered parts that were out of place?

Voice

_____ **5.** Does my voice sound natural?

_____ **6.** Does the dialogue fit the speakers' personalities?

Word Choice

_____ **7.** Have I used active verbs?

_____ **8.** Have I used words with the right feeling?

Sentence Fluency

_____ **9.** Have I varied my sentence beginnings?

_____ **10.** Have I varied the lengths of my sentences?

Make a clean copy. After revising your narrative, make a clean copy for editing.

Editing

Editing is the next step in the writing process. When you edit, you make sure that you have followed the rules for capitalization, punctuation, spelling, and grammar. These rules are called the "conventions" of writing.

Keys to Editing

1. **Use** a dictionary, a thesaurus, and the "Proofreader's Guide" in the back of this book for help.

2. **Edit** on a printed copy if you use a computer. Then make your changes on the computer.

3. **Use** the editing marks shown inside the back cover of this book.

4. **Ask** someone else to check your writing for errors, too.

Editing for Conventions

6 I accurately use conventions, which makes my writing clear and trustworthy.

5 I have a few minor errors in punctuation, capitalization, spelling, or grammar.

4 I need to correct some errors in punctuation, capitalization, spelling, or grammar.

When you edit for *conventions,* you check your writing for errors. The rubric above will help you edit your work.

Are all my subject pronouns clear?

Your subject pronouns are clear when the reader understands which word or words each pronoun replaces. You often find an unclear subject pronoun in a sentence when the pronoun's antecedent is in a previous sentence. (See pages 412–415.)

> Mary and Eva **sprinted to the soccer field.** She **tripped and fell.** She **skinned her knee.** (It is not clear who fell.)

> Mary and Eva **sprinted to the soccer field.** Mary **tripped and fell.** She **skinned her knee.**

Practice

Rewrite each sentence, making any unclear subject pronouns clear.

1. Sam started the lawn tractor near the truck. It had just returned from the shop. It ran smoothly.

2. Mara pulled a banana out of her lunch bag. It felt mushy.

Edit

Check your use of pronouns. Read the examples above to make sure that you used pronouns correctly in your story. If you need more help, see pages 412–415.

3 Some errors may distract the reader. I need to punctuate my dialogue correctly.

2 Many errors make my narrative and dialogue hard to read. I need to correct them.

1 I need to correct numerous errors in my writing.

Have I used verb tenses correctly?

You have used verb tenses correctly if you have stated an action that . . .

- is happening now (or regularly) in **present tense**.

    I walk **to school. We** play **soccer every day.**

- already happened in the **past tense**.

    Shondra performed **in the show. She** sang **well.**

- will take place in the **future tense**.

    I will study **Spanish. We** will buy **a piñata for my birthday party.**

Edit verb tenses. Make sure you have used verb tenses correctly in your narrative. For help, see pages 418 and 584.

Editing in Action

Below, the writer corrects both a subject-pronoun problem and an incorrect verb tense.

My parents ~~decide~~ decided we all watch too much television. So ~~you~~ they made a rule that no one would watch TV for one whole weekend. "What?" I said.

Editing **Using a Checklist**

Edit

Check your editing. On a piece of paper, write the numbers 1 to 10. If you can answer "yes" to a question, put a check mark after that number. If not, continue to edit your writing for that convention.

Conventions

PUNCTUATION

_____ **1.** Do I use end punctuation after all my sentences?

_____ **2.** Do I punctuate my dialogue correctly?

CAPITALIZATION

_____ **3.** Do I start all my sentences with capital letters?

_____ **4.** Do I capitalize all proper nouns?

SPELLING

_____ **5.** Have I spelled all my words correctly?

_____ **6.** Have I double-checked the words my spell-checker may have missed?

GRAMMAR

_____ **7.** Do my subjects and verbs agree in number?
(She and I _were_ going, not She and I _was_ going.)

_____ **8.** Do all my subject pronouns have clear antecedents?

_____ **9.** Do I state all actions in the correct tense?

_____ **10.** Do I use the right words (_their, there,_ and _they're_)?

Adding a Title

- Use strong, colorful words: **A Scary Weekend Without TV**
- Give the words rhythm: **My Shocking Surprise**
- Be imaginative: **I Survived Being Unplugged**

Publishing

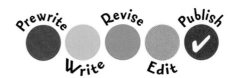

Prewrite · Write · Revise · Edit · Publish ✓

When you're done editing your story, make a neat final copy to share. You may also decide to share your story as a picture book, as a Web page, or in your classroom library. (See the suggestions below.)

Presentation

- Use blue or black ink and write neatly.
- Write your name in the upper left corner of page 1.
- Skip a line and center your title; skip another line and start writing.
- Indent every paragraph and leave a one-inch margin on all sides.
- Write your last name and the page number in the upper right corner of every page after the first one.

Make a Picture Book

Illustrate your story and make it into a book. Share your book with younger children, especially your younger brothers and sisters.

Upload It

If your class has a Web page, you can publish your narrative there.

Add It to a Classroom Collection

Create a cover for your narrative and add it to the class library or writing corner for your classmates to enjoy.

Publish

Make a final copy. Follow your teacher's instructions or use the guidelines above. (If you are using a computer, see pages 43–46.) Write a clean final copy of your essay.

Rubric for Narrative Writing

Use this rubric for guiding and rating your narrative writing.

Ideas

6 Rich ideas and details about an experience create a powerful narrative.

5 Many details are used in the narrative, focused on one experience.

4 The writer tells about one experience. More details are needed.

Organization

6 The order of the writing makes the narrative very easy to read.

5 Details are in order, and transitions are used well throughout.

4 The beginning, middle, and ending are clear. Some transitions are used.

Voice

6 A powerful voice and dialogue create an unforgettable narrative.

5 A strong storytelling voice creates a solid narrative. Dialogue is used.

4 A natural voice creates interest in the story. Some dialogue is used.

Word Choice

6 The exceptional word choice creates a vivid picture.

5 Strong nouns and verbs create a clear picture.

4 Some strong nouns and verbs add to the narrative.

Sentence Fluency

6 The sentences are skillfully written and make the narrative enjoyable to read.

5 The sentences show a variety of lengths and beginnings.

4 Most sentences are varied.

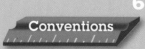

Conventions

6 Accurate use of conventions adds clarity to the writing.

5 The writer shows reasonable control over the conventions.

4 Some errors in spelling, punctuation, or grammar exist.

3 The writer needs to focus on one experience. Some details do not relate to the story.

2 The writer needs to focus on one experience. Details are needed.

1 The writer needs to tell about an experience and use details.

3 Most details are in order. Transitions are needed.

2 The beginning, middle, or ending parts need to be clearer.

1 The narrative needs to be organized.

3 Sometimes a voice can be heard. More dialogue is needed.

2 The voice needs to be stronger. Dialogue is missing.

1 The writer's voice does not come through.

3 Strong nouns and verbs are needed to create a clear picture.

2 Fewer general and overused words would improve the narrative.

1 Some words are confusing or incorrect.

3 A better variety of sentence lengths and beginnings is needed.

2 Many sentences are the same length or begin the same way.

1 Too many sentences sound the same.

3 A number of errors could confuse the reader.

2 Many errors make the narrative hard to read.

1 Help is needed to make corrections.

Evaluating a Narrative

As you read Jonathan's narrative on this page, focus on its strengths and weaknesses. (The essay contains some errors.) Then read the student self-evaluation on page 123.

Out of Gas

One night, Gramps and I were driving in the country when his car died. Chug-a-chug, sput, sput, stop. We were out of gas!

At first, I wasn't worried. We would just use a cell phone to get help. Then I remembered that Gramps doesn't like cell phones. We were stuck without a phone!

"Let's walk, Jonathan," Gramps said. It was a dark, lonely night. I could hardly see two feet in front of me. A tiny beam from gramps flash light hardly cut through the blackness. I held onto Grandpa's jacket. Shinny, little eyes peeked out at me from the woods. I heard strange noises. A small animal wadled across the road in front of me. I didn't like this at all.

We walked forever before we saw a farm house with its lights on. It was the house of some of Gramps friends. We went to the door, and they let us in. Lucky gramps has lived around here forever! The farmer filled a red can with gas, and he drove us back to our car. Soon, we were safe and headed back to the city.

I made Gramps promise to get a cell phone. Walking on that dark road was the scariest thing I have ever done. It's a good thing Gramps had friends nearby. Otherwise, we might have had to walk all night.

Student Self-Assessment

Jonathan used the rubric and number scale on pages 120–121. He made two comments under each trait. First, he wrote something he did well. Then he wrote about something he could have done better.

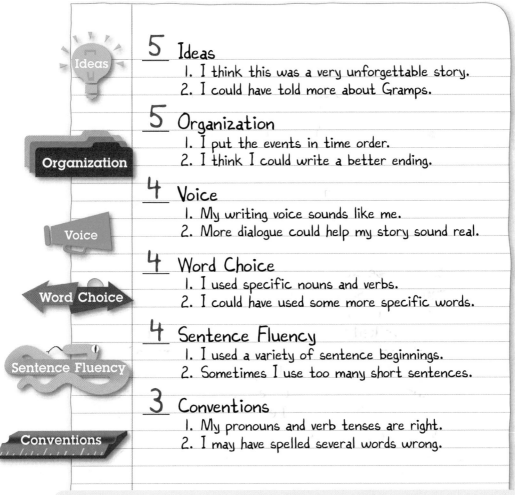

5 Ideas
  1. I think this was a very unforgettable story.
  2. I could have told more about Gramps.

5 Organization
  1. I put the events in time order.
  2. I think I could write a better ending.

4 Voice
  1. My writing voice sounds like me.
  2. More dialogue could help my story sound real.

4 Word Choice
  1. I used specific nouns and verbs.
  2. I could have used some more specific words.

4 Sentence Fluency
  1. I used a variety of sentence beginnings.
  2. Sometimes I use too many short sentences.

3 Conventions
  1. My pronouns and verb tenses are right.
  2. I may have spelled several words wrong.

Use the rubric. Assess your narrative using the rubric on pages 120–121. On your own paper, list the six traits. Write one strength and one weakness for each trait. Number each trait from 1 to 6 to show how well you used it.

Reflecting on Your Writing

You've put a lot of time and effort into writing an interesting and entertaining personal narrative. Now take some time to think about your writing. On your own paper, finish each sentence starter below.

When you think about your writing, you will see how you are growing as a writer.

My Narrative Essay

1. The best part of my narrative is . . .

2. The part that still needs work is . . .

3. The main thing I learned about writing a personal narrative is . . .

4. In my next narrative, I would like to . . .

Narrative Writing
Across the Curriculum

Narrative writing is useful in many classes. In math, you may have to write a story problem about dividing up a pizza. In science, you may be assigned an observation report about hatching chicks. You can also write an e-mail message to a friend about something interesting that happened to you.

In this section, you'll practice narrative writing and also learn how to respond to a narrative prompt on a writing test.

Mini Index

- **Math:** Creating a Story Problem
- **Science:** Writing an Observation Report
- **Practical Writing:** Writing to an E-Pal
- **Assessment:** Writing for Assessment

Math: Creating a Story Problem

In one math class, students wrote story problems based on nutrition labels. Amelia developed her problem based on an orange-drink label.

Liquid Vitamins

BEGINNING

The problem is presented.

Problem: If 1 cup of orange drink has 20% of the daily value of vitamin C a person needs, how many cups of orange drink must a person drink to get 100% of the daily value of vitamin C?

Orange Drink

Nutrition Facts

Serving Size **1 cup**

Amount Per Serving

Calories 116   Calories from fat 0

	% Daily Value*
Total Fat 0 g	**0%**
Sodium 10 mg	**0%**
Potassium 230 mg	**7%**
Total Carb. 25 g	**8%**
Sugars 22g	
Protein 0g	

Vitamin C 20%   •   Iron 2%

Not a significant source of saturated fat, cholesterol, dietary fiber, vitamin A, and calcium.

* Percent Daily Values are based on a 2,000 calorie diet.

MIDDLE

The operation is shown.

Operation: Divide 100% of vitamin C by 20% (the amount in 1 cup).
$100 \div 20 = 5$ cups

ENDING

The solution is given.

Solution: A person would have to drink 5 cups of orange drink each day to get 100% of the daily value of vitamin C.

Prewriting Selecting a Topic

To select a topic for her story problem, Amelia made a "favorite foods" list like the one below.

Ideas List

Favorite Foods

-macaroni and cheese   -eggs
-green beans   -milk *

List favorite foods. Make a list of foods you enjoy that come in a package that shows nutritional information. Put a star (*) beside the food you choose to write about.

Finding Facts on the Food Label

Next, you'll need to study the facts on the label of your favorite food.

2% Milk

Fact Sheet

Food: 2% milk
Serving Size: 1 cup
Nutrient: Calcium
Percentage (or amount): 30%

Nutrition Facts

Serving Size **1 cup** (236ml)
Servings Per Container 1

Amount Per Serving		
Calories 120	Calories from fat 45	
		% Daily Value*
Total Fat 5 g		
Saturated Fat 3g		
Trans fat 0g		
Cholesterol 20 mg		7%
Sodium 120 mg		5%
Total Carbohydrate 11 g		4%
Dietary Fiber 0g		
Sugars 11g		
Protein 9g		
Vitamin A 10%	•	Vitamin C 4%
Calcium 30%	•	Vitamin D 25%

* Percent Daily Values are based on a 2,000 calorie diet. Your daily values may be higher or lower depending on your calorie needs.

Create a fact sheet. List the facts you want to use in your story problem. Include the food, the serving size, one nutrient, and its percentage.

Writing **Creating Your Story Problem**

Your fact sheet will help you to write your story problem. Also use the tips below.

■ **State the Problem**

First, set up the problem by asking a question. Begin with an "if-how" statement.

- **Write *if*** and include the information from your fact sheet:

  If 1 cup of reduced-fat milk has 30% of the calcium a person needs each day, . . .

- **Write *how*** and end with the question you want to ask:

  How much calcium will a person get from 4 cups of milk?

■ **Show the Operation**

Next, write the operation. **Begin with the operation word** *add, subtract, multiply,* or *divide.*

- Then finish writing the problem.

  Multiply the 30% of the daily value of calcium found in 1 cup of milk by 4 cups.

- Write the math problem as an equation.

  30 X 4 = 120

■ **Write the Solution**

Write your solution in a complete sentence.

  A person will get 120% of the daily value of calcium each day by drinking 4 cups of milk.

Create your story problem. Use the directions and examples above to create your own nutritional story problem.

Revising **Improving Your Writing**

After you've written the first draft of your story problem, you'll need to revise it. The following questions can help you revise.

- **Ideas** Do I include the information I need from my fact sheet?

- **Organization** Do I present a problem, an operation, and a solution? Are the facts and the answer correct?

- **Voice** Do I state everything clearly?

- **Word Choice** Do I include specific words such as *percent, milligram,* or *cup?*

- **Sentence Fluency** Do I use complete sentences for each part of my story problem?

Improve your writing. Use the questions above to review your story problem. Also ask a classmate to look over your problem and solve it. Then make any needed changes in your writing.

Editing **Checking for Conventions**

When you have finished revising, it's time to edit for conventions. The following questions can help you.

- **Conventions** Have I checked for errors in punctuation, capitalization, spelling, and grammar? Have I checked all the numbers in my story problem?

Check your work. Write a neat final copy and proofread it before you hand it in.

Science: Writing an Observation Report

When you write a science-class observation report, you will use narrative writing to tell what happened. Justin wrote a report about baby chicks hatching in his classroom.

The beginning introduces the project.

The middle gives dates and records what happened.

The ending summarizes what was learned.

Nov. 5

Baby Chicks Break Out

PURPOSE:
    Ms. Webber brought an egg incubator to class. She carefully put three chicken eggs inside it. Ms. Webber says the eggs are 20 days old. Eggs usually hatch after 30 days. Our class is going to observe how chicks hatch.

OBSERVATIONS:
    <u>November 15</u>
    9:30 The chicks have started hatching! I see a few tiny cracks in the eggshells.
    11:23 The eggshells are covered with cracks. Bits of shell are starting to break off. I can see the beaks of two chicks breaking out.
    2:30 All three chicks are climbing out of their shells. They look slimy. The chicks are weak and clumsy.
    <u>November 16</u>
    9:30 The chicks' feathers have dried. They are balls of fluffy yellow. Now they can walk without wobbling.
    10:25 The chicks are eating food and drinking water on their own.

CONCLUSIONS: I learned chicks have to work hard to break out of their shells. I also learned that at first they are slimy and ugly. Most important, I learned that after chicks hatch, it doesn't take long for them to be ready to live on their own.

WRITING TIPS

Before you write . . .

- **Make careful observations.**
  Pay attention to any changes that take place.
- **Take notes.**
  Write down dates and times of each observation.
  Use specific words to describe shape, size, color,
  texture, movement, and behavior.

During your writing . . .

- **Write the purpose.**
  In the opening paragraph, tell the reason for the
  observation report. Include details by answering
  the 5 W questions.
- **Record your observations.**
  Include the dates and times of important events.
  List details in the order they happened.
- **Write your conclusions.**
  Tell what you have learned.

After you've written a first draft . . .

- **Revise your writing.**
  Make sure the events are in correct
  time order.
- **Edit for conventions.**
  Correct any errors in punctuation,
  capitalization, spelling, and
  grammar.

Write an observation report. Choose a topic you are presently studying in science class.

Practical Writing: Writing to an E-Pal

E-mail connects friends across town or across the world. In this e-mail message, Sal shares a fishing story with his e-pal.

The **subject heading** lists the subject of the message.

The **beginning** tells why the person is writing.

The **middle** tells what happened.

The **ending** closes politely.

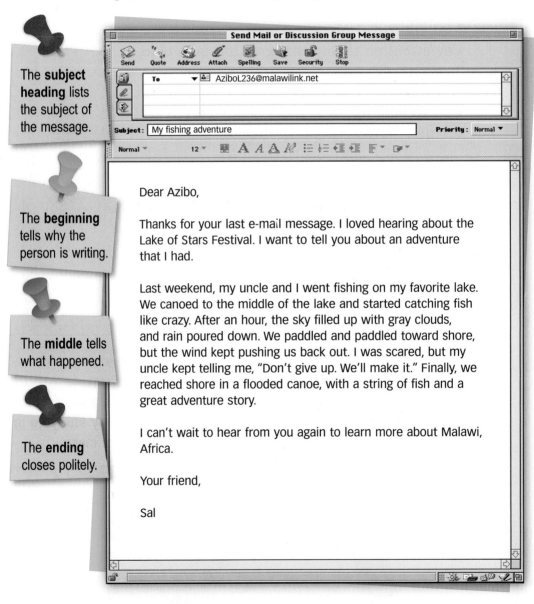

Send Mail or Discussion Group Message

To AziboL236@malawilink.net

Subject: My fishing adventure   Priority: Normal

Dear Azibo,

Thanks for your last e-mail message. I loved hearing about the Lake of Stars Festival. I want to tell you about an adventure that I had.

Last weekend, my uncle and I went fishing on my favorite lake. We canoed to the middle of the lake and started catching fish like crazy. After an hour, the sky filled up with gray clouds, and rain poured down. We paddled and paddled toward shore, but the wind kept pushing us back out. I was scared, but my uncle kept telling me, "Don't give up. We'll make it." Finally, we reached shore in a flooded canoe, with a string of fish and a great adventure story.

I can't wait to hear from you again to learn more about Malawi, Africa.

Your friend,

Sal

WRITING TIPS

Before you write . . .

- **Choose a topic.**
  Select an interesting event that you would like to share.
- **Remember details.**
  Jot down some notes about what you saw, heard, smelled, tasted, and felt.

During your writing . . .

- **Fill in the heading.**
  Double-check the address and write a clear subject line.
- **Connect with your e-pal.**
  Comment on your e-pal's last message before telling your news.
- **Focus on the details.**
  Share interesting details about the event.
  Use words that your reader will understand.
- **Use a friendly voice.**
  Write as if you were talking to your e-pal.

After you've written a first draft . . .

- **Edit for correctness.**
  Read your whole message to catch any errors before hitting *Send*.

Write an e-mail to a friend. Tell him or her about an exciting experience you recently had.

Writing for Assessment

Some writing tests include a narrative prompt that asks you to tell a story about a personal experience.

Narrative Prompt

Every person has been brave at one time or another. Write a narrative essay that tells about a time when you were brave. Tell what you learned from the experience.

Transition Time Line

First   arrived at new school
↓
Then   went to recess
↓
Next   played kickball
↓
After   made a new friend

The beginning gives the focus of the response (underlined) and uses a key word from the prompt.

     My first day of third grade was the scariest day of my life. I was starting at a new school. Mom said, "Just be yourself, and you'll be fine." I didn't feel fine. <u>The only way I would survive this day was to be brave.</u>

     I was most afraid about making new friends. I walked to my classroom without talking to anybody. Then the teacher made me stand up in front of the class while she introduced me. I'm sure I was so red I looked like I had a sunburn. During reading class, I stared at my book. I wouldn't look at anybody.

The middle paragraphs tell about the experience.

     I was nervous when the bell rang for recess. At first, I just watched the other kids play tag, jump rope, and kickball. Then I took a deep breath and walked toward the kickball game.

"Can I play?" I asked a tall boy with red hair.

"Sure, you can go next," he said. "My name is Jeff. What's yours?"

"Anna," I said.

Jeff kicked and got to first base. Then it was my turn. I was shaking! The ball bounced and rolled toward me, and I ran up and blasted it with my foot. The ball sailed over everybody, and Jeff and I ran for home plate. We both scored!

I learned something on my first day at my new school. The biggest thing was that I could be brave and just be myself. After that day, I made lots of new friends.

> The **middle** part is organized by time.

> The **ending** tells what the writer learned.

Respond to the reading. Answer the following questions to see how the traits were used in Anna's response.

- **Ideas** (1) What is the topic of the response? (2) What key words in the prompt are used in the essay?

- **Organization** (3) How does Anna organize the events of her narrative?

- **Voice & Word Choice** (4) What words and phrases show Anna's feelings?

WRITING TIPS

Before you write . . .

- **Understand the prompt.**
  Make sure you understand what
  you are being asked to write.
- **Plan your narrative.**
  Jot down a time line of events.

Time Line

Event
First–
Then–
Next–
Finally–

During your writing . . .

- **Decide on a focus.**
  Use key words from the prompt
  in your focus statement.
- **Choose carefully.**
  Make sure your details keep your story going.
- **End in a meaningful way.**
  Connect the experience to the prompt or tell
  why it was important.

After you've written a first draft . . .

- **Check the prompt and your narrative.**
  Make sure you have done what the prompt asks.
- **Check for conventions.**
  Correct any errors you find.

Narrative Prompts

- Who is the most unforgettable person you have ever met? Show
  what this person did to make him or her so unforgettable.
- Write a letter to a friend and tell about a memorable experience
  during your first day of the school year.

Plan and write a response. Respond to one of the narrative
prompts above within the amount of time your teacher gives you.

Narrative Writing in Review

In narrative writing, you tell a story about something that has happened. You may write about your own personal experiences.

Select a topic from your life experiences. (See page 92.)

Gather important details. Use a graphic organizer to list details for your narrative. (See pages 93–95.)

In the beginning, introduce your story and grab the reader's attention. (See page 99.)

In the middle, tell the events of your story in time order. Use your own words and show your feelings. Use sensory details and dialogue. (See pages 100–101.)

In the ending, tell why the experience was important and what you learned from it. (See page 102.)

First, review your ideas, organization, and **voice**. Then check for **word choice** and **sentence fluency**. (See pages 104–114.)

Check for conventions. Look for punctuation, capitalization, spelling, and grammar mistakes. Also ask a friend to edit your writing. (See pages 116–118.)

Make a final copy and proofread it before sharing it with other people. (See page 119.)

Use the narrative rubric to assess your finished narrative. (See pages 120–121.)

Expository Writing

Expository Writing

Expository Paragraph

What do you enjoy doing? Some people may love to paint pictures. Other people may love to watch birds or build forts. People enjoy different activities. If you write to explain how to do something or to share information about an activity, that's expository writing.

In this chapter, you will have a chance to write an expository paragraph. You'll tell about a favorite activity and explain why you enjoy it. The next best thing to doing your favorite activity is writing about it!

Writing Guidelines

Subject: A favorite activity
Form: Expository paragraph
Purpose: To explain
Audience: Classmates

Expository Paragraph

An expository paragraph starts with a **topic sentence**, which tells what the topic is. The sentences in the **body** support the topic sentence, and the **closing sentence** completes the explanation. In the following paragraph, Rosa tells about her favorite activity.

Topic sentence

Body sentences

Closing sentence

Drawing

Drawing sets my imagination in motion. Sometimes I draw things from my dreams, like a picture of me flying with an eagle. Other times, I imagine grown-ups as kids. It's fun to draw my teacher or my coach as a little kid. My favorite drawings are places I'd like to see someday. I drew Paris with the Eiffel Tower and Notre Dame Cathedral. Maybe someday I'll draw Paris from the top of the Eiffel Tower. For me to be happy, all I need is a pencil, some paper, and my never-ending imagination.

Respond to the reading. On your own paper, answer each of the following questions.

- **Ideas** (1) Why does Rosa like drawing? Find three details that help explain her topic sentence.

- **Organization** (2) Does Rosa start with her strongest detail or lead up to it near the end?

- **Voice & Word Choice** (3) Find the following words in Rosa's essay: *favorite, imagination, dreams, fun, happy.* How do these words make Rosa's voice sound?

Prewriting Selecting a Topic

You can find a topic by completing some sentence starters. Here are Rosa's completed sentences.

Sentence Starters

When I'm inside, I enjoy . . . playing the piano.
When I'm outside, I enjoy . . . hiking in the woods.
When I'm alone, I enjoy . . . drawing in my sketchbook.*
When I'm with friends, I enjoy . . . going to the skate park.

Complete sentences. On your own paper, write the underlined sentence starters above. Complete each one. Put a star (✳) next to the activity you want to write about.

Gathering Details

Rosa wrote a topic sentence that tells why she enjoys drawing. To gather specific details, she completed three *because* statements.

"Because" Completions

Drawing sets my imagination in motion.
because . . . I draw things from my dreams.
because . . . I imagine how grown-ups looked as kids.
because . . . I draw pictures of places I'd like to see.

Do some "because" completions. Write your topic sentence that tells why you enjoy your activity. Under it, write *because* three times. Write three completions.

Writing Creating Your First Draft

The first draft of your paragraph should start with a **topic sentence** that tells what you especially like about your activity. The **body sentences** will include supporting details and examples. Finally, a **closing sentence** will complete your explanation.

Write your first draft. Begin with a topic sentence, include supporting ideas, and end with a thoughtful closing sentence.

Revising Improving Your Paragraph

To decide what to change in your paragraph, check for *ideas, organization, voice, word choice,* and *sentence fluency.*

Revise your paragraph. Use these questions as a guide.

1 Does my topic sentence name a favorite activity and what I like about it?

2 Do the body sentences include details and examples?

3 Does my writing voice show I'm interested in my topic?

4 Do specific words make my topic clear?

5 Do I use complete sentences?

Editing Checking for Conventions

To edit your paragraph, you correct any errors in *conventions.*

Edit your work. Ask yourself the questions below.

1 Does each sentence begin with a capital letter and end with punctuation?

2 Have I checked my spelling?

3 Have I used words correctly *(to, too, two)*?

Expository Writing

Explaining a Career

What do you want to be when you grow up? You've probably heard that question hundreds of times, and you may hear it hundreds more!

In this chapter, you'll write an expository essay that explains the work you want to do when you grow up. Dream big—you might be a jet pilot, a computer-game designer, or even president of the United States!

Writing Guidelines

Subject: A future career
Form: Expository essay
Purpose: To explain
Audience: Classmates

Understanding Your Goal

Your goal in this chapter is to write an expository essay that explains a job you would enjoy doing as a grown-up. The traits listed in the chart below will help you reach your goal.

Your goal is to . . .

Ideas　Select an interesting career (job), write a clear focus statement, and give explanations and examples.

Organization　Begin by grabbing the reader's attention. In the middle, explain the career with details. Write a thoughtful ending.

Voice　Use a writing voice that is knowledgeable and shows your interest in the topic.

Word Choice　Choose words that make every part of your explanation clear.

Sentence Fluency　Write clear, complete sentences, including some compound and complex sentences.

Conventions　Create an essay that has correct punctuation, capitalization, spelling, and grammar.

Get the big picture. Review the rubric on pages 176–177. This rubric can help you measure your progress as you write.

Expository Essay

In the following expository essay, David explains why carpentry is the right job for him.

My Own Two Hands

    My dad is a carpenter, and I want to be one, too. I grew up around hammers and saws. When I was five, Dad and I built a doghouse. <u>Someday, I'll be a carpenter and make things with my own two hands.</u>

    Carpenters build all kinds of things with wood. Carpenters like my dad mostly frame houses, hang drywall, and nail moldings. That's the kind of carpenter I want to be! Other carpenters build furniture. My dad does that, too. He even made my bunk bed.

    I believe that I would be a good carpenter. The most important thing a carpenter needs is experience. I'm

MIDDLE
The second middle paragraph explains why the writer would do the job well.

already an apprentice carpenter since I help Dad with all of his home projects. We built a new closet in my sister's bedroom. Carpenters also need to be strong. I can already pound in a big tenpenny nail in four hits. Finally, carpenters need to love their work. Dad says instead of iron in my blood, I must have sawdust!

ENDING
. . . .
The ending leaves the reader with a final thought.

    I want to make things with my hands. Carpenters can take a pile of boards and make something great. If somebody can dream it, my dad can build it. Someday, I want people to say the same thing about me.

Respond to the reading. On your own paper, answer the following questions about the sample essay.

- **Ideas** (1) What three details show that David would make a good carpenter?

- **Organization** (2) What transition words and phrases help connect the ideas?

- **Voice & Word Choice** (3) What does David mean about having "sawdust" in his blood?

Prewriting

Prewriting is the first step in the writing process. Prewriting helps you decide what to write about and prepares you to write your first draft.

Keys to Prewriting

1. **Select** a career (job) to explain.

2. **Gather** facts and details about the career.

3. **Find** special terms that describe the job.

4. **Write** a focus statement and topic sentences.

5. **Create** an organized list of your facts and details.

Prewriting Selecting a Topic

First, you need to choose a job or career that you would enjoy doing. Sumie made a list of jobs she would like to do.

Ideas List

<u>Jobs I Would Like</u>

sea captain	vet
forest ranger	farmer
firefighter	lion tamer
singer	dolphin trainer*

Create an ideas list. Write "Jobs I Would Like" at the top of a piece of paper. Then list jobs underneath. Put a star (*) next to the job you would like to write about.

Focus on the Traits

Ideas Your topic is the "big idea" of your writing. Choose your topic carefully. If it interests you, it will probably also interest your reader as well. Also, if you like your topic, you will enjoy gathering details about it.

Finding Details

Now it's time to gather details about the job you have chosen. Sumie used some questions to help her gather details. She checked articles in encyclopedias and on Web sites to find answers.

Questions and Answers

<u>What job would I like?</u> dolphin trainer

<u>Why am I interested in this job?</u> I would like to swim with and work with these amazing animals. I saw how much fun the trainer was having at a dolphin water show.

<u>What are three main duties for this job?</u>
1. A dolphin trainer feeds and cares for the dolphins.
2. The trainer must teach the dolphins tricks.
3. Trainers need to clean the dolphin tank.

<u>Why would I be good at this job?</u>
1. I love dolphins.
2. I am patient.
3. I work hard.

Prewrite

Gather details. Copy and answer each of the underlined questions above. Try to find at least three answers for each of the last two questions.

Prewriting Finding Special Words

In an expository essay, you can show your knowledge of a topic by using special words, or terms, that are related to it. You can find these terms in the articles you read.

Practice

Read the following article about dolphin trainers. Then write down at least three special terms that Sumie could use in her essay.

Trainers Teach Tricks for Health

Dolphin tricks aren't just showstoppers. Trainers teach some behaviors that help veterinarians keep the animals healthy. For example, dolphins need to learn to open their mouths for a dental checkup. They also must learn how to show their dorsal fin, flippers, and tail flukes for inspection. As with any animal, dolphins that are familiar with people are easier to check for injury or disease. This is important because by instinct dolphins hide any illness or disease so that they don't look like easy prey.

Prewrite

Find special words. Read about your topic and write down special terms that you could use in your essay.

Focus on the Traits

Voice When you use special terms, the reader feels confident that you know your subject well.

Writing a Focus Statement

Your focus statement should name the job you chose and tell why you are interested in it.

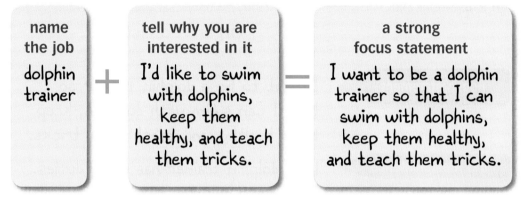

name the job		tell why you are interested in it		a strong focus statement
dolphin trainer	+	I'd like to swim with dolphins, keep them healthy, and teach them tricks.	=	I want to be a dolphin trainer so that I can swim with dolphins, keep them healthy, and teach them tricks.

Prewrite

Write your focus statement. Follow the formula above to write your own focus statement. You may need to try it a few times before you find the one that works for you.

Writing Topic Sentences

Your essay will have two middle paragraphs, and each will start with a topic sentence. Here are the topic sentences Sumie wrote.

Topic Sentence 1: Write a sentence about the main duties of the job.

A dolphin trainer has many duties.

Topic Sentence 2: Write a sentence about why you would be good at the job.

I have the right personality to be a dolphin trainer.

Prewrite

Write your topic sentences. Use Sumie's sentences as models for your own topic sentences.

Prewriting Organizing Your Ideas

Your focus statement, topic sentences, and details can be put into an organized list that will guide your writing.

Organized List

Focus statement

I want to be a dolphin trainer so that I can swim with dolphins, keep them healthy, and teach them tricks.

First topic sentence

1. A dolphin trainer has many duties.

Details
- keep dolphins healthy
- teach tricks
- clean the tanks

Second topic sentence

2. I have the right personality to be a dolphin trainer.

Details
- love dolphins
- patient
- work hard

Prewrite **Organize your essay.** Follow the model above to make your own organized list. (Refer to your work from pages 149–151.)

Focus on the Traits

Organization Your organized list shows you what you should include in each part of your essay.

Writing

Now that you've selected a career, gathered details, and made an organized list, you are ready to create a first draft. This is your chance to put all your ideas on paper or in a computer file.

Keys to Writing

1. **Write** a strong beginning paragraph that ends with your focus statement.

2. **Start** each middle paragraph with a topic sentence.

3. **Include** explanations and examples in your middle paragraphs to support each topic sentence.

4. **Write** a thoughtful ending paragraph.

Writing Getting the Big Picture

The chart below shows how the parts of an expository essay fit together. (The examples are from the sample essay on pages 155–158.) You are ready to write your essay when you have . . .

- gathered details and special terms,
- written your focus statement and topic sentences, and
- created an organized list.

Beginning

The **beginning** gets the reader's attention and gives the focus statement.

Focus Statement

I want to be a dolphin trainer so that I can swim with them, keep them healthy, and teach them tricks.

Middle

Each **middle** paragraph explains a different part of the focus.

Topic Sentences

- A dolphin trainer has many duties.
- I have the right personality to be a dolphin trainer.

Ending

The **ending** leaves the reader with a final thought.

Closing Sentence

Maybe, if I become a trainer, dolphins will dream about swimming with me.

Starting Your Essay

Your beginning paragraph should catch the reader's attention. Here are some ways to do that.

> **Beginning**
>
> Middle
>
> Ending

- **Start with an interesting fact.**
  Dolphins have bigger brains than humans do.

- **Ask a question.**
  Have you ever trained an animal?

- **Tell how you became interested in the job.**
  Last year, I saw a dolphin show on television.

Beginning Paragraph

Sumie used the third strategy to start her beginning paragraph.

> Last year, I saw a dolphin show on television. The dolphins jumped so high! It was exciting, and I learned a lot about dolphins. They are amazing animals. I want to be a dolphin trainer so that I can swim with them, keep them healthy, and teach them tricks.

The last sentence is the focus statement (underlined).

Write

Write your beginning paragraph. Try one of the ideas at the top of this page to get started. Then lead into your focus statement.

Writing Developing the Middle Part

Each middle paragraph in your essay begins with one of your topic sentences (page 151). The body sentences should contain supporting details and terms (pages 149–150).

Beginning
Middle
Ending

Using Transitions

Make sure to connect your ideas with transition words and phrases like those shown below. They make your ideas easy to follow.

The most important . . .	To start,	To begin with,
Secondly,	Also,	In addition,
The third thing . . .	Finally,	In conclusion,

Middle Paragraphs

Topic sentence 1

What are the three main duties?

Transitions are underlined.

A dolphin trainer has many duties. <u>The most important</u> duty is to take care of the dolphins. That means feeding them and making sure they don't get sick. <u>Secondly</u>, trainers teach dolphins tricks. Tricks are used in shows, but some tricks actually help veterinarians keep the dolphins healthy. Tricks also keep dolphins from being bored. <u>The third thing</u> trainers do is clean the tanks. It's hard work, but it's important!

Topic sentence 2

Why would you be good at this job?

Transitions are underlined.

I have the right personality to be a dolphin trainer. <u>To begin with,</u> I love dolphins. As a trainer, I could help other people love and protect dolphins. I am <u>also</u> patient. I have two little brothers, and I've helped them learn to swim and taught them how to do special dives and somersaults! <u>Finally,</u> I work hard and get along with others. Trainers have to work long days with each other and the public.

 Write

Write your middle paragraphs. Use your organized list from page 152. Include one topic sentence and its supporting details in each paragraph. Connect your ideas with transitions.

FIRST DRAFT TIPS

- Write freely to get your ideas on paper.
- Arrange details by order of importance.
  (Go from most important to least or least to most).

Writing **Ending Your Essay**

Your ending paragraph gives you one last chance to speak to the reader. Here are some ways to write a strong ending.

Beginning
Middle
▶ Ending

- **Connect the end to the beginning.**
  Someday people may see me on a dolphin TV show!

- **Give the reader a final thought.**
  If a dog is our best friend on land, a dolphin is our best friend in the sea.

- **Connect with the reader.**
  Everybody has a dream, and my dream is to swim with dolphins.

- **End with a surprise.**
  Maybe, if I become a trainer, dolphins will dream about swimming with me.

Ending Paragraph

The writer ends with a surprise.

Dolphins are our water friends. Training dolphins is an important job. It's one way to encourage people to enjoy and protect these amazing animals. At night, I even dream about swimming with dolphins. Maybe, if I become a trainer, dolphins will dream about swimming with me.

Write your ending. Use one of the four ways above to give your essay a strong ending.

Form a complete first draft. Write a complete copy of your essay on every other line to make room for your revising changes.

Revising

Once you have completed your first draft, you are ready to make changes to improve your writing. When you revise, you check your essay for *ideas, organization, voice, word choice,* and *sentence fluency.*

Keys to Revising

1. **Read** your essay out loud once to see how you feel about it.

2. **Review** each part: the beginning, the middle, and the ending.

3. **Ask** a classmate to read your first draft, too.

4. **Change** any parts that need to be improved.

Revising for Ideas

6 My topic, focus, explanations, and examples make my essay truly memorable.

5 My essay is informative with a clear focus. I include explanations and examples.

4 My essay has a clear focus. I need more explanations or examples.

When you revise for *ideas,* you make sure your paragraphs include explanations and examples. The rubric above can help you revise.

How can I use explanations in a paragraph?

You can use explanations to support your topic sentence, which focuses on the question for that paragraph. (See page 55.)

Middle Paragraph 1: What are three main duties for this job?

Middle Paragraph 2: Why would I be good at this job?

Practice

Read the following middle paragraph. Find three sentences that explain the topic sentence (in black). Find three sentences that do not do this.

Movie actors have three main duties. (1) Most importantly, actors have to learn their lines. (2) It's really hard work to be an actor. (3) Secondly, actors need to say their lines and move like their character would. (4) They get to wear different costumes as well. (5) Lastly, actors must listen to the director. (6) After shooting a movie, an actor can celebrate with a party.

Revise

Check your explanations. In each middle paragraph, make sure your sentences explain the topic sentence. Cross out any sentences that do not explain the topic sentence.

3 My focus needs to be clear, and I need more explanations and examples.

2 I need a focus and more details.

1 My topic is unclear.

How can I use examples to explain my topic?

You can use an example to give the reader a clearer picture. An example is something that has happened or could happen.

Topic Sentence: I could be a good movie actor.

Explanation: For one thing, I have a terrific memory.

Example 1: Some actors must memorize very long parts.

Example 2: I had the lead in our class play and remembered all of my lines!

Revise

Add examples. Read your essay and check your explanations. Try to add an example or two to make each explanation clearer.

Revising in Action

The writer adds an example to make the explanation clearer.

A dolphin trainer has many duties. The most
important duty is to take care of the dolphins. ʌ That means
feeding them and making sure they don't get sick.

Secondly, trainers teach dolphins tricks. . . .

Revising for  Organization

| 6 | My essay is clear and easy to read, with every part in just the right place. | 5 | I have a strong beginning, middle, and ending, and my explanations are in order. | 4 | My essay has a clear beginning, middle, and ending, but I need to reorder one explanation. |

When you revise for *organization,* you make sure each part of your essay is in the right spot and does its job. Make sure your explanations appear in the best order, too. The rubric strip above can help you revise your writing.

How can I check my organization?

You can check the overall organization of your essay by doing the following scavenger hunt.

Organization Scavenger Hunt

1. Place a ⅊ beside each paragraph indent.

2. If your focus statement is in your beginning paragraph, put a ✳ next to it.

3. If a middle paragraph starts with a topic sentence and has three more sentences with explanations or examples, put a ☺ next to it.

4. Add another ✳ if you have a strong ending paragraph.

Revise

Do the scavenger hunt. Mark your own essay or exchange papers with a partner. Then, add up how many marks you have made (⅊ , ✳ , ☺). You should have 8 points. If you don't, go back and make changes until you do.

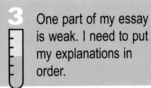

3 One part of my essay is weak. I need to put my explanations in order.

2 I need to put my beginning, middle, and ending into paragraphs.

1 I need to completely reorganize my essay.

How should I organize my explanations?

You should organize your explanations by putting your most important explanation first (or last).

Practice

Which explanation below is most important for the topic sentence "I want to work on fishing boats? Tell why.

1. I love riding in boats.   **3.** I want to travel around the world.
2. Waves don't bother me.   **4.** I have always liked fishing.

Revise

Check the organization of your explanations. Make sure you have put your strongest explanation first (or last).

Revising in Action

The writer moves an explanation to a better place.

> To begin with, I am ∧also patient. I have two little
> brothers, and I've helped them learn to swim.
> ~~Also,~~ I love dolphins. As a trainer, I could help
> other people love and protect dolphins.

Revising for Voice

| **6** | My voice is strong and lively. I sound knowledgeable and enthusiastic. | **5** | I sound well informed and interested. | **4** | I sound well informed and interested most of the time. |

When you revise for *voice,* make sure you sound knowledgeable and interested. The rubric strip above can help you.

How can I make my voice sound knowledgeable?

Your voice will sound knowledgeable if you include interesting facts about your topic.

Practice

Read the following job facts about firefighters. Which three facts could a writer include to sound more knowledgeable?

1. Firefighters open high-pressure hydrants, attach hoses, and turn on the water.
2. They fight fires that are caused by many different things.
3. It takes several firefighters to handle a hose since a person can be knocked down by the water pressure.
4. Firefighters use water.
5. Firefighters must sometimes climb tall ladders or enter burning buildings.

Check your facts. Make sure you include some facts that the reader might not know. Add more facts to your essay if necessary.

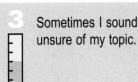

3 Sometimes I sound unsure of my topic.

2 I sound unsure of my topic.

1 I need help understanding what my writing voice is.

How can I make my voice sound more interested?

Your voice will sound interested if you care about your topic.

Practice

Read the following paragraph about firefighters. Write down three words or phrases that show how the writer feels.

> I would make a good firefighter for many reasons. Most importantly, I like to help people. When my neighbor broke his leg, I walked his dog every day. Also, firefighters need to be in great shape. I love sports, and I lift weights three times a week. Finally, a firefighter has to work well under pressure. When the kids play football in my neighborhood, I love being in the middle of a blitz.

Revise

Review your voice. Look for words or phrases that show that you care about your topic. Add a few more if you can.

Revising in Action

The writer adds a sentence to show that she cares about the topic.

Tricks also keep dolphins from being bored. The third
     It's hard work, but it's important!
thing trainers do is clean the tanks./

Revising for Word Choice

6 The words I use make my essay very clear, informative, and fun to read.

5 I use specific nouns and only the best modifiers.

4 I use specific nouns, but I should cut a few extra modifiers.

When you revise for *word choice,* you make sure you use specific nouns and modifiers (adjectives and adverbs). The rubric strip above will help you revise.

How can I use specific nouns?

You can replace general nouns with specific nouns to make your writing more informative. (Also see page **410**.)

GENERAL NOUNS	singer	music	place	people
SPECIFIC NOUNS	soprano	jazz	concert hall	fans

Practice

For each sentence below, decide which noun in parentheses is more specific.

1. A rock band always has a lead *(musician, guitarist).*
2. Pop bands can play different *(things, songs).*
3. Some band members play *(horns, trumpets).*
4. If I were in a band, I would play *(an instrument, the drums).*
5. A band can sell *(stuff, souvenirs)* to the fans.

Revise

Replace general nouns. Read your essay and look for nouns that are too general. Replace them to make your writing more informative.

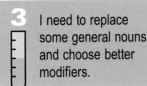

3 I need to replace some general nouns and choose better modifiers.

2 Most of my nouns are general, and my modifiers are not well chosen.

1 I need help with my word choice.

How can I use the best modifiers?

The best modifiers (adjectives and adverbs) make your ideas clearer. Words like *really, very,* or *totally* are empty modifiers. If an idea is clear without the modifying word, remove the modifier.

Practice

Rewrite the following sentences, removing any empty modifiers.

1. I would be very excellent as a pop music performer.
2. I really have a lot of talent and am totally terrific on stage.
3. A pop star needs a very lovely voice and a really trendy look.
4. I totally imagine myself as a world-famous singer.

Check your modifiers. Read your work and look for empty modifiers. Remove any that you find.

Revising in Action

The writer replaces a general noun and cuts an empty modifier.

>   personality
> I have the right ~~stuff~~ to be a dolphin trainer. To
> begin with, I ~~totally~~ love dolphins. As a trainer, . . .

Revising for Sentence Fluency

| 6 | My sentences are well written and flow smoothly. People will enjoy reading them. | 5 | My sentences flow smoothly, and I use compound and complex sentences. | 4 | Most of my sentences flow well, but I need to combine a few more short sentences. |

When you revise for *sentence fluency,* you combine short, choppy sentences into compound or complex sentences. The rubric strip above can help you.

How can I write compound sentences?

You can write a compound sentence by joining two choppy sentences using a comma and a coordinating conjunction. (See page 443.)

Coordinating Conjunctions   and, but, or, nor, for, so, yet

> **SHORT, CHOPPY SENTENCES**
> I like hot-air balloons. Someday I'll fly one.

> **COMPOUND SENTENCE**
> I like hot-air balloons, and someday I'll fly one.

Practice

Combine each set of sentences using a comma and a coordinating conjunction: *and, but, or, nor, for, so,* or *yet.*

1. Hot-air balloons are huge. The baskets can carry 10 people.
2. The pilot controls altitude. Direction depends on the wind.
3. The pilot can make the balloon rise with heat. He can release weights.
4. People like the gentle ride. Balloon rides are very quiet.

Combine short, choppy sentences. Look for short, choppy sentences and combine them into compound sentences.

Editing

Prewrite   Revise   Publish
Write   Edit

Once you have revised your essay, editing is the next step in the writing process. When you edit, you check to make sure you have followed the rules of English. These rules are called "conventions."

Keys to Editing

1. **Use** a dictionary, a thesaurus, and the "Proofreader's Guide" in the back of this book for help.

2. **Edit** on a printed copy if you use a computer. Then make your changes on the computer.

3. **Use** the editing marks shown inside the back cover of this book.

4. **Ask** someone else to check your writing for errors, too.

Editing for Conventions

| **6** I accurately use conventions that make my writing exact and clear. | **5** I have few errors in punctuation, spelling, or grammar. | **4** I have several errors in punctuation, spelling, or grammar. |

When you edit your writing for *conventions,* you need to check for punctuation, capitalization, spelling, and grammar errors. The rubric strip above can guide you.

How can I check subject-verb agreement?

You can check subject-verb agreement by making sure that your singular subjects have singular verbs and your plural subjects have plural verbs. Remember that *singular verbs* usually end in *s,* but *plural verbs* usually do not. (See pages **438** and **439**.)

| SINGULAR | A librarian helps. | A reader asks. | A book informs. |
| PLURAL | Librarians help. | Readers ask. | Books inform. |

Practice

Tell which verb in parentheses agrees with the subject of the sentence.

1. Librarians (*organize, organizes*) books using the Dewey decimal system.
2. Library journals (*tell, tells*) what new books are available.
3. During a story hour, an adult (*read, reads*) a book out loud.
4. Librarians (*is, are*) experts on all kinds of books.

Check your subject-verb agreement. Review your essay. Make sure singular subjects have singular verbs and plural subjects have plural verbs.

3 My errors may confuse the reader. I need to fix them.

2 Many errors make my essay hard to read. I need to correct them.

1 I need to correct numerous errors in my writing.

How can I be sure my verb tenses are correct?

Check your verbs to make sure you don't change tenses accidentally. There are three basic tenses. Most of your essay should be written in the present tense. However, if you give examples that happened in the past, past tense is correct. Also, when you talk about something that hasn't happened yet, you will use future tense. (See page 418.)

Present	*Past*	*Future*
carry	carried	will carry

Practice

Rewrite each sentence below, first in the past tense and then in the future tense.

1. Librarians sort books and place them on the shelves.
2. People with overdue books pay fines.
3. Libraries organize fiction books by the author's last name.
4. Reference librarians help students find articles.

Editing in Action

The writer fixes subject-verb agreement and verb tense errors.

> Training dolphins ~~are~~ *is* an important job. . . . At night, I even ~~dreamed~~ *dream* about swimming with dolphins. . . .

Editing **Using a Checklist**

Check your editing. Number a piece of paper from 1 to 10. If you can answer "yes" to a question, put a check mark after that number. If not, continue to edit for that convention.

Conventions

PUNCTUATION

_____ **1.** Do I use end punctuation after all my sentences?

_____ **2.** Do I use commas after introductory word groups?

_____ **3.** Do I use commas in all my compound sentences?

CAPITALIZATION

_____ **4.** Do I start all my sentences with capital letters?

_____ **5.** Do I capitalize all names (proper nouns)?

SPELLING

_____ **6.** Have I spelled all my words correctly?

_____ **7.** Have I checked for words my spell-checker might miss?

GRAMMAR

_____ **8.** Do all my subjects and verbs agree?

_____ **9.** Are my verb tenses correct?

_____ **10.** Do I use the right word *(to, too, two)*?

Adding a Title

Here are some suggestions for writing a title.

■ Name the topic: **Being a Dolphin Trainer**

■ Use an expression: **Jumping Through Hoops**

■ Repeat a sound: **Dreaming About Dolphins**

Publishing

It's time to proofread your essay and make a neat final copy to share. You can also turn your writing into a résumé, a skit, or a poster. (See the suggestions below.)

Presentation

- Use blue or black ink and write neatly.
- Write your name in the upper left corner of page 1.
- Skip a line and center your title; skip another line and start writing.
- Indent every paragraph and leave a one-inch margin on all sides.
- Write your last name and the page number in the upper right corner of every page after the first one.

Create a Résumé

Pretend you are applying for the job you chose. Write your name and address and then list the skills you have that make you right for the job.

Perform a Skit

Team up with a partner and act out a skit about the jobs you chose.

Make a Poster

Create an informative poster about the career you chose. Make sure to include the main duties of the job.

Publish

Make a final copy. Follow your teacher's instructions or use the guidelines above to format your essay. (If you are using a computer, see pages 44–46.) Create a clean final copy of your essay and carefully proofread it.

Rubric for Expository Writing

Use this rubric for writing and assessing expository essays.

Ideas

6 The topic, focus, and details make the essay truly memorable.

5 The essay is informative, with a clear focus and supporting details.

4 The essay is informative, with a clear focus. More supporting details are needed.

Organization

6 The organization makes the essay easy to read.

5 The beginning, middle, and ending work well. Transitions are used.

4 The essay's beginning, middle, and ending use some transitions.

Voice

6 The writer's voice sounds confident, knowledgeable, and enthusiastic.

5 The writer's voice sounds informative and confident.

4 The writer's voice sounds well informed most of the time.

Word Choice

6 The word choice makes the essay clear, informative, and interesting.

5 Specific nouns and action verbs make the essay clear and informative.

4 Some nouns and verbs could be more specific.

Sentence Fluency

6 The sentences flow smoothly and will hold the reader's interest.

5 The sentences flow smoothly and read well aloud.

4 Most of the sentences read smoothly, but some are short and choppy.

Conventions

6 Mastery of conventions gives this essay authority.

5 The essay has few errors in punctuation, spelling, or grammar.

4 The essay has several errors in punctuation, spelling, or grammar.

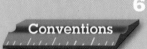

3 The focus of the essay needs to be clearer, and more supporting details are needed.

2 The topic needs to be narrowed or expanded. Many more supporting details are needed.

1 The topic has been chosen but needs to be developed.

3 The middle needs transitions and a paragraph for each main point.

2 The beginning, middle, and ending all run together. Paragraphs are needed.

1 The essay is hard to follow.

3 The writer sometimes sounds unsure.

2 The writer sounds unsure in many parts.

1 The writer needs to sound much more confident.

3 Too many general words are used. Specific nouns and verbs are needed.

2 General or missing words make this essay hard to understand.

1 The writer needs help finding specific words.

3 Many short, choppy sentences need to be rewritten to make the essay read smoothly.

2 Many sentences are choppy or incomplete.

1 Many sentences are difficult to follow.

3 Some errors confuse the reader.

2 Many errors make the essay confusing and hard to read.

1 Help is needed to make corrections.

Evaluating an Expository Essay

Read through Charley's essay, focusing on its strengths and weaknesses. (The essay contains several errors.)

Call Me "Copter Charley"

"Choppa, choppa, choppa, choppa!" What's that sound? It's a helicopter. There the very coolest flying machines ever. I want to be a helicopter pilot.

Helicopter pilots have many different duties. Some work for the military. They go on secret missions and fly to places where planes can't go. Other helicopter pilots work for the police. They chase down criminals. Once the "Eye in the Sky" spots people, they don't get away. I want to be a pilot that flies into volcanoes.

I could fly a helicopter, no problem. First of all, helicopter pilots need good eyesight. I have a perfect 20/20 on my school sight test. Also, pilots need nerves of steel. Whenever my friends and I play flinch, I win. Third, helicopter pilots need to study hard, and I'm on the A-B honor roll. Last of all, pilots should not get motion sick. I never get dizzy on the merry-go-round.

So, sometime when you want to fly into a volcano, give me a call. Maybe you'd rather join me for one of my high-speed police chases! You can do just about anything when your a helicopter pilot!

Student Self-Assessment

Charley rated his writing. Under each trait, he wrote a positive comment and then something he could improve on. (He used the rubric and the number scale on pages 176–177.)

Ideas

4 Ideas
1. I have a great beginning.
2. I included some information that I didn't explain.

Organization

5 Organization
1. I used transitions in my last two paragraphs.
2. I forgot to list my ideas in order of importance.

Voice

4 Voice
1. I sound excited about my topic.
2. I don't always sound knowledgeable.

Word Choice

4 Word Choice
1. I used specific nouns.
2. I used some modifiers I didn't need.

Sentence Fluency

5 Sentence Fluency
1. I have combined my short, choppy sentences.
2. Some parts don't read smoothly.

Conventions

4 Conventions
1. I spelled my words right.
2. I have trouble with <u>there</u> and <u>they're</u> and <u>your</u> and <u>you're</u>.

Use the rubric. Rate your essay using the rubric shown on pages 176–177. On your own paper, list the six traits. Leave room after each trait to write one strength and one area that needs work. Then choose a number (from 1 to 6) to rate each trait.

Reflecting on Your Writing

Now that you've finished your expository essay, take a moment to reflect on the job you have done. On your own paper, complete each sentence starter below.

> Take a moment to reflect on the essay you wrote!

My Expository Essay

1. The best part of my essay is . . .

2. The part that still needs work is . . .

3. The main thing I learned about expository writing is . . .

4. Next time I write an expository essay, I would like to . . .

Expository Writing
Across the Curriculum

Sometimes expository writing answers the question "Can you explain that?" For example, your science book might explain how to make a pinhole camera. Your math book might explain what division is. Those are both forms of expository writing.

Throughout your school day, textbooks give you the explanations you need. With practice, you can develop your expository writing skill . . . and explain things yourself!

Mini Index

- **Science:** Writing a How-To Essay
- **Math:** Explaining a Math Concept
- **Practical Writing:** Taking Two-Column Notes
- **Assessment:** Writing for Assessment

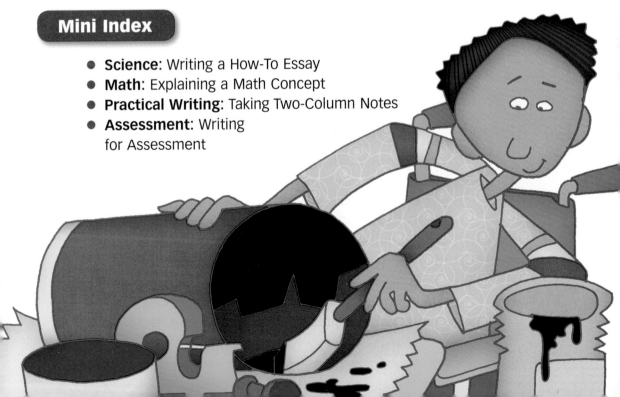

Science:
Writing a How-To Essay

A how-to essay explains how to do something. In this essay, a student gives step-by-step instructions for making a pinhole camera.

BEGINNING

The beginning gives the focus statement (underlined).

MIDDLE

The middle lists materials and leads the reader through each step.

ENDING

The ending leaves the reader with a final thought.

How to Make a Pinhole Camera

If you like taking pictures, you might like making a pinhole camera. You need just a few supplies and some patience. <u>Making a pinhole camera is easy and fun for camera lovers.</u>

Start by gathering your supplies. You need a round oatmeal carton, black spray paint, black paper, tape, scissors, and a needle. You also need film paper from a camera store.

Next, get your oatmeal carton ready. Spray-paint it black, inside and out. Then poke the needle through the middle of the bottom. This hole is your "lens." Cut out a small piece of black paper and tape it over the lens so it can flip up. This is your "shutter." Last, go into a dark room and tape your film paper inside the box top. Seal the box tight.

Now you can take a picture! Go outside on a sunny day and prop up your camera to take a picture. Open the shutter for two seconds (count 1,000-one, 1,000-two) and close it again. Then take your camera to the camera store to develop your film or learn to develop your own film.

Experiment with your camera. See what great pictures you can take. The only thing more fun than making a pinhole camera is using it!

Prewriting **Choosing a Topic**

First, you need to pick a topic for your explanation, or how-to essay. A cluster can help you think about things you know how to do.

Cluster

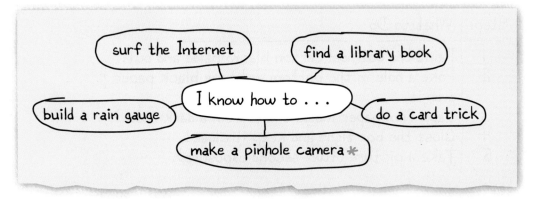

surf the Internet

find a library book

I know how to . . .

build a rain gauge

do a card trick

make a pinhole camera ✳

Prewrite

Create a cluster. Write *I know how to . . .* and circle it. Then write things you know how to do. Choose a topic that has steps.

Listing Materials and Tools

Now you should list the necessary materials and tools.

List

Materials	Tools
oatmeal carton	scissors
black spray paint	sewing needle
black paper	
film paper	
tape	

Prewrite

Create a list. Write *Materials* and *Tools* at the top of a piece of paper. Under them, list materials that are needed.

Prewriting **Organizing Your Steps**

Next, write down the steps (include at least three) in the order you do them. A time line can help you organize your steps.

Time Line

Steps	What to Do
1	Paint the oatmeal carton black inside and out.
2	Poke a hole in the bottom and tape black paper over it.
3	Tape film paper inside the top (in a dark room).
4	Close the box tight and keep it closed.
5	Take a picture (two-second exposure).

Create a time line. Write *Steps* and *What to Do* on a piece of paper. Then list each step in order. If you forget a step, write it beside the others and draw a line to show where it goes.

Prewriting **Writing a Focus Statement**

Your focus statement names your topic and gives the reader a reason to try it. Here is a formula for writing your focus statement.

topic		reason to try it		a strong focus statement
how to make a pinhole camera	+	easy and fun for camera lovers	=	Making a pinhole camera is easy and fun for camera lovers.

Write your focus statement. Use the formula above. Write several versions until you have a good focus statement.

Writing Creating Your First Draft

The main parts of your first draft should do these things:

- **Beginning:** Introduce your topic and state your focus.
- **Middle:** Describe materials and explain each step.
- **Ending:** Encourage the reader to try the process.

Write your first draft. Use your list and time line from pages 183 and 184 to guide your writing.

Revising Improving Your Writing

Next, you'll probably need to make some changes.

- **Ideas** Is my focus clear? Have I listed materials and all the steps?
- **Organization** Are my steps in the right order?
- **Voice** Do I sound interested?
- **Word Choice** Do I use specific nouns and active verbs?
- **Sentence Fluency** Do my sentences read smoothly?

Revise your work. Use the questions above to make changes in your first draft. Then make a clean copy for editing.

Editing Checking for Conventions

It's also important to follow the rules of English.

- **Conventions** Have I checked for punctuation, capitalization, spelling, and grammar errors?

Edit your work. Edit your essay using the question above. Then make a clean final copy and proofread it.

Math: Explaining a Math Concept

Writing about a concept you learn in math class can often help you understand it better. In this example, Josie explained division.

The **beginning** names the idea.

The **middle** gives explanations and examples.

The **ending** shows a picture of the idea.

What Is Division?

Division is taking something and dividing it into equal parts. At home, I share a big room with my little sister. Mom said we should divide it in two. We also use division to cut up a pizza. We divide the round pizza into 8 slices for everyone to eat.

Sometimes, you divide a big number. Maybe you have 24 lines. If you divide them into 2 equal groups, you have 12 lines in each half, or 2 equal parts. If you divide the 24 lines into 4 equal groups, you have 6 lines in each fourth, or 4 equal parts.

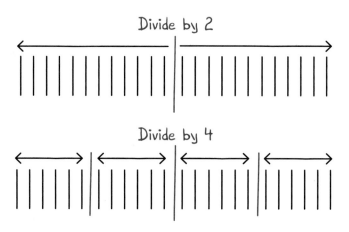

Divide by 2

Divide by 4

WRITING TIPS

Before you write . . .

- **Choose a math concept.**
  Use a math concept or process you've studied or the concept your teacher gives you.
- **Talk about the concept.**
  List the steps you need to explain and then explain them to a partner. Jot down some of the thoughts from your discussion.

During your writing . . .

- **Define the concept or process.**
  Write an opening sentence that defines the concept.
- **Share examples.**
  Tell how the concept or process can be used in daily life. Use examples to help the reader understand the concept.
- **Make a math picture.**
  Give another example and use a math picture to explain it.

After you've written a first draft . . .

- **Edit your work.**
  Check for errors in punctuation, capitalization, spelling, and grammar.

Explain a math concept or process. **Follow the tips above and remember to include a drawing.**

Practical Writing:
Taking Two-Column Notes

Being able to take notes will help you in your classes. In the sample below, Mark took notes while studying a book about his state's history.

Mark

TRAIL OF TEARS

"Nunna daul Tsuny"	– Cherokee for "Trail where they wept"
1835–Treaty of New Echota	– President Jackson wanted the Cherokee land. – legalized removing Native Americans from Georgia
1838–General Scott arrives to remove the Cherokees.	– Cherokees are forced to march 800 miles west to Oklahoma. – Not enough food/shelter on the trail – Over 4,000 Cherokees died.
Some didn't want removal.	– John Ross, Davy Crockett, Henry Clay, Daniel Webster

Main ideas are listed on the left, and details are on the right.

A drawing helps to explain the details.

Oklahoma   Georgia

800 Miles

WRITING TIPS

Before you write . . .

- **Create a heading.**
  Write your topic heading at the top of your paper.
- **Divide your paper into two columns.**
  Create a narrower column on the left.
- **Write neatly.** You must be able to read your notes later.

During your writing . . .

- **Write the main ideas on the left side.**
  Leave room between each main idea so that you have plenty of room to fit the details on the right side.
- **Write the details on the right side.**
  Use words and phrases instead of complete sentences.
- **Use drawings.**
  Add pictures to your notes to make information clear.

After you've written . . .

- **Review your facts.**
  Be sure the facts are correct and complete.
- **Write any questions you still have.**
  Jot down questions in your notes. Then check your book or ask your teacher for help to find the answers.
- **Use your notes to help you study.**
  Read over your notes before a test. Have a friend or family member ask you questions from your notes.

Take notes. Use the tips above as you take notes in your classes.

Writing for Assessment

Some writing tests include prompts that ask you to explain something or share information. This sample expository prompt asks the student to write an essay.

Expository Prompt

Most people have a favorite object. Write an essay naming your favorite thing and explaining why it is your favorite.

> Basketball
>
> well made | gift from dad
>
> helps me stay fit

The beginning gives the focus statement (underlined).

My dad's favorite thing is his cell phone because of all its functions. My brother's favorite thing is his stereo because he loves loud music. <u>My favorite thing is my basketball.</u>

First of all, my basketball is really well made. It has a cover of orange leather, like a regulation NBA ball. It feels great, and I love the smell of the leather. The extra-wide channels give me a great grip. The sound it makes bouncing on the cement and on the backboard is like music to me. The ball even has Yao Ming's signature on it, and he's my favorite player.

The middle gives important details.

My basketball also helps me stay fit. Instead of sitting in front of the TV, I go outside to shoot hoops for hours. I also go one-on-one with my brother. I feel good after a fast game.

Still, the best thing about my basketball is that my dad gave it to me. We play together whenever I spend a weekend with him. The rest of the time, that basketball makes me feel like he's still with me. Dad says if I keep studying and practicing, I might get a college scholarship just like he did.

My basketball is my favorite thing for a lot of reasons. It's well made, it helps me stay in shape, and it's from my dad. When I feel that leather and hear that special bounce sound, I start dreaming about making three-pointers as my dad shouts from the bleachers.

The ending wraps up the explanation.

Respond to the reading. Answer the questions below about the response you just read.

- **Ideas** (1) What is the focus of the writer's response? (2) What details support the focus?

- **Organization** (3) How does the writer introduce the topic? (4) How does he restate the topic in the ending?

- **Voice & Word Choice** (5) What sentences show the writer's strong feelings? (6) What key words from the prompt also appear in the essay?

WRITING TIPS

Planning your response . . .
- **Understand the prompt.**
  Read the prompt carefully and look for key words.
- **Gather your ideas.**
  Make a list or fill in a simple graphic organizer.
- **Form a focus statement.**
  Write your main point in a single sentence.
- **Use your time wisely.**
  Save a few minutes at the end to check your work.

Writing your response . . .
- **Begin with a strong opening paragraph.**
  Clearly state your main idea.
- **Organize your details.**
  Divide your details into two or three well-organized paragraphs.
- **End effectively.**
  Leave the reader with something to think about.

Checking your response . . .
- **Check for correctness.**
  Rewrite any confusing parts and correct any errors.

Expository Prompts

- Imagine that a new student has come to your school and needs to learn the class rules. Write an essay that explains the main rules.
- Most people have a favorite activity. Choose an activity that you enjoy doing and write an essay that explains how the activity is done. Remember to discuss any equipment or training needed.

 Respond to an expository prompt. Write a response to one of the prompts above. Finish within the time your teacher gives you.

Expository Writing in Review

In expository writing, you explain something to a reader.

Prewrite

Select a topic that truly interests you and will also interest your reader. (See page 148.)

Gather and organize details about your topic using a graphic organizer. (See pages 149–150.)

Write a focus (thesis) statement, naming your topic and a special part of it that you plan to cover. (See page 151.)

Write

In the beginning, introduce your topic and state your focus. (See page 155.)

In the middle, give the details that explain or support the focus. (See pages 156–157.)

In the ending, summarize your main points and make a final comment about the topic. (See page 158.)

Revise

Review the ideas, organization, and **voice** of your writing first. Then review for **word choice** and **sentence fluency.** Make changes to improve your first draft. (See pages 160–170.)

Edit

Check your writing for conventions. Also have a trusted classmate edit your writing. (See pages 172–174.)

Publish

Make a final copy and proofread it for errors before sharing it. (See page 175.)

Use the expository rubric to assess your finished writing. (See pages 176–177.)

Persuasive Writing

Persuasive Writing

Persuasive Paragraph

How would you complete the next sentence? "The best event at school is . . . ." Would you say hat day, grandparents' day, the school carnival? A special event can make a whole week, or even a whole year, more fun.

In this chapter, you'll write a paragraph that uses reasons to convince others to agree with your opinion about a special school event.

Writing Guidelines

Subject: A special event at school

Form: Persuasive paragraph

Purpose: To persuade (convince the reader to do something)

Audience: Parents and students

Persuasive Paragraph

A persuasive paragraph starts with a **topic sentence**, which states an opinion about something. The **body** sentences give reasons that support the opinion, and the **closing sentence** may state the opinion in a new way. In the following paragraph, Willis tells about a favorite school event and gives reasons why everyone should attend.

Topic sentence

Body

Closing sentence

Have Some Summer Fun!

Our school carnival is a special event everyone should attend. One Friday night in January, our whole school becomes a summer carnival. Each classroom has a game or an activity. Students help in their own rooms and then visit the other rooms. First of all, there are activities for everyone. This year our room had a fishpond for the little kids. Another room painted a clown with a huge mouth for a beanbag toss. I like the shoe scrambles and relay races. Secondly, each room gives prizes like yo-yos, bug-eye glasses, and light-up pens. The best part is the clown contest. Old clothes, face paint, wigs, big clunky shoes, and wild ties make it pretty funny. Adults and kids laugh and laugh. For a little summer fun in January, come to our school carnival.

Respond to the reading.
On your own paper, answer each of the following questions.

- **Ideas** (1) What does Willis like about the school carnival?
- **Organization** (2) What reason is most important to him?
- **Voice & Word Choice** (3) What words or phrases show excitement about the topic?

Prewriting **Selecting a Topic**

Think of events you enjoy at school. Making a quick list will help you find an idea for your persuasive paragraph.

Quick List

Create a quick list. List events at your school. Star (✳) the one you choose.

- field day
- school carnival ✳
- Arbor Day tree planting
- student-teacher basketball game

Writing an Opinion

Next, form your opinion. An opinion is something you believe.

Formula: A specific subject (our school carnival)
+ your opinion (is a special event everyone should attend)
= a good opinion statement

Write your opinion statement. Use the formula above to write your own opinion statement.

Gathering Reasons

You'll need to give good reasons to support your opinion.

First of all, there are activities for everyone.
Secondly, each room gives prizes.
The best part is the clown contest.

Complete sentence starters. Copy and complete the underlined sentence starters above to find three reasons that support your opinion.

Writing **Creating Your First Draft**

The first draft of your paragraph should start with your topic sentence, which states your opinion about a special school event. The body sentences should give your reasons along with details and examples. The closing sentence can restate your opinion.

Write your first draft. Follow the suggestions above. Remember that your audience includes adults and students. Use your topic sentence and reasons from page 197.

Revising **Improving Your Paragraph**

When you revise, check your paragraph for *ideas, organization, voice, word choice,* and *sentence fluency.*

Revise your paragraph. Use these questions as a guide.

1. Does my topic sentence give an event and my opinion about it?
2. Do my body sentences give reasons for my opinion?
3. Is my writing voice convincing?
4. Do I use specific nouns and strong verbs?
5. Do I use complete sentences?

Editing **Checking for Conventions**

Editing means looking for errors in *conventions.*

Edit your work. Ask yourself the following questions.

1. Does each sentence end with punctuation?
2. Have I checked my spelling?
3. Have I used the right words *(threw, through)*?

Persuasive Writing

Promoting an Event

When a circus comes to town, performers try to convince people to come see the show. They parade elephants down Main Street, put up posters, and appear on TV. There are many ways to promote a circus.

You can promote an event by writing a persuasive essay. In the essay, you name the event or activity and give the reader reasons to become involved. This chapter will help you write an essay that will make an event a big success!

Writing Guidelines

Subject:	An event or activity
Form:	Persuasive essay
Purpose:	To promote an event
Audience:	Classmates

Understanding Your Goal

Your goal in this chapter is to write a persuasive essay that promotes an event or activity. The traits listed in the chart below will help you reach your goal.

Your goal is to . . .

Ideas
Select an event or activity and gather strong reasons for people to become involved in it.

Organization
Create a clear beginning, middle, and ending, and lead up to your most important reason.

Voice
Use a writing voice that sounds clear and convincing.

Word Choice
Choose words that make your writing persuasive.

Sentence Fluency
Write complete sentences that flow smoothly from one to another.

Conventions
Check your essay for correct punctuation, capitalization, spelling, and grammar.

Get the big picture. Look at the rubric on pages 232–233. It can help you measure your progress as you write.

Persuasive Essay

In the following persuasive essay, Desirée promotes a contest at her school. The side notes tell what each part of the essay does.

Help Make History

BEGINNING

The beginning gets the reader's attention and gives the opinion statement (underlined).

Sometimes at recess, I stand by the mural wall. I like the people painted there. One girl is my favorite because my mom painted her 20 years ago. Now, the old mural has to go. The paint is all faded and flaking off. Jones Elementary is having a new mural contest, and every student should get involved.

The first reason kids should help out is that the mural represents Jones Elementary. Students will decide what kind of picture they want. Then they can draw pictures and enter them in the contest. The artist hired by the school will choose pictures that tell the city something about us.

MIDDLE

Each middle paragraph gives reasons to support the opinion.

Also, kids need to help because the new mural is going to take a lot of work. The artist can't do it all alone. She needs a whole crew of kids to help paint the new mural. Some kids can help during recess. Other kids can help on

MIDDLE
Transition
words and
phrases
help show
which
reason
is most
important.

Saturdays. If we all help, the mural will get done quickly.

The most important reason to get involved is that this mural is going to be around for 20 years. When we are grown up, we will want to point to the wall and tell which parts we painted. As Mom says, "The mural is part of our history and part of our future."

ENDING

The ending asks the reader to do something (a call to action).

The mural wall is important to everybody at Jones Elementary, so everybody should help with the mural contest. Start dreaming of a new mural, draw your best ideas, and send them in. Then get ready to put on a painting shirt, grab a paintbrush, and help make history!

Respond to the reading. On your own paper, answer the following questions about the sample essay.

- **Ideas** (1) What reasons does Desirée use to promote the mural contest?

- **Organization** (2) What transition words or phrases does Desirée use to connect her middle paragraphs?

- **Voice & Word Choice** (3) What verbs does Desirée use to make her voice sound convincing?

Prewriting

The writing process starts with prewriting. During this step, you decide on a topic and get ready to write your first draft.

Keys to Prewriting

1. **Select** an event or activity to promote.

2. **Gather** reasons people should be involved in the event.

3. **Write** an opinion statement and topic sentences.

4. **Write** a call to action.

5. **Create** an organized list of your opinion and reasons.

Prewriting Selecting a Topic

To find a topic, you need to think about events and activities in your school or community. Jerome used a T-chart to list possible topics for his essay.

T-Chart

Special Events

School	Community
book fair	fishing contest
zoo field trip	St. Patrick's Day parade
young author contest	boat races
summer reading *	food drive

Prewrite

Create a T-chart. Label your chart like the one above. In each column, list events or activities you could promote. Put a star (✳) next to the topic you choose.

Focus on the Traits

Ideas Remember to select an event that students aren't required to attend. You don't need to promote an event that every student has to go to. For example, Jerome did not pick the zoo field trip because the whole class would be going anyway.

Gathering Reasons

Your essay must tell people why they should get involved in the event you chose. A table diagram can help you gather reasons. The tabletop names the event, and the table legs answer the question "Why should people get involved?" Here is Jerome's table diagram.

Table Diagram

 Create a table diagram. Draw a tabletop like the one above and write your special event or activity in it. Then draw at least three table legs. In each one, answer the question "Why should people get involved?"

Focus on the Traits

Organization Reasons support your opinion just as legs support a table. A table with two legs won't stand up. You need at least three reasons before you have strong support.

Prewriting Writing an Opinion Statement

Your opinion statement should name the event and tell people to get involved. Use the word *should* to make a strong opinion statement.

name the event Befford reading program	+	tell how people should get involved students should sign up for summer reading	=	a strong opinion statement Students at Befford School should sign up for summer reading.

Prewrite

Write your opinion statement. Follow the formula above to write your own opinion statement. Try a few different versions.

Writing Topic Sentences

Each of your topic sentences will be about one of the reasons in your table diagram from page 205. The sentences will begin the three middle paragraphs of your essay. Here are Jerome's topic sentences.

1. To start with, reading is fun.
2. Also, the summer reading program gives out great prizes.
3. The best reason is that the summer reading program keeps your brain strong.

Prewrite

Write your topic sentences. Include one reason from your table diagram in each topic sentence. Use transition words and phrases to connect your ideas.

First of all,	The first reason	To start with,
In addition,	Another reason	Also,
Most importantly,	The biggest reason	The best reason

Creating a Call to Action

Persuasive writing tries to convince the reader to do something. A **call to action** is usually written as a command, with the understood subject, *you,* referring to the reader. Jerome wrote this call to action in his essay.

(You) Go to the library, sign up, and start reading!

Practice

Change the following statements into commands (remove the subject and helping verb). Begin your command with the main verb.

1. Students should come to band information night.

2. People should bring canned food for the local food pantry.

3. Students should volunteer for the school cleanup day.

4. Everyone should donate money to the Arbor Day fund.

5. Kids should get pledges for the jump rope fund-raiser.

6. Students should take part in the reading challenge.

Prewrite

Write a call to action. Write a command sentence about your event that tells the reader what to do. Make sure to start your sentence with a verb.

Focus on the Traits

Voice Writing your call to action as a command makes your voice more persuasive. A command tells the reader how to respond to your idea—with action.

Prewriting Organizing Your Ideas

An organized list of your ideas gives you a final plan for writing your essay. The list contains your opinion statement, topic sentences with details, and a call to action.

Organized List

Opinion statement

Students at Befford School should sign up for summer reading.

First topic sentence

List of details

1. To start with, reading is fun.
   - amazing books
   - lots of titles to choose from

Second topic sentence

List of details

2. Also, the summer reading program gives out great prizes.
   - pizza
   - mini-golf and go-carts
   - Adventure Island

Third topic sentence

List of details

3. The best reason is that the summer reading program keeps your brain strong.
   - exercises your brain
   - helps you succeed next year

Call to action

Go to the library, sign up, and start reading!

Prewrite

Organize your essay. Make your own organized list, using the example above as a guide.

Writing

Now that you've completed your prewriting, you are ready to write your first draft. Your main job is to put all your ideas on paper or in a computer file.

Keys to Writing

1. **Write** a strong beginning paragraph that includes your opinion statement.

2. **Start** each middle paragraph with a topic sentence that gives one reason.

3. **Include** details in each paragraph to support the topic sentence.

4. **Write** an ending paragraph that includes your call to action.

Writing Getting the Big Picture

The chart below shows how the parts of a persuasive essay fit together. (The examples are from the sample essay on pages 211–214.) You are ready to write your essay when you have . . .

- written your opinion statement and topic sentences,
- written a call to action, and
- created an organized list.

Beginning

The **beginning** gets the reader's attention and gives the opinion statement.

Opinion Statement
Students at Befford School should sign up for summer reading.

Middle

Each **middle** paragraph starts with a topic sentence that gives one reason for the opinion. The body sentences provide details.

Topic Sentences
To start with, reading is fun.

Also, the summer reading
P   gives out great prizes.

The best reason is that the summer reading program keeps your brain strong.

Ending

The **ending** tells the reader to do something (call to action).

Call to Action
Go to the library, sign up, and start reading!

Starting Your Essay

Your first paragraph should get the reader's attention and provide your opinion statement. Here are several ways to get your reader's attention:

- **Start with a question.**
  Where did you go on your last summer vacation?

- **Surprise your reader.**
  Last summer, I traveled to faraway Treasure Island!

- **Be creative.**
  Books invite you into a time machine.

- **Use a quotation.**
  "Sign up for summer reading!" shouts the poster in the library.

Beginning Paragraph

> The first sentence catches the reader's attention.
>
> The last sentence includes the opinion statement (underlined).

"Sign up for summer reading!" shouts the poster in the library. I can just imagine my friends saying that summer is for being outside! I agree with both. Summer is for exercising your body, but it's also for exercising your brain. <u>Students at Befford School should sign up for summer reading.</u>

Write your beginning paragraph. Try one of the strategies above to get your reader's attention. End your paragraph with your opinion statement.

Writing Developing the Middle Part

In your first paragraph, you got the reader's attention and led up to your opinion statement. Each of your middle paragraphs should focus on one reason people should get involved with your event, arranged by order of importance. Write at least three body paragraphs that begin with a topic sentence. Use your organized list as a guide.

Beginning

Middle

Ending

Understanding Order of Importance

Order of importance simply means that you share ideas from most to least important or from least to most important. The transition words and phrases you use with each topic sentence help to show this order of importance.

Middle Paragraphs

Topic sentence 1
Details support the first reason.

To start with, reading is fun. Sure, it's great to play basketball and soccer with friends. It's also great to dig a tunnel to the center of the earth and fly to Jupiter. Books let you do things like that. When the weather's nice, go out and ride your bike. When it's too hot or rainy, stay in and take a trip in a rocket!

Topic sentence 2
Details support the second reason.

Also, the summer reading program gives out great prizes. The prize for reading 5 books is a free pizza. Just think of every chapter as a small slice! The prize for reading 10 books is a free ticket for mini-golf and go-carts. If you read 20 books, you get to go to Adventure

Island for free! Last summer, I got to go to Adventure Island.

> The best reason is that the summer reading program keeps your brain strong. The poster in the library says, "Brains need exercise!" If you keep reading all summer, you'll put thousands of miles on your imagination. Your brain will also be geared up for heading back to school in the fall.

Topic sentence 3
Details support the third reason.

Arrange your paragraphs by order of importance, ending with the most important reason.

Write **Write your middle paragraphs.** Use your organized list from page 208.

Writing **Ending Your Essay**

The last paragraph should review your reasons and give your call to action. Here are three ways to review your reasons.

- **Create a list.**
  If you want to have fun, win prizes, and develop a first-class brain, you should join the Befford summer reading program.

- **Sum up the reasons.**
  Summer reading is fun and keeps your mind in shape.

- **Ask a question.**
  Are you looking for a way to have fun and give your brain a good summer workout?

Ending Paragraph

The writer ends with a call to action.

> If you want to have fun, win prizes, and develop a first-class brain, you should join the Befford summer reading program. It's free, and so are the library books. <u>Go to the library, sign up, and start reading!</u>

Write your ending. Use one of the strategies above to give your essay a strong ending. Remember to include your call to action.

Form a complete first draft. Write a complete copy of your essay. Write on every other line to make room for changes when revising.

Revising

After completing your first draft, it's time to revise your work using the steps below. When you revise, you check your essay for *ideas, organization, voice, word choice,* and *sentence fluency.*

Keys to Revising

1. Read your essay once to see how you feel about it.

2. Review each part: the beginning, the middle, and the ending.

3. Ask a classmate to read your first draft and respond to it.

4. Change any parts that need to be improved.

Revising for  Ideas

6 My essay strongly promotes my topic. I use many convincing details.	**5** I convince the reader by using different kinds of details.	**4** My essay is somewhat convincing, but adding an anecdote or a quotation would make it stronger.

When you revise for *ideas,* you check the kinds of details (including anecdotes and quotations) you have used. The rubric above can help you revise.

How can I use an anecdote in my essay?

You can use an anecdote to gain your reader's interest or to support a reason. An anecdote is a little story that makes an idea clearer.

To capture the reader's interest in the beginning . . .

Two years ago, I heard my brother play in the fourth-grade band.

To support one of your reasons in a paragraph . . .

When I first tried the trombone, I couldn't believe how loud it was.

Practice

Find three anecdotes for an essay about joining the band.

1. When my brother joined the band, he didn't know how to read music, but now he plays saxophone like a pro.
2. I started school a week late because I had the flu.
3. Last Fourth of July, I heard the band play in the park.
4. When I went to band information night, the school stage had stands with flutes, clarinets, trumpets, and drums.
5. Most parades have marching bands.

Revise

Think of anecdotes. List brief stories that are related to the event or activity you are writing about. Add one to your beginning or to support a reason.

3 I need to remove fuzzy thinking, which makes my essay less convincing.

2 My thinking is confusing and unconvincing.

1 My opinion and reasons are unclear.

How can I recognize exaggerations?

Exaggerations stretch the truth. They make your writing less convincing. (See page 464.)

Practice

Read the following paragraph. Tell which sentence is an exaggeration.

The best reason to come to open swim night is to use the diving boards. The low board is three feet off the water and has great spring. The high board must be 100 feet high. Some kids who go to open swim night learn how to do tricks off the diving boards.

Watch for exaggerations. Read your essay to find places where you may have stretched the truth. Rewrite those parts.

Revising in Action

The writer rewrites an exaggeration to make the essay more convincing.

Also, the summer reading program gives out great
The prize for reading 5 books is a free pizza.
prizes. ~~One kid won a thousand pizzas~~ Just think of

each chapter as a small slice! The prize for . . .

Revising for Word Choice

6 The words I use in my essay are strong and convince the reader.

5 I use synonyms and modifiers to make my writing persuasive.

4 My essay is persuasive, but more synonyms or modifiers would help.

When you revise for *word choice,* you use synonyms and modifiers to make your essay more persuasive. The rubric strip above will help you revise.

How can synonyms improve my writing?

Synonyms can help you avoid using the same word again and again. A synonym is a word that has the same meaning (or nearly the same meaning) as another word. A thesaurus can help you find synonyms. (See page 332.)

Practice

Read the following paragraph. Decide which word is being used too often. Then find two synonyms for the word. Use a thesaurus if you need help.

Most importantly, kids should work at the rummage sale because the money helps the fourth-grade classes. Some of the money pays for field trips. The rest of the money pays for the classroom supplies and room decorations. Last year's sale made so much money that some of the money paid for snacks for this year!

Revise

Replace overused words. Read your essay. Watch for words that you use again and again. Replace some of them with synonyms.

3 I need more synonyms and modifiers to be persuasive.

2 I need to replace many repeated or confusing words.

1 My word choice does not fit a persuasive essay.

How can I write strong statements?

You can write strong statements by using persuasive words that send a clear message to the reader.

Weak Statements (weak words are underlined):

It would probably be a good idea to have a collection for the community food pantry. I think every student could bring one food item.

Strong Statements (persuasive words are underlined):

We need to have a collection for the community food pantry. Every student should bring one food item.

 Review your sentences. Make sure you have used persuasive words that make strong statements.

Revising in Action

The writer cuts weak words to make the call to action stronger.

~~If you want to take part in~~ summer reading, ~~you could~~
go to the library, sign up, and start reading. !

Revising for Sentence Fluency

6 My sentences read smoothly. They are complete, correct, and enjoyable to read.

5 My sentences read smoothly and are well written.

4 Most of my sentences are easy to read.

When you revise for *sentence fluency,* you fix sentence errors such as fragments and rambling sentences. Use the rubric strip above as a guide.

How can I fix sentence fragments?

You can fix fragments by making sure that each sentence has a subject and a predicate and expresses a complete thought. (See page 436.) Here are some sentence fragments:

> **Often work hard on a science-fair project.** (missing a subject)
>
> **Milo and his whole class.** (missing a predicate)
>
> **Because they have done research.** (not a complete thought)

Practice

Change each sentence fragment into a complete sentence. Use your own words and ideas to add whatever is missing.

1. Topics from the science textbook.
2. A diorama of the earth's layers.
3. When all of the projects have been judged.
4. Ribbons for each project in the fair.
5. After the science fair.

Revise

Check for sentence fragments. Make sure each of your sentences has a subject and a predicate and expresses a complete thought. Revise to fix any fragments you find.

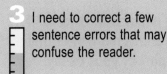

3 I need to correct a few sentence errors that may confuse the reader.

2 Many sentence errors will confuse the reader. I need to correct my sentences.

1 My essay is hard to read. I need to rewrite most of my sentences.

How can I fix rambling sentences?

You can fix rambling sentences by splitting them into smaller sentences. Rambling sentences are often connected with words such as *or, but, and,* or *so.* Remove the extra conjunctions and add end punctuation and capital letters as needed.

Practice

Rewrite this rambling sentence as three sentences.

Kids should enter the science fair because it lets them learn about a science topic and students get to learn about other people's projects by looking at the exhibits and it is also great to get a ribbon!

Fix rambling sentences. Look for sentences that ramble on and on. Fix them by breaking them up into shorter sentences.

Revising in Action

The writer splits a rambling sentence into three sentences.

Sure, it's great to play games with friends, but it's also

great to dig a tunnel to the center of the earth and

fly to Jupiter, and books let you do things like that.

Revising Using a Checklist

Check your revising. Number a piece of paper from 1 to 10. If you can answer "yes" to a question, put a check mark after that number. If not, continue working on that part of your essay.

Ideas

_____ **1.** Do I have a clear opinion statement?

_____ **2.** Do my middle paragraphs have topic sentences?

_____ **3.** Do I use different kinds of details (such as anecdotes and quotations) to help persuade the reader?

Organization

_____ **4.** Do my opinion statement and call to action work together?

_____ **5.** Do I have my reasons in order of importance?

Voice

_____ **6.** Have I avoided bandwagon thinking and exaggeration?

Word Choice

_____ **7.** Have I replaced repeated words with synonyms?

_____ **8.** Have I used persuasive words?

Sentence Fluency

_____ **9.** Have I fixed fragments?

_____ **10.** Have I fixed rambling sentences?

Make a clean copy. When you've finished revising your essay, make a clean copy for editing.

Editing

The next step in writing your essay is editing. When you edit, you make sure you have used the rules of English, called "conventions," correctly.

Keys to Editing

1. **Use** a dictionary, a thesaurus, and the "Proofreader's Guide" in the back of this book for help.

2. **Edit** on a printed copy if you use a computer. Then make your changes on the computer.

3. **Use** the editing marks shown inside the back cover of this book.

4. **Ask** someone else to check your writing for errors, too.

Editing for ⟨Conventions⟩

6 My strong control of conventions makes my writing clear and persuasive.

5 I have a few errors in punctuation, spelling, or grammar.

4 I have several errors in punctuation, spelling, and grammar.

When you edit for *conventions,* you check for punctuation, capitalization, spelling, and grammar errors. The rubric strip above can guide your revision.

When do I use an apostrophe to show ownership?

Use an apostrophe after nouns to show ownership. (See page 492 for more information.)

Singular nouns: Add an apostrophe and an *s*—dog's collar.

Plural nouns ending in *s*: Add just the apostrophe—dogs' collars.

Plural nouns not ending in *s*: Add an apostrophe and an *s*—men's ties.

Practice

For each word below, write the correct possessive form.

1. pet
2. car
3. greyhounds
4. students
5. trainer

6. gymnasium
7. children
8. judges
9. contest
10. women

Edit

Check your possessive forms. Read your essay to be sure you have used apostrophes correctly to show possession. (Also see page 229.)

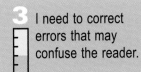

3 I need to correct errors that may confuse the reader.

2 My errors make my essay difficult to read. I need to correct them.

1 I need to correct numerous errors in my writing.

How do pronouns show ownership?

Pronouns show ownership without using an apostrophe. Some possessive pronouns come before a noun, and some stand alone.

Before a noun: my   your   his   her   our   their   its

Stand alone: mine   yours   his   hers   ours   theirs

Greg left his book at school.

(The pronoun *his* comes before the noun *book*.)

Can Greg borrow yours for the assignment?

(The pronoun *yours* stands alone.)

tip When a possessive pronoun comes before a noun, the pronoun functions as an adjective. (See **578.3**.)

Practice

Use each of the possessive pronouns correctly in a sentence.

1. my
2. mine
3. her
4. hers
5. their
6. theirs

Editing in Action

The writer corrects a pronoun to show ownership.

When the weather's nice, go out and ride ~~you's~~ your bike.

Editing **Using a Checklist**

Check your editing. Number a piece of paper from 1 to 10. If you can answer "yes" to a question, put a check mark after that number. If not, continue to edit for that convention.

Conventions

PUNCTUATION

_____ **1.** Do I use end punctuation after all my sentences?

_____ **2.** Do I use commas after introductory word groups?

_____ **3.** Do I correctly use apostrophes to show ownership?

CAPITALIZATION

_____ **4.** Do I start all my sentences with capital letters?

_____ **5.** Do I capitalize all names (proper nouns)?

SPELLING

_____ **6.** Have I spelled all my words correctly?

_____ **7.** Have I checked for words my spell-checker might miss?

GRAMMAR

_____ **8.** Do my subjects and predicates agree?

_____ **9.** Have I checked my use of possessive pronouns?

_____ **10.** Do I use the right word *(to, too, two)*?

Adding a Title

Here are some suggestions for writing a title.

- Repeat a sound: **Sign Up for Summer Reading**
- Be creative: **Befford Summer Brain Workout**
- Use an expression: **Put Some Miles on Your Imagination**

Publishing

It's time to proofread your essay and make a neat copy to share. Present your work on a Web page, in a newsletter or newspaper, or as a morning announcement. (See the suggestions below.)

Presentation

- Use blue or black ink and write neatly.
- Write your name in the upper left corner of page 1.
- Skip a line and center your title; skip another line and start writing.
- Indent every paragraph and leave a one-inch margin on all sides.
- Write your last name and the page number in the upper right corner of every page after the first one.

Make a Web Page

Get your teacher's help to post your work on your class or school Web page.

Create an Editorial

Turn your paper into an editorial for your school newsletter or a community newspaper.

Make a Morning Announcement

Ask permission to promote your event in the school's morning announcements. Base your announcement on your opinion statement and topic sentences.

Create a final copy. Follow your teacher's instructions or use the guidelines above to format your essay. (If you are using a computer, see pages 44–46.) Create a clean final copy of your essay and carefully proofread it.

Rubric for Persuasive Writing

Use the following rubric for rating your persuasive writing.

Ideas

6 The clear opinion and strong reasoning inform and convince the reader.

5 The essay has a clear opinion statement. Logical reasons support the writer's opinion.

4 The opinion statement is clear, and most reasons support the writer's opinion.

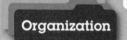
Organization

6 The organization is logical, and ideas flow smoothly from beginning to end.

5 An opening opinion statement is clearly supported in the middle. Transitions connect ideas.

4 The opening has an opinion statement. The middle adds support. Most transitions work.

Voice

6 The writer's voice is confident, positive, and very convincing.

5 The writer's voice is clearly confident and persuades the reader.

4 The writer's voice is confident and somewhat persuasive.

Word Choice

6 Strong, engaging, positive words add to the main message. Every word counts.

5 Strong, positive words help make the message clear.

4 Strong words are used, but some may be too negative.

Sentence Fluency

6 The sentences flow smoothly, and readers will enjoy their variety.

5 Variety is seen in both the types of sentences and their beginnings.

4 Sentence beginnings are varied. A little more variety in types would add interest.

Conventions

6 Mastery of conventions adds persuasive power to the essay.

5 One or two grammar and punctuation errors do not distract the reader.

4 Grammar and punctuation errors in a few sentences may distract the reader.

3 The opinion statement is clear. Reasons and details are not as complete as they need to be.

2 The opinion statement is unclear. Reasons and details are needed.

1 An opinion statement, reasons, and details are needed.

3 There is a beginning, a middle, and an ending. Transitions are needed.

2 The beginning, middle, and ending run together.

1 The writing needs to be organized to avoid confusion.

3 The writer's voice needs to be more confident to persuade the reader.

2 The writer's voice sounds unsure.

1 The writer needs to learn more about voice.

3 Many words need to be stronger and more positive.

2 The same general words are used throughout the essay.

1 Help is needed to find better words.

3 Several sentences begin the same way. Sentence fragments need to be rewritten.

2 Too many sentences begin the same way. Fragments and rambling sentences need to be rewritten.

1 Choppy or incomplete sentences need to be rewritten.

3 There are enough errors to confuse the reader.

2 Errors make the essay difficult to read.

1 Help is needed to make corrections.

Evaluating a Persuasive Essay

Rosa's persuasive essay appears below. Read through it, focusing on its strengths and weaknesses. (The essay contains several errors.)

Walk for a Cure!

Last year, I camped by the high school track and stayed up late and walked with friends. I also helped people with cancer. The Walk for a Cure lets people do all of these things! <u>Kids from Rosewood School should join the Walk for a Cure.</u>

To begin with, walk for a cure is fun. Hunderds of people come out. Some walk, some ride in wagons, and some even ride their bikes. Last year, there was a high school student on a unicycle and people camped around the track and on the football field and they barbecued food and sang songs.

Also, Walk for a Cure is like a huge sleepover outside. Friends and families get to hang out. My sister Christina and I hung out all night with our friends. It's like hanging out at a camp in the middle of the city!

Of course, the biggest reason kids should come out. They can help stop cancer. People plege money for miles or hours. Grandmas, grandpas, uncles, and aunts love to give money. All the money helps people with cancer and helps sceintists find a cure.

So, if you like to stay up late and be with friends, join the Walk for a Cure. You'll even help cure cancer! Come on out! Everybody's doing it!

Student Self-Assessment

Rosa rated her writing. Under each trait, she wrote a positive comment and then something she could improve on. (She used the rubric and the number scale on pages 232–233.)

Ideas

4 Ideas
1. I love my topic, and I tell three reasons.
2. I should use a quotation.

Organization

5 Organization
1. My reasons are in order.
2. My ending could be stronger.

Voice

4 Voice
1. I don't use exaggeration.
2. I guess the end has bandwagon thinking.

Word Choice

4 Word Choice
1. My word choice is pretty good.
2. I should find a synonym for "hang out."

Sentence Fluency

3 Sentence Fluency
1. Most of my sentences read smoothly.
2. I have some sentence errors.

Conventions

3 Conventions
1. I punctuated my long sentences correctly.
2. I have trouble with spelling.

Use the rubric. Rate your essay using the rubric shown on pages 232–233. On your own paper, list the six traits. Leave room after each trait to write one strength and one weakness. Then choose a number (from 1 to 6) that shows how well you used each trait.

Reflecting on Your Writing

Congratulations! You've finished your persuasive essay. Now take a moment to reflect on the job you have done. On your own paper, complete each sentence starter below.

> Take some time to reflect on the experience of writing persuasively.

My Persuasive Essay

1. The best part of my essay is . . .

2. The part that still needs work is . . .

3. The main thing I learned about persuasive writing is . . .

4. The next time I write a persuasive essay, I would like to . . .

Persuasive Writing
Across the Curriculum

Persuasive writing is useful in all your classes as well as in extracurricular activities. In science, a problem-solution essay may convince others to work at fixing a problem in the environment. In math, a graph that tracks a fund-raising project can persuade people to contribute. And a polite letter can bring in donations for a worthy cause.

Mini Index

- **Science**: Writing a Problem-Solution Essay
- **Math**: Creating a Thermometer Graph
- **Practical Writing**: Drafting a Letter of Request
- **Assessment**: Writing for Assessment

Science:
Writing a Problem-Solution Essay

In the following essay, Michael names a problem and suggests how kids can help solve it.

BEGINNING

The problem is introduced, and an opinion statement (underlined) is given.

MIDDLE

One middle paragraph tells why people should care about the problem. The other paragraph describes a solution.

ENDING

The ending asks the reader to help.

Silence in the Swamp

Last week, my dad and I went to the park at night to hear the frogs sing. Their song was not as loud as it used to be. Frogs are dying out because wetlands are disappearing or being poisoned by chemicals. <u>People should do something to save the frogs.</u>

If frogs disappear, people will have problems. Frogs eat insects like flies and mosquitoes. Without frogs, bugs will be everywhere! Also, frogs are food for animals like cranes, herons, raccoons, opossums, and snakes. If frogs die out, other animals may die out, too. Finally, frogs sing, and their night songs would be missed.

Kids can help by joining a group called "A Thousand Friends of Frogs." Members do frog counts near their homes. The counts help scientists keep track of how the frogs are doing. Kids also help dig new ponds for frogs. The group has contests for writing essays and making posters that convince people to stop polluting wetland areas.

This problem can't be fixed by one or two people. To give frogs a fighting chance, everyone concerned about wildlife needs to get involved. Join "A Thousand Friends of Frogs," and help the frogs keep singing!

Prewriting Selecting a Topic

An ideas cluster can help you find a topic.

Ideas Cluster

littering

noisy traffic

Environmental
Problems

frogs disappearing *

old landfill

Prewrite

Make an ideas cluster. Write *Environmental Problems* on a piece of paper. Around this heading, list problems that you know of where you live. Put a star (✳) next to the problem you want to write about.

Gathering Details

Your problem-solution essay should show *why the problem is serious* and *how people can solve it*. A why-how chart can help.

Why-How Chart

Problem: Frogs are disappearing

Why is the problem serious?

Frogs eat bugs.
Frogs are food for other animals.
Frogs make music.

How can people solve it?

Count frogs.
Dig new ponds.
Write essays.
Make posters.

Prewrite

Create a why-how chart. Write your problem and the same underlined questions above on your own paper. Find at least three answers for each question.

Prewriting Writing an Opinion Statement

In a problem-solution essay, your opinion statement should name the problem and the solution.

the problem		the solution		an effective opinion statement
Frogs are disappearing.	+	People need to get involved.	=	People should do something to save the frogs.

Write your opinion statement. Use the formula above to create a strong focus for your persuasive essay.

Writing Topic Sentences

Each of the middle paragraphs in your essay needs a topic sentence. Your topic sentences will sum up the answers on your why-how chart (page 239). Here are Michael's topic sentences.

Topic Sentence 1: If frogs disappear, people will have problems.

Topic Sentence 2: Kids can help by joining a group called "A Thousand Friends of Frogs."

Write your topic sentences. Follow the instructions below.

1 Write topic sentence 1 to answer this question: Why is the problem serious?

2 Write topic sentence 2 to answer this question: How can people solve it?

Writing **Creating Your First Draft**

The beginning of your essay should introduce the problem. It must also get the reader's attention and include your opinion statement (page 240). Your middle paragraphs will begin with your topic sentences (page 240) and include details from your why-how chart (page 239). In the ending, ask the reader to do something (page 207).

Create your first draft. Use all of the ideas you have gathered so far to write your first draft.

Revising **Improving Your Writing**

You can improve your essay by thinking about these questions:

- **Ideas** Have I stated the problem and shared a solution?
- **Organization** Does my beginning get the reader's interest? Does my ending ask the reader to do something?
- **Voice** Do I sound concerned about the problem?
- **Word Choice** Do I use strong nouns and action verbs?
- **Sentence Fluency** Do I use different sentence beginnings?

Revise your essay. Use the questions above as a guide to make changes to your essay.

Editing **Checking for Conventions**

Before you make a final copy, you must correct any errors.

- **Conventions** Have I checked for errors in punctuation, capitalization, spelling, and grammar?

Check your work. Correct the errors you find. Then write a clean final copy and carefully proofread it.

Math: Creating a Thermometer Graph

Many fund-raisers use a thermometer graph. It shows how much money has been raised and how much money is still needed. Ahmad made this poster to persuade people to donate money for a new skate park. He used math calculations to divide his thermometer graph into 10 equal parts.

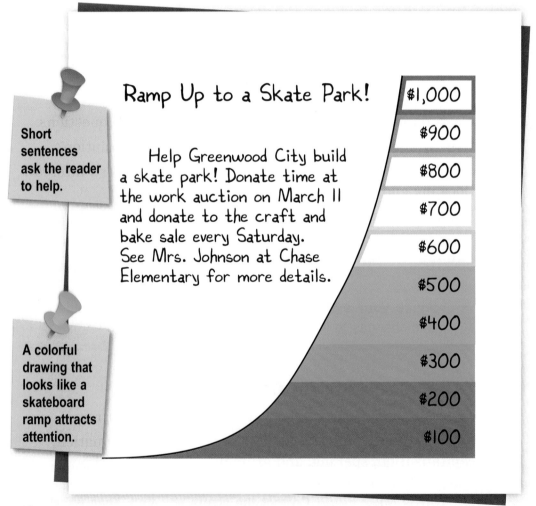

Ramp Up to a Skate Park!

Short sentences ask the reader to help.

Help Greenwood City build a skate park! Donate time at the work auction on March 11 and donate to the craft and bake sale every Saturday. See Mrs. Johnson at Chase Elementary for more details.

A colorful drawing that looks like a skateboard ramp attracts attention.

$1,000
$900
$800
$700
$600
$500
$400
$300
$200
$100

Note: The chart shows that $500 has been raised so far.

WRITING TIPS

Before you write . . .

- **Select a topic.**
  List fund-raisers in your school or community. Choose one that could be shown with a thermometer graph.
- **Think of a fun item related to your topic.**
  Create an interesting thermometer. Use math calculations to divide the thermometer graph into equal parts.

During your writing . . .

- **Start with a sketch.**
  Plan your poster on a piece of paper. Fill the page with the art.
- **Explain your topic.**
  Write a short paragraph that tells the purpose of your poster.
- **Give suggestions.**
  Tell people how they can help.
- **Use color.**
  Use bold colors. Make your words clear and large enough to read.

After you write a first draft . . .

- **Check for errors.**
  Make sure that you have used proper punctuation, capitalization, spelling, and grammar.
- **Make a final version.**
  Make your poster on a large sheet of poster board.

Make a poster. Use these writing tips to make a thermometer graph for the topic you've chosen.

Practical Writing:
Drafting a Letter of Request

A letter of request asks someone to do something. In this example, Gabriel asks for a contribution from a local organization.

8711 Snake Road
Little Rock, AR 72200
March 15, 2005

Mr. Jules Hernandez
Little Rock Rotary Club
2131 E. Main Street
Little Rock, AR 72200

Dear Mr. Hernandez:

The **opening** introduces the topic.

My elementary school is having a "Jump Rope for Fitness" program during April. The money we earn will help buy computers for the school. I am writing to ask your organization to sponsor our class for one hour during the contest.

The **body** asks the reader to act.

Would you be willing to give a penny for each time a student in my class can jump rope in that hour? Another plan is to give a dime, a quarter, or a dollar for each minute a student can each jump rope without stopping. My class has 20 students participating.

The **ending** thanks the reader.

With your help, the contest can be a big success. I hope you can help us out! Thank you.

Sincerely,

Gabriel Vasquez
Gabriel Vasquez

WRITING TIPS

Before you write . . .

- **Choose a person to write to.**
  Think of a person who could help you in some way.
- **Think of what you need.**
  Write down what you want the person to do.

While you write . . .

- **Start with a first draft.**
  Write the body of your letter first. (Don't think about the letter format yet.)
- **Introduce your topic.**
  In the opening paragraph, tell why you are writing.
- **Make your request.**
  Ask the person for help.
- **Write a strong closing.**
  Explain how important the help will be and thank the person.

After you write a first draft . . .

- **Make a final version.**
  Follow the letter format shown on pages 246–247.
- **Check for errors.**
  Read over your letter to be sure you used proper punctuation, capitalization, spelling, and grammar.

Write a letter. Follow the directions above to write a letter of request to an adult, a business, or an organization.

Parts of a Business Letter

1 The heading includes your address and the date. Write the heading at the left margin, at least one inch from the top.

2 The inside address includes the name, title, and address of the person or organization you are writing to.

■ Put short titles on the same line as the name. Put longer titles on the next line.

■ If you are writing to an organization, use the name of the organization.

3 The salutation is the greeting. Put a colon after it.

■ If you know the person's name, use it.

Dear Mr. Smith:

■ Otherwise, use a salutation like one of these:

Dear Manager:

Dear Editor:

Dear Salem Soccer Club:

4 The body is the main part of the letter. Do not indent your paragraphs; instead, skip a line between them.

5 The closing is placed after the body. Use **Yours truly** or **Sincerely**. Capitalize only the first word and put a comma after the closing.

6 The signature ends the letter. If you are using a computer, leave four spaces after the closing; then type your name. Write your signature between the closing and the typed name.

tip Turn to page 477 for more information about writing letters and about addressing envelopes properly.

Business-Letter Format

See page **477** for a model business letter.

1

———————————
———————————
———————————

)—— **Four to Seven Spaces**

2

———————————
———————————
———————————
———————————
———————————

3

——————————— :)—— **One Space**

)—— **One Space**
——————————————————
——————————————————
——————————————————

)—— **One Space**
——————————————————

4

——————————————————
——————————————————
——————————————————

)—— **One Space**
——————————————————
——————————————————
——————————————————

)—— **One Space**

5

——————————— ,)—— **One Space**

6

)—— **Four Spaces**

———————————

(Leave a one-inch margin on all sides.)

Writing for Assessment

Some writing tests include a persuasive prompt that asks you to convince the reader to agree with you and take some action. In the example below, Shawna responds to a proposed change at her school.

Persuasive Prompt

To save money, your principal wants to cancel all field trips for the rest of the year. Write a letter to the principal to express your opinion about canceling field trips. Support your opinion with reasons.

Table Diagram

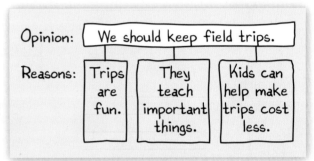

Opinion: We should keep field trips.

Reasons: Trips are fun. | They teach important things. | Kids can help make trips cost less.

The beginning introduces the topic and gives an opinion statement (underlined).

Dear Principal Lane,

Do you remember being in grade school? Do you remember hayrides and visits to apple orchards? Do you remember trips to the Museum of Science and Industry? On field trips, kids get to see things they've only read about. <u>Seymore School should keep its field trips.</u>

Field trips help students learn. Some kids learn best from experiences. One day at a dairy farm could teach kids more than reading a whole unit on dairy farms would. Field trips also help kids know how

Each **middle** paragraph gives reasons to support the opinion.

things work in real life. When our class went to the steel mill, I finally understood what my dad does at work all day.

Kids can help pay for the field trips. We could have craft and book sales and do chores to earn money. Also, we could ask our parents if their companies would let our class visit for free. Some field trips, like a walk to the hospital, would not cost anything.

The **ending** sums up the reasons and asks the reader to act.

Field trips add to our classroom learning by letting us experience what we are being taught. Please keep field trips. They make learning fun!

Sincerely,
Shawna Parks

Respond to the reading. Answer the questions below to learn more about the response you just read.

- **Ideas** (1) What is Shawna's opinion? (2) What reasons support her opinion?

- **Organization** (3) In what order does Shawna give her reasons?

- **Voice & Word Choice** (4) What key words show Shawna's enthusiasm?

WRITING TIPS

Planning your response . . .

- **Understand the prompt.**
  Read the prompt carefully and watch for key words that tell you what to write.
- **Gather your ideas.**
  Use a graphic organizer to plan your response.

Writing your response . . .

- **Include an opinion statement.**
  Write your opinion statement at the end of your first paragraph.
- **Organize your reasons.**
  List your reasons by order of importance.
- **Write a strong ending.**
  Sum up your reasons and ask the reader to act.

Checking your response . . .

- **Check for errors.**
  Be sure you have used proper punctuation, capitalization, spelling, and grammar.

Persuasive Prompt

■ Your school is going to start requiring two hours of homework every night. Write a persuasive essay to let the school board know your opinion of this idea. Give reasons to support your opinion.

Respond to a persuasive prompt. Respond to the prompt above or to a prompt that your teacher gives you.

Persuasive Writing in Review

In persuasive writing, you try to *convince* people to agree with you.

Select a topic that you feel strongly about. Be sure it will also interest your reader. (See page 204.)

Gather and organize reasons to support your opinion. You may use a graphic organizer. (See pages 205 and 208.)

Write an opinion statement that names your cause and your feeling about it. (See page 206.)

Plan a call to action that asks your reader to respond in a specific way. (See page 207.)

In the beginning, get your reader's attention and state your opinion. (See page 211.)

In the middle, each paragraph should list one reason with facts and examples to support it. (See pages 212–213.)

In the ending, repeat your opinion and give a call to action. (See pages 207 and 214.)

Review your ideas, **organization**, and **voice** first. Then review for **word choice** and **sentence fluency**. Make other changes to improve your first draft. (See pages 216–226.)

Check your writing for conventions. Also have a trusted classmate edit your writing. (See pages 227–230.)

Make a final copy and proofread it for errors before sharing it. (See page 231.)

Use the persuasive rubric to assess your finished writing. (See pages 232–233.)

Response to Literature

Response to Literature

Response Paragraph

Sam started telling Kaitlyn about a book he had read. "Don't tell me everything!" Kaitlyn said. She knew that if Sam told her everything, the book would be less fun for her to read. Kaitlyn only wanted to hear enough to decide if she would enjoy reading the book.

Writing a response to literature is much like telling someone about a good book. You want to encourage that person to read the story without giving away the most important parts, especially the ending.

Writing Guidelines

Subject: Key parts of a fiction book
Form: A paragraph
Purpose: To preview a fiction book
Audience: Classmates

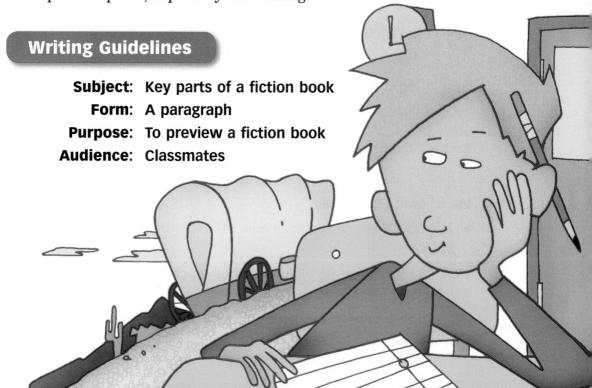

Response Paragraph

A response paragraph begins with a **topic sentence** that names the book's title and author. The **body sentences** share important ideas from the story. The **closing sentence** includes the book's message, or theme.

Topic sentence

Body sentences

Closing sentence

Little House on the Prairie

Little House on the Prairie is a book by Laura Ingalls Wilder. In the story, Laura and her family move from Wisconsin to Kansas. They travel by covered wagon and have many adventures, too. For example, they cross wide rivers in their wagon. They see packs of howling wolves, and they fight a prairie fire that is coming right at their new house. You will have to read the book to find out about Laura's other adventures. *Little House on the Prairie* is a great book that tells how the Ingalls family faces many challenges in nature, works together, and has fun in the days of the pioneers.

Respond to the reading. On your own paper, answer each of the following questions.

- **Ideas** **(1) Which sentence tells about the theme of the book?**
- **Organization** **(2) Which part of the paragraph shares important ideas from the story?**
- **Voice & Word Choice** **(3) Find two sentences that make you want to read this book.**

Prewriting **Selecting a Topic**

First, you need to choose a book to write about. Creating a list can remind you of books that you have read.

List

Fiction Book	Author
James and the Giant Peach	
Harriet the Spy	
Little House on the Prairie	Laura Ingalls Wilder *
Grizzly	Gary Paulsen

Choose a fiction book. Make a list like the one above. List books that you have enjoyed. Include authors' names if you know them. Put a star (*) next to the book you choose.

Remembering the Plot

The plot tells important details about the story. These details answer the questions *who, what, where,* and *when.*

Plot Chart

Who?	What?	Where?	When?
The Ingalls family	they had many adventures	from Wisconsin to Kansas	during pioneer days

Make a plot chart. Write the most important details from your book.

Writing Creating Your First Draft

Your paragraph should have three parts. The topic sentence names the book and its author. The body tells a few important ideas from the story. The closing sentence shares the book's theme, or message.

Write the first draft of your paragraph. *Remember:* Your goal is to tell just enough about the book to make others want to read it.

Revising Improving Your Paragraph

Next, you'll need to make improvements in your first draft.

Revise your paragraph. Use the following questions to guide your changes.

1. Do I name the book and its author?
2. Do I include some of the most important details?
3. Do I sound interested in my book?
4. Do my sentences read smoothly?

Editing Checking for Conventions

Finally, you'll need to correct any errors in your paragraph.

Edit and proofread your work. Use the questions below to help you. Then make a neat copy and proofread it again.

1. Have I checked my punctuation, spelling, and grammar?
2. Are the words in the book title capitalized correctly?
3. Have I underlined the title?

Response to Literature

Writing a Book Review

Reading a new book is like making a new friend. Each time you turn a page, you learn more about the book's story. When you finish the book, you know it well enough to tell others about it. One way to do this is to write a book review.

In this chapter, you will write a review of a fiction book you have read. You will share important parts of the story without giving away the whole story. You will also tell about the main character and explain why you like the book.

Writing Guidelines

Subject: Review of a fiction book
Form: An essay
Purpose: To show your understanding of a book and its main character
Audience: Classmates

Writing a Book Review

The beginning paragraph in a book review gives the book's title, names the author, and includes a sentence or two to introduce the book. The middle paragraphs tell about the story and the main character's personality. The ending paragraph tells why the writer likes the book.

How to Eat Fried Worms

How to Eat Fried Worms by Thomas Rockwell is one of the best books I have ever read. It is a disgusting but funny story about a boy named Billy Forrester, who accepts a bet.

"I'll bet you fifty dollars you can't eat fifteen worms," says Billy's friend, Alan. Billy answers that he will do it, but he will only eat one worm a day for fifteen days. The first worm is boiled and covered with tons of ketchup, mustard, salt, pepper, and horseradish. Billy gulps it down. He is determined to win the bet. Billy tries to find different ways to eat worms so they taste better. He eats them rolled in cornmeal and fried like fish. He even eats one buried in an ice-cream cake! Of course, Alan tries everything to get Billy to lose the bet, but

Billy won't give up. That is what makes this book so funny.

MIDDLE
The second middle paragraph tells about the main character's personality.

The best thing about Billy's personality is that he is stubborn about winning. One day, Billy almost forgets to eat his worm. When he discovers his mistake, he chomps down a raw worm just minutes before midnight. Yuck! That took courage.

ENDING

The final paragraph tells what the writer likes about the book.

I like this book because the characters are very real. It seems like everything is happening in my own backyard. Anyone who likes funny books should read How to Eat Fried Worms. I know I liked it. I will never forget Billy Forrester.

Respond to the reading. Answer the following questions about the sample book review.

- **Ideas** **(1)** What main idea or feeling about the book does the writer share in the beginning paragraph?

- **Organization** **(2)** What is the purpose of each middle paragraph?

- **Voice** & **Word Choice** **(3)** What words and phrases show you that the writer liked this book?

Prewriting Selecting a Topic

The first step in writing a book review is choosing a book. You must be able to tell about the important parts of the book and explain why you like it. One way to choose a book is to make a topic matrix.

Make a topic matrix. Use the sample below as a guide.

- In the first column, list books that you have read and enjoyed.

- In the second column, write one sentence that tells what each book is about.

- In the last column, write one sentence that tells why you like the book.

Topic Matrix

What is the book's title?	What is the book about?	Why do you like the book?
Because of Winn-Dixie ✓	It is about a girl named India Opal Buloni and her dog Winn-Dixie.	I like reading about dogs, and I like characters that remind me of people I know.
Sarah Plain and Tall	A long-ago family gets a new mom.	My family has a new dad, so I know how the children in this story feel.

Choose your topic. Review your completed matrix. Put a check mark next to the book you want to write about.

Gathering and Organizing Details

When you explain what a book is about, you should put the events in time order. A beginning-middle-ending map can help you.

Beginning-Middle-Ending Map

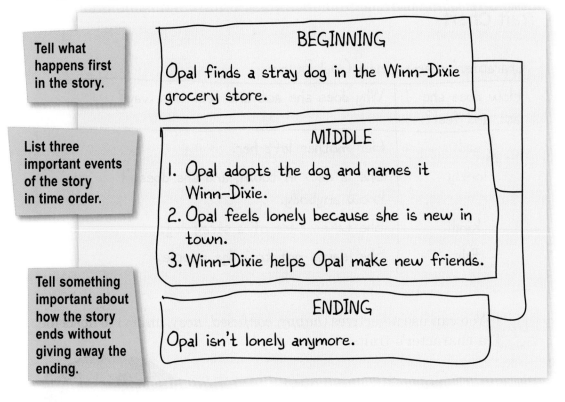

Tell what happens first in the story.

BEGINNING

Opal finds a stray dog in the Winn-Dixie grocery store.

List three important events of the story in time order.

MIDDLE

1. Opal adopts the dog and names it Winn-Dixie.
2. Opal feels lonely because she is new in town.
3. Winn-Dixie helps Opal make new friends.

Tell something important about how the story ends without giving away the ending.

ENDING

Opal isn't lonely anymore.

 tip Be sure that your book review doesn't give away any of the story's surprises or the ending.

 Prewrite **Create your beginning-middle-ending map.** As you think about your book, write down the main events from beginning to end. Try to include at least three events from the middle part, and don't give away the ending.

Prewriting Identifying Character Traits

Character traits include how a character looks, acts, and behaves. A trait chart, like the one below, can help you identify the personality traits of the characters in your book.

Trait Chart

Character's name: India Opal Buloni	
How does she act and feel?	Why does she act and feel this way?
sad	Her mother left her.
lonely	She is new in town, and she doesn't know anybody.
kind	She takes care of a stray dog.
fair	She learns not to judge people.

 tip You can use adjectives (*happy, confused, nosy, angry*) to describe a character's traits.

Prewrite **Identify character traits.** Make a trait chart for the main character in your book. List at least four personality traits and tell why you think the person acts or feels that way.

Writing **Starting Your Book Review**

The beginning paragraph of your book review should name the book's title (underlined) and the author. It should also share something interesting about the story to get the reader's attention.

Telling About the Book

Answer the 5-W and H questions to find something interesting to tell about your book.

- *Who* is the story about?
- *What* is the main character's problem?
- *Why* does the main character have this problem?
- *When* does the story happen?
- *Where* does the story happen?
- *How* does the story make you feel?

Beginning Paragraph

Review the paragraph below and the beginning paragraph in the sample review on page 258.

The beginning paragraph names the book and its author and introduces the story.

> Sad and sweet things get mixed together in <u>Because of Winn-Dixie</u> by Kate DiCamillo. India Opal Buloni feels sad because her mama left her when she was only three. Then something sweet happens to make Opal feel better. That sweet thing is a dog named Winn-Dixie.

Write your beginning. Write the first paragraph of your book review. Include the book's title, its author, and a sentence or two that tells something interesting about the story.

Writing Developing the Middle Part

The middle paragraphs should tell the important events of the story and talk about the main character's personality. Look at your beginning-middle-ending map and trait chart from pages 261–262 to help you write these paragraphs.

| Beginning |
| Middle |
| Ending |

First Middle Paragraph

Share the main events of the story in the first middle paragraph. Do not tell the most surprising parts or the ending, in case your reader chooses to read the book. (Review the paragraph below and the one on page 258.)

The first middle paragraph includes important events from the story.

Opal is lonely after she moves to a new town. Soon she finds a big stray dog in a Winn-Dixie grocery store. She names him Winn-Dixie. Opal's life changes because of her new pet. Winn-Dixie helps Opal make friends. One of them is the town librarian. She gives Opal a hard candy that tastes like root beer and strawberry. It has a secret ingredient that makes whoever eats it think of sad things. Opal decides that life is like that candy. It is sweet and sad all mixed together.

Write

Write the first middle paragraph of your review. Use your beginning-middle-ending map to guide you. Share the main events in time order.

Second Middle Paragraph

Name the main character's strongest personality trait in the second middle paragraph. Show the character's personality by including details from the book. (Review the second middle paragraph below and the one on page 259.)

| Beginning |
| Middle |
| Ending |

The second middle paragraph shares the character's strongest trait.

I like India Opal Buloni because she is friendly. In fact, I think I would like to be her friend. You can always count on Opal to start up a friendship. One day she is talking with the town librarian, Miss Franny. "You, me, and Winn-Dixie, we could all be friends," Opal says. By the end of the book, Opal has all kinds of friends.

Write

Write the second middle paragraph of your review. Look over your trait chart to guide your writing. Name the character's strongest trait and support it with an example or two.

Present-tense verbs make your writing more lively.

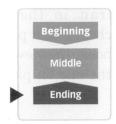

Writing Ending Your Book Review

In the ending paragraph, you should tell why you like the book. The following questions will help you write this paragraph.

- How am I like or different from the main character?

- What did I learn from the story?

- Why is this a good book?

 tip End your story by giving the reader something to think about.

Ending Paragraph

Read the ending paragraph below. The writer shares what she learned from the story. (Also review the ending paragraph on page 259.)

> **The writer shares what she learned from the story.**
>
> I like <u>Because of Winn–Dixie</u> because it has a happy ending. In my life, just like Opal, I learned that sad things get better because of good things. Special friends and pets like Winn–Dixie can change even the saddest times.

 Write your ending. Try answering one of the questions at the top of this page to help you write your ending paragraph. If that doesn't work, try another question. Keep trying until your ending sounds just right.

Form a complete first draft. Write a complete copy of your first draft. (You may want to write on every other line.)

Revising **Using a Checklist**

Revise your first draft. Number a piece of paper from 1 to 9. If you can answer "yes" to a question, put a check mark after that number. If not, work with that part of your essay.

Ideas

_____ **1.** Do I name the book and the author?

_____ **2.** Do I share three important events from the story?

_____ **3.** Do I tell about the main character's personality?

Organization

_____ **4.** Do I have a beginning, a middle, and an ending?

_____ **5.** Are events from the story in time order?

Voice

_____ **6.** Do I sound interested in the book?

Word Choice

_____ **7.** Have I used specific nouns and present-tense verbs?

Sentence Fluency

_____ **8.** Do I use a variety of sentence lengths?

_____ **9.** Are my sentences clear and easy to understand?

Make a clean copy. After revising your review, make a clean copy for editing.

Editing Using a Checklist

Edit **Edit your revised copy.** Number a piece of paper from 1 to 9. If you can answer "yes" to a question, put a check mark after that number. If not, edit for that convention.

Conventions

PUNCTUATION

_____ **1.** Do I use end punctuation in all my sentences?

_____ **2.** Do I use commas between items in a series?

_____ **3.** Do I use commas with quotations from the story?

CAPITALIZATION

_____ **4.** Do I start all of my sentences with capital letters?

_____ **5.** Do I capitalize proper nouns and words in titles?

SPELLING

_____ **6.** Have I spelled all my words correctly?

_____ **7.** Have I double-checked the words my spell-checker may have missed?

GRAMMAR

_____ **8.** Do my subjects and verbs agree (*Ky tries,* not *Ky try*)?

_____ **9.** Do I use the right words (*to, too, two*)?

Create a Title

- Use the title of the book: ***Because of Winn-Dixie***
- Focus on the main character: **New Girl in Town**
- Be creative: **Lost and Found**

Publish **Make a clean final copy.** Check your paper one last time.

Reflecting on Your Writing

Now that you've finished your book review, take a moment to reflect on it. Complete each sentence starter below on your own paper.

> Your thoughts about your writing will help you prepare for your next review.

My Book Review

1. The prewriting activity that worked best for me was . . .

2. The best part of my review is . . .

3. The part that still needs work is . . .

4. The main thing I learned about writing a book review is . . .

5. In my next book review, I would like to . . .

Additional Ideas for Book Reviews

Listed below are sentence starters that will help you gather details for other book reviews.

Plot (the action of the story)

- Several surprising events in the story are . . .
- The most important event of the story is . . .
- An event in the ending of the story is important because . . .
- The ending is (surprising, believable, unbelievable) because . . .

Characters (the people—and sometimes the animals—in the story)

- The main character changes by the end of the story because . . .
- The main character's behavior is changed by (a person, place, or thing) . . .
- The main character's most important personality trait is . . .

Setting (the time and place of the story)

- The setting affects the main character because . . .
- The setting (in a historical-fiction book) helped me to understand . . .
- The setting (in a science-fiction book) is believable or unbelievable because . . .

Theme (the author's statement or lesson about life)

- The theme of this book is . . . (overcoming a challenge, courage, survival, friendship)
- The moral (in a fable) is . . . ("Look before you leap," "Haste makes waste")
- The lesson I learned from this book is . . .

Writing in a Response Journal

One way to respond to a book is to keep a response journal. In your journal, you may write freely about the characters in the book, jot down what you think will happen next, or look for parts of the story that remind you of your own life.

How to Respond

Write in your journal several times as you read a book. For example, make an entry after you have read the first few chapters, about halfway through the book, and after you finish it. Use the following questions to help you respond as you read. (You will find more questions on page 272.)

■ **First Feelings**

What do you like best about the first few chapters? Do you like the characters? Why?

■ **On Your Way**

Are the events in the story clear? What do you think will happen next? Have your feelings changed about the characters?

■ **The Second Half**

Has anything surprising happened? Is the book still interesting? How do you think it will end?

■ **Summing Up**

How do you feel about the ending? How has the main character changed? What do you like most about the book? What do you like least? Why?

■ **Reflections**

How does the book relate to your own life? Does the book connect to today's world? Why or why not?

Additional Questions for Responding

Whenever you need a starting point for writing in your response journal, check this page for ideas. Not every idea will work for every book you read.

Before and After

- What are your feelings after reading the first part of the book?
- What is one important thing that happens in the middle of the book? Why is it important?
- What are your overall feelings about this book?

Favorites

- What is the best part of this book? Explain.
- Which illustration in the book is your favorite? Describe it in detail.

Making Changes

- Would you like to write a new ending for this book? What would it be?
- Do you think the title of the book is a good one? Why?

Author! Author!

- What do you think the author wants you to learn from this story?
- What would you say in a short friendly letter to the author?

Cast of Characters

- What is the main character in the story like? Write about him, her, or it.
- Are you like any of the characters in the book? Write a story about how you and the character are alike.
- Do any of the characters remind you of people you know? Explain by writing a comparison.
- Would you like having one of the characters in the story as a friend? Explain why or why not.

Response to Literature

Other Forms of Responding

As you go from class to class, you'll find many different kinds of literature. Literature includes short stories, articles, reports, poems, and plays. Just think of all the things you can read.

In this section, you will learn how to respond to four different forms of literature: a biography, a poem, a nonfiction article, and a tall tale.

Mini Index

Responding to a Biography

A **biography** is a book about a person's life. One way to respond to a book is to write to the author. In the sample below, Jeff responded to a biography he had read by sending an e-mail message to the author.

The **beginning** introduces the writer, the book, and the reason for liking the book.

The **middle** explains a favorite part of the book.

The **ending** includes something the writer wonders about and asks the author a question.

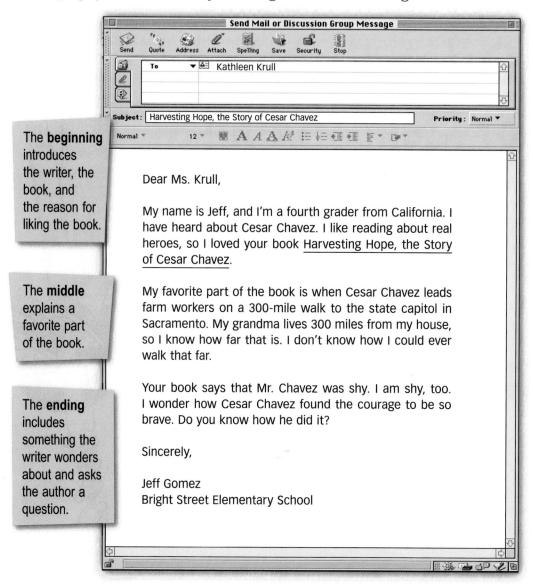

Send Mail or Discussion Group Message

Send   Quote   Address   Attach   Spelling   Save   Security   Stop

To ▾   Kathleen Krull

Subject: Harvesting Hope, the Story of Cesar Chavez   Priority: Normal ▾

Normal ▾   12 ▾

Dear Ms. Krull,

My name is Jeff, and I'm a fourth grader from California. I have heard about Cesar Chavez. I like reading about real heroes, so I loved your book Harvesting Hope, the Story of Cesar Chavez.

My favorite part of the book is when Cesar Chavez leads farm workers on a 300-mile walk to the state capitol in Sacramento. My grandma lives 300 miles from my house, so I know how far that is. I don't know how I could ever walk that far.

Your book says that Mr. Chavez was shy. I am shy, too. I wonder how Cesar Chavez found the courage to be so brave. Do you know how he did it?

Sincerely,

Jeff Gomez
Bright Street Elementary School

Prewriting Planning Your Response

To plan an e-mail response to a biography, follow these three steps.

1 **Select a biography.** Choose a book that you have read and enjoyed.

2 **Gather information for your message.** A gathering grid like the one below can help you plan your e-mail message. List why you like the book, your favorite part, and a question you would like to ask the author.

Gathering Grid

Title: <u>The Daring Nellie Bly</u>   Author: Bonnie Christensen

Why I like this book	My favorite part	My question for the author
I like to write. I'd like to be a reporter someday.	Nellie's trip around the world and the map that shows where she went	How can I become a great writer?

3 **Find out where to send your message.** Many authors have Web sites that include their e-mail addresses. Another way to contact an author is through the book publisher. Your teacher or school librarian can help you find the publisher's e-mail address.

Prewrite

Plan your response. Follow the three steps above to get ready to write your e-mail message.

Writing Developing Your Response

In the **beginning**, you should greet the author, introduce yourself, name the book, and tell why you like the story. Be sure to use the title of the book in your subject heading.

> Dear Ms. Christensen,
>
> My name is Angie. I'm a fourth grader from Virginia. I like reading about famous women. That is why I liked your book The Daring Nellie Bly.

In the **middle**, you can tell about your favorite part of the book.

> My favorite part is Nellie's trip around the world. I was surprised that she did it in 80 days. There were no airplanes back then, so she had to travel by boat and train. I loved the map you drew to show where she went.

In the **ending**, you can tell what you still wonder about and ask the author a question. Sign your e-mail message with your name and the name of your school.

> I still wonder why it was so hard for women to be reporters in Nellie's time. I would like to be a famous writer someday. Can you tell me how to get started?

Write a first draft. Write your e-mail response using the information from your gathering grid (page 275) and the guidelines above.

Revising and Editing Checklist

Once you finish your first draft, the following checklist can help you revise and edit your response.

Ideas

_____ **1.** Does my writing show that I understand the book?

_____ **2.** Do I include examples when I tell about my favorite part?

Organization

_____ **3.** Do I include a clear beginning, middle, and ending?

Voice

_____ **4.** Do I sound like I enjoyed reading the book?

Word Choice

_____ **5.** Do I use specific nouns and verbs?

Sentence Fluency

_____ **6.** Do my sentences read smoothly?

Conventions

_____ **7.** Do I use correct capitalization and punctuation?

_____ **8.** Do I spell all my words correctly?

Revise

Revise and edit your response. Make the necessary changes in your response. Proofread your final message and double-check the address before sending it.

Writing for Assessment

On a test, you may be asked to respond to a biography you have read. Study the following prompt and student response.

Prompt: *Think about a biography you have read. Write a letter to the author. Tell why you liked the book, share your favorite part, and ask the author a question.*

Notes

Title	Author	Facts	Question
On the Field with Derek Jeter	Matt Christopher	–always wanted to be a shortstop –almost got cut from his high school baseball team	Did you ever meet him?

The **beginning** introduces the writer, the book, and the reason for liking the book.	Dear Mr. Matt Christopher, My name is Steven. I'm a fourth grader from Colorado. Baseball is my favorite sport in the world. That is why I liked your book On the Field with Derek Jeter.
The **middle** explains a favorite part of the book.	My favorite part of your book is the interesting facts about Derek Jeter. He cared a lot about his family, and he wanted to be a shortstop for the Yankees ever since he was a little boy. I was surprised to find out that when he was in high school, he almost got cut from the school baseball team.
The **ending** asks the author a question.	I wonder what it would be like to meet Derek Jeter. When you wrote your book, did you get to meet him in person? Sincerely, Steven Chan Martin Luther King Elementary School

WRITING TIPS

Before you write . . .

- **Choose a book that you know and enjoy.**
  Make sure you know who the author is.
- **Make a graphic organizer.**
  Jot down notes in a simple chart to organize ideas
  for your response.

Title	Author	Facts	Question

During your writing . . .

- **Name the book and tell why you liked it.**
  Be sure to underline the book title.
- **Develop the middle.**
  Share your favorite part. Include an example.
- **End with a question.**
  In the last paragraph, mention something that you
  still wonder about and ask the author a question.

After you've written your response . . .

- **Review your writing for ideas and organization.**
  Make sure your message is clear.
- **Edit and proofread.**
  Check for errors in punctuation, capitalization,
  spelling, and grammar.

 Respond to a biography. Choose a favorite biography and write
a letter or an e-mail to the author in the time your teacher allows.

Responding to a Poem

A **poem** creates a word picture using sights, sounds, smells, tastes, and feelings. To respond to a poem, you consider its form, its sound, special words the poet uses, and the main idea of the poem. In the essay below, the writer responds to a limerick, a humorous, rhymed poem.

Toucan

There once was a toucan named Sue
Who lived in an Illinois zoo.
She dined on green peas
And swatted at bees
While she dreamed about life in Peru.

The **beginning** names the form and the topic of the poem.

"Toucan" is a limerick. A limerick has five lines that follow a pattern. The last words of lines one, two, and five rhyme with each other. The last words of lines three and four rhyme with each other. There is a special rhythm to the sound of the poem.

The **middle** explains how the words are used.

The poet uses rhyming words to create a funny story. The words make me laugh because the toucan has a huge bill, but it's trying to eat tiny, little peas. How could a toucan ever swat a bee with that big awkward bill? I think this poet enjoyed choosing the rhyming words for this poem.

The **ending** explains the main idea of the poem.

Even though "Toucan" is a funny poem, I think the main idea is that Sue wishes she were in the jungles of Peru instead of in a zoo. It makes me wonder about all animals who have to live in zoos instead of in their natural habitat.

Prewriting Planning Your Response

1 **Choose a poem.** Select one that you enjoy and understand.

2 **Read the poem out loud several times.**

> **State Flower**
> California
> Golden poppies, bright yellow
> Like flaming sunshine.

3 **Name the form of the poem** (*limerick, haiku, cinquain, free verse*). Ask yourself these questions: How many lines does the poem have? Do the words rhyme? Does the poem follow a pattern?

4 **List ideas for your response.** Make a graphic organizer like the one below to gather ideas.

Gathering Chart

Form	Special Words	Main Idea
Haiku—nature poem first line—5 syllables second line—7 syllables third line—5 syllables	golden poppies— state flower of California bright yellow color like flaming sunshine	Golden poppies look like sunshine.

Plan your response. Use the guidelines above to choose a poem and gather ideas about it. If you have trouble finding a poem, you may use this one:

Early Evening
The night is blazing
With a swarm of fireflies
Dancing a ballet.

Writing Developing Your Response

The **beginning** paragraph names and describes the poem's form and subject.

> "State Flower" is a haiku poem about California poppies. Haiku poems are three lines long. The first and third lines have five syllables. The second line has seven syllables. Haiku poems are about nature.

The **middle** paragraph explains how the poet uses special words in the poem. Examples from the poem support your ideas.

> The first line of the poem names the state of California. The other lines describe what the golden poppy looks like. For example, golden poppies are "bright yellow." They look "like flaming sunshine." The last line reminds me that the sun is bright because it's a huge ball of fire. I think a field of poppies might look like it's on fire with sunshine!

The **ending** paragraph explains the poem's main idea.

> The poem's main idea is that golden poppies are cheerful and bright like sunshine. I think the poet loves looking at the poppies. In this poem about the Golden State's flower, I can feel that "flaming sunshine," too.

Write a first draft. Use the explanations above and your planning from page 281 to create your response. Include a beginning, a middle, and an ending.

Revising and Editing Checklist

Once you finish your first draft, use the following checklist to revise and edit your response.

Ideas

_____ **1.** Do my ideas show that I understand the poem?

_____ **2.** Do I name the form and quote words from the poem?

Organization

_____ **3.** Do I include the beginning, middle, and ending parts?

Voice

_____ **4.** Do I sound like I understand and enjoy the poem?

Word Choice

_____ **5.** Do I use specific nouns and verbs?

Sentence Fluency

_____ **6.** Do my sentences read smoothly?

Conventions

_____ **7.** Do I use correct capitalization and punctuation?

_____ **8.** Do I spell all my words correctly?

Revise and edit your response. Make the necessary changes to your response. Proofread your final copy before sharing it.

Writing for Assessment

On a test, you may be asked to respond to a poem. Study the following prompt and student response.

Prompt: *Respond to the following poem. In your essay, name the topic, explain the poem's form, point out special words the poet uses, and share the poem's main idea or message.*

> **Spider**
> Smart, quick
> Weaving a web
> To trap its prey
> Arachnid.

The **beginning** names the poem and explains the form.

"Spider" is a word cinquain poem about spiders. It has five lines that follow the pattern one word, two words, three words, four words, and one word. The first line and the last line are synonyms.

The **middle** describes special words the poet uses.

The poet uses different kinds of words to help the reader see the spider. <u>Smart</u> and <u>quick</u> are adjectives. They describe the spider and how it moves. <u>Weaving</u> is a verb that shows the spider in action. The line "to trap its prey" shows the spider as a hunter. The last word, <u>arachnid</u>, is a synonym for spider. I like the word because it sounds scary. I think being caught in a web would be scary, especially for a bug.

The **ending** explains the main idea of the poem.

The poem's main idea is that spiders are very clever. This poem shows a spider setting a trap for its prey.

WRITING TIPS

Before you write . . .

- **Read the poem several times.**
  Think about its form and
  how the words are used.
- **Make a graphic organizer.**
  Use a gathering chart to organize
  ideas for your response.

Gathering Chart

Form	
Special words	
Main idea	

During your writing . . .

- **Name and describe the form of the poem.**
  Name the kind of poem (*haiku, cinquain, free verse, limerick*) and explain how it is put together.
- **Develop the middle part.**
  Tell how the poet uses special words in the poem.
- **Share the meaning of the poem.**
  In the ending, explain the poem's main idea or message.

After you've written your response . . .

- **Review your writing for ideas and organization.**
  Make sure your ideas are clear.
- **Edit and proofread.**
  Check for errors in punctuation, capitalization, spelling, and grammar.

Respond to a poem. Respond to the following poem or to a poem selected by your teacher.

> **Mid-Summer Night**
> Summer moon rising
> Turns the sleeping lake to gold
> Echoing loon calls.

Responding to a Nonfiction Article

A **nonfiction article** shares information about a real person, place, or thing. One way to respond to a nonfiction article is to write a summary of it.

Sample Article

Whiskers—A Cat's Antennae

Whiskers are an important part of a cat's body. They help a cat to move around. These long, thick hairs on a cat's face can sense even the smallest changes in air movement. As a cat gets close to an object, its whiskers sense a change in the air. This allows a cat to move about in the dark without bumping into things.

The tips of whiskers contain many nerve endings. This means that a cat can judge the width of an opening by feeling the edges with its whiskers. It can decide if it can fit through tight spaces.

You should never trim a cat's whiskers. Without them it is much harder for a cat to move around safely.

Sample Summary

The **topic sentence** names the article's main idea.

The **body** includes the most important information from the article.

The **closing sentence** includes the final important point.

A cat's whiskers help it to move around. Whiskers can sense any small movement in the air. They help a cat tell when an object is near. A cat can judge how wide a space is by feeling the edges with its whiskers. Without whiskers it would be hard for a cat to move around safely.

Prewriting Planning Your Summary

Follow these steps when you plan to write a summary of an article.

1 Select an interesting article to read, like this one:

> ### Ah . . . Ah . . . Ah-choo!
>
> A sneeze results from a chain of events that takes place in a matter of seconds. It may be a response to particles in the air, like dust, or to a sudden change in temperature.
>
> First, your nose gets a tickle. The tickle tells your brain to create a sneeze. Your brain then sends a message to all the muscles that make up a sneeze. These include muscles in and near your belly, chest, lungs, vocal cords, throat, face, and eyes. All of these muscles work together, in just the right order, to build a sneeze. Ah-choo!
>
> The sneeze sends tiny particles from your nose flying at speeds of up to 100 miles per hour. This is why you should always cover your mouth and nose when you sneeze (and wash your hands afterward). A sneeze often results in germs being spread from one person to another.

2 Make an idea cluster like the one below to name the topic. Add the most important information in your own words.

Idea Cluster

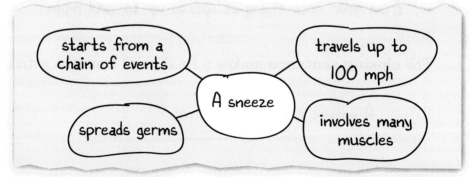

starts from a chain of events

travels up to 100 mph

A sneeze

spreads germs

involves many muscles

Plan your summary. Follow the steps above to get started on your summary. If you can't find an article, ask your teacher for help.

Prewrite

Writing **Developing Your Summary**

Your summary paragraph will have three main parts: a topic sentence, the body, and a closing sentence. (See pages 333–336.)

The **topic sentence** should state the article's main idea.

> A sneeze results from a chain of events.

Tips for finding the main idea

- Look for the main idea at the beginning or end of the first paragraph in an article.
- Ask yourself, "What main message is the author communicating?"

The **body** includes *only* the most important information from the article. All of the sentences in the body should support the topic sentence. Arrange your ideas so that they are easy to follow.

> These events take only a few seconds. Many muscles work together to make a sneeze. Sneezing sends particles from your nose flying at speeds up to 100 mph.

The **closing sentence** makes a final point from the article.

> A sneeze can spread germs.

Write a first draft. Write your summary paragraph using the information above and your idea cluster (page 287).

Revising and Editing Checklist

Use the following checklist to revise and edit your summary.

Ideas

_____ **1.** Do I share the article's most important ideas?

Organization

_____ **2.** Does my topic sentence state the article's main idea?

_____ **3.** Do the body sentences include the most important ideas from the article?

_____ **4.** Does the last sentence make a final point about the topic?

Voice

_____ **5.** Do I sound confident, like I understand the article?

Word Choice

_____ **6.** Have I put the information in my own words?

Sentence Fluency

_____ **7.** Do my sentences flow smoothly?

Conventions

_____ **8.** Do I use correct capitalization and punctuation?

_____ **9.** Do I spell all my words correctly?

Revise

Revise and edit your summary. Make the necessary changes and corrections. Proofread your final copy before sharing it.

Writing for Assessment

On a test, you may be asked to respond to a nonfiction article. Study the following prompt and student response.

Prompt: *Carefully read the following article. Then briefly summarize the article. Include the most important details.*

The Unstoppable Franklin D. Roosevelt

Franklin D. Roosevelt was the 32nd president of the United States. He was also disabled. As an adult, he had an illness called polio that left him unable to move his legs.

Roosevelt never gave up. He fought hard to walk again. Even though he regained some strength in his legs, he was never able to walk without help.

He wore leg braces, and he used crutches and a wheelchair.

Polio did not stop President Roosevelt. He was elected for four terms. While in office, he created programs for disabled American citizens. Roosevelt was determined. He would not let a disability stop him from doing great things.

Sample Summary

The **topic sentence** states the subject of the article.

The **body** includes the most important details in the writer's own words.

The **closing sentence** sums up the information.

As an adult, Franklin D. Roosevelt got polio. He could not move his legs. Even with hard work, for the rest of his life, he was able to walk only with help. He was elected president of the United States four times. He also came up with programs to help other people with disabilities. Roosevelt never let his disability stop him.

WRITING TIPS

Before you write . . .

- **Read the prompt and the article.**
  Be sure you understand what the prompt asks you to do.

Idea Cluster

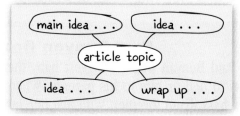

- **Make a graphic organizer.**
  Create a cluster about the article to collect details for your summary.

During your writing . . .

- **Organize your summary.**
  In the topic sentence, state the article's main idea. Use the body sentences to share other important information. End with a final important point.

After you've written your summary . . .

- **Review your writing for ideas and organization.**
  Make sure that your summary includes *only* information from the article.
- **Edit and proofread.**
  Check for errors in punctuation, capitalization, spelling, and grammar.

Respond to the following prompt.
Read a brief nonfiction article about a person. Write a summary of the article that includes the main idea and the most important information. Complete your work in the time your teacher allows.

Responding to a Tall Tale

Tall tales are filled with humor and exaggeration. They are often about superhuman characters doing amazing things. One way to respond to a tall tale is to compare yourself to one of the characters. Read this tall tale and the student response.

Paul Bunyan Grows Up and Up

Paul Bunyan was the biggest baby there ever was. Moreover, it took five giant storks to deliver him to his parents. When he arrived, his cry was like a buzz saw and a bass drum together. With just one holler, Paul emptied a whole pond of frogs. He had a giant appetite, too. He ate 40 bowls of porridge at a time, and he grew faster than bamboo. He grew so fast that before long his clothes had wagon wheels for buttons. One day, Paul's daddy gave him a blue ox named Babe. Babe grew just as fast as Paul. In fact, the two were so big that the tracks they made walking around Minnesota made 10,000 lakes.

The **beginning** names the story and tells what it's about.

The **middle** compares the responder to the tall-tale character.

The **ending** leaves the reader with something to think about.

When I read "Paul Bunyan Grows Up and Up," I discovered that Paul was a very big, strong baby. Paul and his pet ox became giants.

In some ways, I am like Paul. I can be loud like him. I have never scared frogs out of a pond, but sometimes I yell loud enough to scare my dog. I also have a big appetite. I don't eat porridge, but I can gobble up a couple bowls of cereal and three pieces of toast.

I am different from Paul because I'm not a giant. I have a pet dachshund, but she's tiny compared to Babe. Sometimes I make muddy tracks on the kitchen floor, but they turn into little brown puddles, not lakes.

When I read this tall tale, I thought about my baby brother. He is growing very fast. I guess we had better watch him. I hope he's not another Paul Bunyan!

Prewriting **Gathering Details**

Follow these steps when you plan a response to a tall tale.

1 Read an interesting tall tale, like this one:

> ### Pecos Bill Rides a Twister
>
>   Pecos Bill was up in Kansas one day. He wanted to ride something mean and fast, so he decided to ride a tornado. He waited for the biggest, meanest tornado to come along. When it did, it turned the sky to pea soup, and it roared so loud you could hear it clear to China. As it spun, it whipped and whirled and tied rivers into knots. Bill rode that twister all the way to California. Along the way, it made so much rain that it washed out the Grand Canyon. Finally, the tornado gave out in California, and Bill fell to the ground. He landed so hard that he sank below sea level. Today that spot is called Death Valley.

2 Use a Venn diagram to show how you are like and how you are different from the main character.

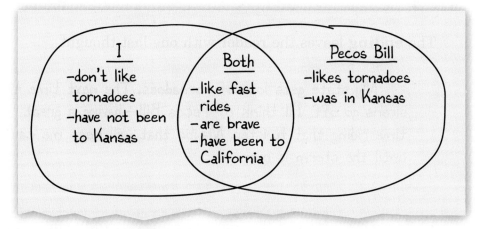

I
- don't like tornadoes
- have not been to Kansas

Both
- like fast rides
- are brave
- have been to California

Pecos Bill
- likes tornadoes
- was in Kansas

Prewrite

Plan your response. Follow the steps above to get started. If you can't find a tall tale, ask your teacher for help.

Writing Developing Your Response

The **beginning** names the story and tells what it is about.

> In "Pecos Bill Rides a Twister," I found out that Pecos Bill was brave. He even went looking for danger.

The **middle** tells how you are like and how you are different from the tall-tale character.

> I think I'm a little like Pecos Bill. I sure love to ride fast things, although I prefer scooters and roller coasters. Bill liked riding tornadoes. Now that's brave! I was brave, too, when I had to get 15 stitches in my leg. We've both been to California, too.
>
> Pecos Bill and I are different because he likes tornadoes, and I don't. Twisters do way too much damage. Also, I've never been to Kansas like Pecos Bill has.

The **ending** leaves the reader with one last thought.

> My state gets lots of tornadoes. The next time the sirens go off, I'll think of Pecos Bill—having a great time riding that twister. Maybe that will keep me calm until the storm is over.

Write a first draft. Write the beginning, the middle, and the ending of your response. Use the information above and your Venn diagram (page 293.)

Revising and Editing Checklist

Once you finish your first draft, use the following checklist to revise and edit your response.

Ideas

_____ **1.** Do I include important details from the story?

Organization

_____ **2.** Does the beginning name the story and tell what I discovered?

_____ **3.** Does the middle make a comparison?

_____ **4.** Does the ending give the reader a final thought?

Voice

_____ **5.** Do I make a personal connection to the tall tale?

Word Choice

_____ **6.** Have I used strong nouns and vivid verbs?

Sentence Fluency

_____ **7.** Do my sentences flow smoothly?

Conventions

_____ **8.** Do I use correct capitalization and punctuation?

_____ **9.** Do I spell all my words correctly?

Revise

Revise and edit your response. Make the necessary changes and corrections. Proofread your final copy before sharing it.

Writing for Assessment

On a test, you may be asked to respond to a tall tale. Study the following prompt and student response.

Prompt: *Write a response to this tall tale, comparing the main character to yourself. Show how you are the same and how you are different.*

Jack and the Popcorn Stalk

One day, a farmer sent his son to see how the popcorn was growing. Jack was small, so he took a ladder with him, just in case the popcorn was taller than he was. He found the tallest stalk, and using the ladder, he climbed to the top and hung on. Before he knew it, the stalk had grown so high that Jack couldn't get back down to the ladder. He was stuck up there. Jack's father and all the other farmers tried to get him down, but the stalk was growing too fast. Poor Jack. He had to stay there till the stalk nearly reached the sun. Then the popcorn started popping. That gave Jack an idea. He jumped back down to earth—into a mountain of popcorn.

The beginning names the story and restates the prompt.

The middle compares the responder to the tall-tale character.

The ending gives the reader something to think about.

As I read "Jack and the Popcorn Stalk," I compared myself to Jack. He's the main character in the tall tale.

Jack and I are alike because we are both small. We also both live in the country. Jack seems to help out at home, and so do I.

We are different for two reasons. First, I am too heavy to climb up a popcorn stalk. Second, I would not be patient enough to wait for the corn to pop. I would scream and yell if I were stuck somewhere and couldn't get down.

This tall tale reminds me of the story of Jack and the beanstalk. The difference is that jumping into a mountain of popcorn is much more fun than being chased by a giant.

WRITING TIPS

Before you write . . .

- **Read the tall tale and the prompt.**
  Be sure you know what the prompt is asking you to do.
- **Make a graphic organizer.**
  Create a Venn diagram to collect details for your comparison.

Venn Diagram

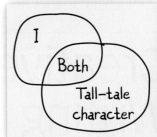

During your writing . . .

- **Organize your response.**
  In the first paragraph, name the story and tell what you discovered. In the middle part, tell how you are like and how you are different from the tall-tale character. In the ending paragraph, give the reader something to think about.

After you've written your response . . .

- **Review your writing for ideas and organization.**
  Make sure your ideas are clear.
- **Edit and proofread.**
  Check for errors in punctuation, capitalization, spelling, and grammar.

Respond to the following prompt.
Read a tall tale. Write a response comparing yourself to the tall-tale character. Show how you are the same and how you are different.

Creative Writing

Creative Writing

Writing Stories

Fictional stories let us experience life from someone else's point of view. They can make us feel strong emotions—happiness, sadness, or even fear. After reading the best stories, we may even feel changed in some important way.

In this chapter, you will learn to write a realistic fictional story. This kind of story seems real, but it is made up. You can also try writing a fantasy story or a play.

Writing Guidelines

Subject:	Realistic fictional story
Form:	Short story
Purpose:	To entertain
Audience:	Classmates

Realistic Fictional Story

The story below focuses on the real-life problem of being messy. The main character, Jessica, discovers why she should be more organized.

A Messy Lesson

BEGINNING

The beginning introduces the main character, the setting, and the problem.

Jessica danced into her room. She couldn't wait for tomorrow's field trip. She plopped her bulging backpack on her desk, on top of all the papers and junk. Her mother was always complaining about the messy bedroom, but Jessica didn't think it was that bad.

The phone rang, and Jessica ran to answer it. "Hello?"

Her best friend, Lacey, squealed, "Hi, Jess! I'm so excited about tomorrow!"

"Me, too!" Jessica said. "I've never been to the aquarium!"

"Did you get your permission slip signed? If you don't have it, you can't go."

"My permission slip! Sorry, Lacey, I've got to go!" Jessica hung up and rushed back to her room. "Where's that blue slip?"

RISING ACTION

The character tries to solve the problem.

Jessica started digging through stacks of books, papers, old magazines, granola-bar wrappers, broken jewelry, and piles of clothes on her desk. She started throwing away trash and sorting out important papers. Slowly, the desktop appeared, but the permission slip wasn't there.

Jessica turned to the rest of her messy room. "It could be anywhere."

She picked things up, searching for the blue slip of paper. As she looked, she filled her clothes hamper and tossed out more junk. Soon, she could see the floor, but she couldn't see that little blue paper.

Jessica's mother came to the doorway and looked around the room. "Wow, this looks great!"

"But I can't find my permission slip. If I don't have it, I can't go to the aquarium tomorrow." Jessica sat down on her newly made bed and started to cry. "I guess there is a reason to be neat."

HIGH POINT
The problem gets solved.

Her mother smiled. "There's one more messy place to check. Have you looked in your backpack?"

ENDING

The ending tells how the character changes.

Jessica lifted the pack and unzipped it. She emptied the whole mess onto her bed. Jessica started sorting through all the papers. Suddenly, she found the slip. Waving it, she said, "Here it is! Here it is! And from now on, I promise to do better! I guess neatness is important, after all."

Respond to the reading. On your own paper, answer the following questions about the story.

- **Ideas** **(1) What does Jessica want? (2) What problem does she face?**

- **Organization** **(3) What element of fiction does the writer use to share the characters' thoughts and feelings? (See pages 309–310.)**

- **Voice & Word Choice** **(4) What words or phrases help create a picture of Jessica's room? List three.**

Prewriting Selecting a Topic

One way to create a character is to combine traits of people you know. LaToya, the writer of "A Messy Lesson," made the chart below.

Character Chart

Name	Age	Hair	Wears	Personality
Kenny	(10)	spiky blond	headphones	(messy)
Rosa	11	(long brown)	heart pin	quiet
Bette	22	short black	(lots of rings)	kooky

Create a character chart. Make a chart like the one above. List friends and fill in each column. Circle the traits you want to use for your character. Decide on a name for your character.

Selecting a Problem

Next, you need a problem for your character to solve. To think about different everyday problems, LaToya made the following chart.

Problem Chart

School	Friends	Home	Neighborhood
-tough art class	-Sasha's move	-Billy tattles	-Busy street
-long bus ride	-Trouble on scout trip	(-Mom says I'm too messy)	-Noisy neighbors

Create a problem chart. Make a chart like the one above. Fill it in with problems and choose one problem for your story.

Creating a Plot

The actions that take place during a story make up the plot line. Each part of the plot plays an important role in the story.

- The **beginning** introduces the characters and setting.
- The **rising action** gives the main character a problem to solve.
- The **high point** is the most exciting part.
- The **ending** tells how everything works out.

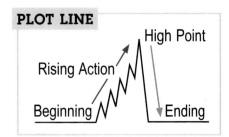

PLOT LINE

Rising Action

High Point

Beginning

Ending

LaToya planned her story by making the plot chart below.

Plot Chart

Beginning	Rising Action	High Point	Ending
Jessica is excited about a field trip. Lacey reminds her of the permission slip.	Jessica looks for the slip, but her room is too messy. She starts to clean up.	Jessica's room is clean, but she still can't find the slip. Her mother suggests one more place to look.	Jessica finds the slip in her backpack. She decides to be neater.

Prewrite

Create a plot chart. In each column, write what will happen in the beginning, during the rising action, at the high point, and in the ending.

Writing **Creating Your First Draft**

You're ready to begin your story. Follow the tips below.

1 Set the scene by *showing* instead of *telling*.

Instead of . . . **Jessica was happy.**

    Write . . . Jessica danced into her room.

2 Use action to show the reader what is happening.

Instead of . . . **She cleaned up.**

    Write . . . She started throwing away trash and sorting out important papers.

3 Use dialogue to let characters speak for themselves.

Instead of . . . **Lacey was excited about the field trip.**

    Write . . . Lacey squealed, "Hi, Jess! I'm so excited about tomorrow!"

4 Use sensory details to make the story come alive.

Instead of . . . **The desk was messy.**

    Write . . . Jessica started digging through stacks of books, papers, old magazines, granola-bar wrappers, broken jewelry, and piles of clothes on her desk.

5 Build the tension to a high point.

Instead of . . . **Her mom told her where to look, and Jessica found it.**

    Write . . . Her mother smiled. "There's one more messy place to check. Have you looked in your backpack?"

Write your first draft. Use your prewriting and the tips above to write the first draft of your realistic story.

Revising Improving Your Writing

Once you have finished your first draft, set it aside for a while. When you are ready to revise, the following questions can help you.

- **Ideas** Have I included an interesting character and problem?
- **Organization** Have I gradually built up to the high point?
- **Voice** Have I used dialogue?
- **Word Choice** Have I used action verbs to show, not tell?
- **Sentence Fluency** Do my sentences read smoothly?

Improve your writing. Use the questions above to guide your changes.

Editing Checking for Conventions

The following questions can help you edit your story.

- **Conventions** Have I corrected spelling and capitalization errors? Have I included end punctuation for each sentence? Have I checked for easily confused words *(its, it's)*?

Check your story. Use the questions above to guide your editing. After correcting any errors, use the tips below to write a title. Then make a clean final copy and proofread it.

Creating a Title

- Use a repeated sound: **A Messy Lesson**
- Be playful: **Jess vs. the Mess**
- Use a line from the story: **A Reason to Be Neat**

Creating a Fantasy

Another type of fictional story is a fantasy. In a fantasy, animals can talk, people can fly, and anything can happen. Here are some hints to help you write a story that is fantastic yet believable.

1 **Pretend impossible things are possible.**

Write as if your imaginary world actually exists.

Roger shook his shiny mane and stomped his hoof. "I don't like this," he snorted. His tail angrily flicked away a fly.

2 **Give the character a fantastical problem.**

Introduce your main character, set the scene, and give the character a problem that is out of this world.

One night, Luc jumped out of bed and ran to the window. Outside, a spaceship was landing. What should he do?

3 **Decide what feeling you want the story to give.**

Create the mood you want—happy, sad, funny, or so on.

Name's Snuffy. I'm a police bloodhound. I'm supposed to sniff out criminals, but I always have a cold and can't smell anything. That caused a big problem one day when . . .

Write a fantasy. Imagine a very different world. Create an interesting character and a fantastical problem. Let your imagination run free as you write.

Creating a Play

A story can also be told in a play. Plays use **dialogue** (what people say) to tell the story. The **action** (what people do) is written in parentheses. Here is the start of LaToya's play.

What a Mess!

Characters: Jessica, 10 years old
             Lacey, 10 years old
             Mom

Setting: Jessica's room

ACT I

(Jessica and Lacey enter her room. Jessica drops her backpack on her messy desk.)

Lacey: (Moves papers off a chair and sits down.) Wow, Jess, how can you find anything in here?

Jessica: (Flops on her bed, scattering stuff.) I know where everything is. I'm just too busy to clean up.

Lacey: I can't wait for tomorrow's field trip!

Jessica: Yeah! I've never been to the aquarium.

Lacey: Well, don't forget your permission slip!

Jessica: It's right here on my desk (she looks at the messy desk) somewhere. I know I had it. . . .

Write your story as a play. Use the sample above as a guide. List your characters, set the scene, and then write dialogue to tell your story.

Story Patterns

Stories follow different patterns. Here are five popular story patterns that you could try.

The Rivalry
Two characters face each other in competition, with a prize at stake.

> Two friends compete for the chance to attend the state science fair.

The Change
A character overcomes a challenge or a personal weakness and changes or grows in some way.

> A girl must overcome her fear of heights to save her sister stranded on a cliff.

The Obstacle
Two characters are kept apart and must find a way to be together.

> The dog is left behind by mistake when a family moves, and he must find his way to the new home.

The Rescue
A character must either be rescued or must rescue someone else who is in trouble.

> A girl searches for her grandfather, who is lost in a crocodile-filled bayou in Louisiana.

The Pursuit
A character chases another character with a goal in mind.

> A detective must hunt down a jewel thief before she can steal the world's largest diamond.

Check the story pattern. Think of a favorite story. Does it fit one of the story patterns above? If not, how would you describe its story pattern?

Elements of Fiction

Writers use specific terms to talk about the parts of a story. In the following list, you'll find words that will help you talk about the stories you write and read.

Action   The **action** is everything that happens in a story.

Antagonist   An **antagonist** (sometimes called a villain) is a person or thing that fights against the hero.

> The wolf is the antagonist of the three little pigs.

Character   A **character** is a person or humanlike animal in a story.

Conflict   **Conflict** is a problem or challenge for the characters. There are five basic types of conflict:

- **Person vs. Person:**
  Two characters have opposite goals.
  > A supervillain wants to sink a ship, but a superhero wants to save it.

- **Person vs. Society:**
  A character has a problem with a group of people.
  > A student has trouble fitting in at a new school.

- **Person vs. Himself or Herself:**
  A character has an inner struggle.
  > A young student wonders what to do when he discovers his best friend cheating on a test.

- **Person vs. Nature:**
  A character has to battle an element of nature.
  > A mountain climber gets caught in a blizzard.

- **Person vs. Fate:**
  A character faces something he or she can't control.
  > After falling from a horse, an injured man fights to learn to walk again.

Dialogue   **Dialogue** refers to the words characters speak to each other in a story.

Mood   **Mood** is the feeling a reader gets from a story—happy, sad, frightened, peaceful.

Moral   A **moral** is a lesson the writer wants the reader to learn from a story. The moral of "The Boy Who Cried Wolf" is that if you tell lies, no one will believe you even when you tell the truth.

Narrator   The **narrator** is the one who tells the story. Harold the dog tells the story in the book *Bunnicula*, so Harold is the narrator (even though he is a dog!).

Plot   The **plot** is the action or series of events that make up the story. Most plots have four parts: beginning, rising action, high point, and ending. (See page 303.)

Point of View   **Point of view** is the angle from which a story is told.

- A story told by the main character uses *first-person point of view.*

  I danced into my room and plopped my backpack on my desk.

- A story told by a narrator uses *third-person point of view.*

  Jessica danced into her room and plopped her backpack on her desk.

Protagonist   The **protagonist** is the hero of the story.

Setting   The **setting** is the time and place of a story.

Theme   A **theme** is a main message of a story. One theme of *Charlotte's Web* is the importance of friendship.

Tone   The **tone** is the feeling the author creates in a story. For example, the tone of a story may be serious, funny, or angry.

Creative Writing
Writing Poems

Some words make pictures: *shimmer* and *shine, spiky* and *sharp, yellow* and *green*. Other words make sounds: *whistle* and *toot, blare* and *bray, rumble* and *crash*. Poems use words to help the reader see, hear, feel, and experience something new.

Writing a poem can let you describe someone you know. The details you choose and the way you put them together will reveal a lot about the person. This chapter will help you write in this special way about someone interesting.

Writing Guidelines

Subject: An interesting person
Form: Free-verse poem
Purpose: To entertain
Audience: Classmates and family

Free-Verse Poem

Free-verse poems do not follow a rhyming pattern. However, they still use language in a special way. Brant wrote the following free-verse poem about his grandfather.

Grandpa Mac

My grandpa has sawdust in his beard
whenever I visit.
He always brushes off his clothes
before he opens the door, but he never
remembers his beard and hair.
When he grins,
sawdust trembles on his chin.
When he bends down to hug me,
I smell sawdust
and peppermint gum.
He hands me a stick of gum
on the way to his workshop.

Respond to the reading. On your own paper, answer the following questions about the traits of writing in this poem.

- **Ideas** **(1)** What smells are mentioned in the poem?

- **Organization** **(2)** The poem tells a little story. List the main events of this story in order.

- **Word Choice** **(3)** What words tell you something about Grandpa Mac's personality?

Prewriting Selecting a Topic

In order to write a poem, you need a topic. Brant brainstormed ideas by making a list of interesting people in his life.

List

my friend Chasidy	Mr. Green, my soccer coach
✓ Grandpa Mac	Mrs. Gill at Dobrin's Bakery
my Spanish teacher	TJ, my youth-group leader

Make a list. Make a list of interesting people in your life. Choose one you would like to write about.

Gathering Details

Poems use sensory details to create an image. Brant gathered details about his grandfather in a sensory chart.

Sensory Chart

See	Hear	Smell	Taste	Touch
kind of short	chuckling laughter	peppermint gum	sawdust in the air	rough hands
gray whiskers	Grandpa scratching his beard when he's thinking	sawdust from his shop	peppermint gum he gives me	prickly beard
gray work clothes		machine oil on his tools		tight hug
light blue eyes				
laugh wrinkles				
sawdust shaking on his chin				

Gather sensory details. Make a chart like the one above and list details about the person you are writing about.

Prewriting Using Poetry Techniques

Poets use special techniques in their writing. Brant used line breaks and repetition to make his poem special.

- **Repetition** is the use of the same word, idea, or phrase. This creates rhythm or emphasis.

    When he **grins,**

    sawdust trembles on his chin.

    When he **bends down to hug me, . . .**

- **Line breaks** make the reader slow down and pay attention to certain words and phrases.

    I smell sawdust

    and peppermint gum.

Use poetry techniques. Find important words in your sensory chart. You can emphasize them with repetition and line breaks.

Writing Developing Your First Draft

The following tips will help you write your poem.

- **Imagine being with this special person.** Review your sensory chart for details. Focus on your feelings.

- **Write whatever comes to mind.** Write descriptive words, phrases, and sentences about the person. You can organize your ideas and add line breaks later.

- **Play with words.** Have fun. Don't worry about writing a perfect poem.

Write the first draft of your poem. Using the tips above, show the reader the special person you are writing about.

Revising Improving Your Poem

You can revise your poem by thinking about the traits of writing.

- **Ideas** Do I use sensory details to *show* the person? Do I share my feelings?
- **Organization** Do I arrange my ideas in an interesting way?
- **Voice** Is my poem original, or fresh?
- **Word Choice** Do I use repetition for emphasis?
- **Sentence Fluency** Do my line breaks help make my poem interesting and easy to read?

Revise your writing. Change your poem until you're happy with every word.

Editing Fine-Tuning Your Poem

Free-verse poems don't always follow all the capitalization and punctuation rules.

- **Conventions** Are the words in my poem spelled correctly? Did I use punctuation effectively?

Edit your work. Correct any errors in your poem.

Publishing Sharing Your Poem

There are many ways to share your poetry.

- **Perform it** or read it aloud to friends and family.
- **Display it** on a bulletin board or on the fridge at home.
- **Send it out** to a newspaper, magazine, or Web site. Ask your teacher to help you submit it.

Present your work. Use an idea above or one of your own.

Writing a "Where I'm From" Poem

A "Where I'm From" poem tells interesting details about your background. In the process, it reveals something about who you are. Aleshia wrote this poem about her own background.

Where I'm From

I'm from a house downtown,
near the library, town square, and fairgrounds,
a great place for skateboards, bikes, and squirrels.

I'm from a family with four daughters,
between one older sister and two younger,
a great place for sharing music, books, and dolls.

I'm from green parks, fresh air, giggling sisters, and happy songs.

WRITING TIPS

- **Select a topic.** This is easy. Just write about yourself.
- **Gather details.** Make a list of unusual or interesting details about at least two of the following ideas.
  - The area near your home
  - Your family and its history
  - Your friends
  - Your favorite things
- **Follow the form.** Write two stanzas (group of lines), one for each of the ideas you chose above. Use line breaks and repetition to change the rhythm and emphasis of your words. Add a final line to summarize your feelings.

 Create your "Where I'm From" poem. Follow the tips above to write your own poem. Let it show your unique personality.

Writing Rhymed Poetry

Rhyme can add fun and interest to a poem. It is important to find rhymes that fit your ideas naturally.

Split Couplet

A couplet is two rhyming lines of about the same length. A split couplet, however, has a long first line and a short second line. The first line has five stressed syllables; the second has two. You can put several split couplets together to make a longer poem.

> **Moira**
>
> Moira listens to my secret fears,
> And shares her tears.
> Moira stands up for me when kids say
> That I can't play.
> She forgot to bring a pen one time.
> I lent her mine.
> Now you know how this poem will end.
> She's a true friend.

WRITING TIPS

- **Select a topic.** Choose an interesting person you know.
- **Gather details.** Make a list of details about that person. How does he or she look? What is his or her personality like? How does the person touch your life?
- **Follow the form.** Write sentences or phrases that use details from your list. Write the first line of a couplet; then think of a rhyming word to end the second line.

 Write a split-couplet poem. Follow the tips above to write a poem containing at least two split couplets.

Using Special Poetry Techniques

These two pages explain some special techniques that poets use.

Figures of Speech

- A **simile** *(sĭm'ə-lē)* compares two different things using *like* or *as*.

    The picket fence looked like a toothy smile.

- A **metaphor** *(mĕt'ə-fôr)* compares two different things without using *like* or *as*.

    The picket fence is a friendly guard.

- **Personification** *(pər-sŏn'ə-fĭ-kā'shən)* makes an object seem human.

    The picket fence grinned with bright white teeth.

- **Hyperbole** *(hī-pûr'bə-lē)* is an exaggeration.

    The picket fence even kept the birds out of our yard.

Sounds of Poetry

Poets use the following techniques to add interesting sounds to their work. (Also see page 314.)

- **Alliteration** *(ə-lĭt'ə-rā'shən)* is the repeating of beginning consonant sounds.

    green parks, fresh air, and giggling sisters

- **Assonance** *(ăs'ə-nəns)* is the repeating of vowel sounds in words.

    giggling sisters

- **Consonance** *(kŏn'sə-nəns)* is the repeating of consonant sounds anywhere in words.

    peppermint gum

- **Line breaks** slow down the reader and bring attention to individual words and phrases.

  > He hands me a stick of gum
  >
  > on the way to his workshop.

- **Onomatopoeia** *(ŏn´ə-măt´ə-pē´ə)* is the use of words that sound like what they name.

  > The iron hisses, sizzles, and pops as it heats.

- **Repetition** is the use of the same word, idea, or phrase for rhythm or emphasis.

  > They kept me waiting, waiting, waiting.

- **Rhyme** *(rīm)* is the use of words whose endings sound alike.

  End rhyme happens at the ends of lines.

  > Now you know how this poem will end.
  >
  > She's a true friend.

  Internal rhyme happens within lines.

  > And trails of snails.

- **Rhythm** *(rĭth´əm)* means the pattern of accented and unaccented syllables.

  > I lent her mine.

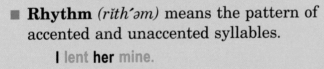

 Write a poem. Write about a favorite person. Use one figure of speech and at least one special sound technique.

Research Writing

Research Writing

Building Skills

Research means investigating. Like a detective, when you search for information, you may find something interesting. That might give you an idea about another place you can look. Along the way, you take notes to keep track of what you learn. Finally, you pull it all together into a report.

In this chapter, you'll learn about where and how to search for information—in books, magazines, encyclopedias, and other sources. Using all these skills, you are sure to become a great research detective!

Mini Index

- **Gathering Information**
- **Researching on the Internet**
- **Using the Library**
- **Using Reference Materials**

Gathering Information

A good researcher uses more than one source of information. Checking different sources helps you to get "the big picture."

- **Reading** . . . Books, encyclopedias, and magazines hold many facts and details about your topic.
- **Surfing** . . . The Internet often has the latest information about a topic.
- **Viewing and Listening** . . . Television and videos can help you understand a topic.
- **Interviewing** . . . Talking to an expert is another way to learn. (See below.)

Guidelines for Interviewing

- Before the interview, prepare a list of questions. Ask questions that need more than a "yes" or "no" answer. You need information from this expert.
- During the interview, take notes on important details. Politely say, "Let me write that down," so that the person will pause.
- If the person uses any special terms, ask how to spell them.

Evaluating Your Sources

Some sources are more valuable than others. Always ask yourself these questions:

- Is the site published by an institution, an organization, or a person who knows the subject well?
- Is there background information about the authors of the site?
- Is the information on the site up to date?
- Is the point of view or purpose of the site stated? If there is more than one side of an issue, are both sides presented?
- Is the information complete and dependable?

Researching on the Internet

You can use the Internet to browse the World Wide Web and send e-mail. To find the Web pages you need, use a search engine like www. Google.com or www.Yahoo.com. When you type in keywords related to your topic (see page 325), the search engine will list Web pages for you to look at. Many Web pages also give an e-mail address where you can send questions.

> Check the Write Source Web site (www.thewritesource.com) for a list of search engines.

Helpful Hints

- **Be safe.** Know your school's Internet policy and follow it. Also follow any guidelines your parents may have given you.

- **Be smart.** Look for trustworthy Web sites. Sites with *.edu, .org,* or *.gov* in the address are usually the best. These are educational, nonprofit, or government Web sites. When you find a good page, watch for links to other helpful pages.

- **Be patient.** Sometimes finding the best sources takes time. If a search doesn't give the results you need, try again with different keywords.

Practice

Use a search engine to find information about an invention. Write down the Internet addresses of at least two Web sites where you found details about that invention.

Using the Library

The library has helpful resources you can use to do research. Most libraries have books, magazines, encyclopedias, audio and video recordings, and computers, as shown on the sample map below.

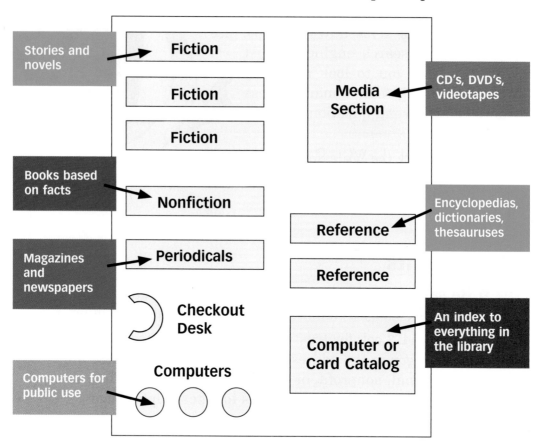

Practice

Visit your school or public library and look for each of the sections shown above. Then make a map of your library.

Searching a Computer Catalog

A **computer catalog** lets you search for library books in three different ways.

1 You can search by **title** if you know the book's title.

2 You can search by **author** if you know the author's name.

3 Or you can search by **subject** if you want to find several books on the same topic.

Using Keywords

To find a book by subject, use keywords. A keyword is a word or phrase about the subject.

If your subject is . . .	your keywords might be . . .
wool,	wool, knitting, or sheep.

Computer Catalog Screen

Author:	Nelson, Robin
Title:	From Sheep to Sweater
Published:	Lerner, 2003
Subjects:	Wool, knitting, sheep

STATUS:	**CALL NUMBER:**
Available	J.746.43 NEL

LOCATION:
Juvenile collection
Nonfiction

Practice

Create a computer catalog screen like the one above for a book you have read.

Searching a Card Catalog

A **card catalog** is a cabinet of drawers that holds title, author, and subject cards in alphabetical order.

1 If you know the book's **title**, look up its first word. (If the first word is *A, An,* or *The,* look up the second word instead.)

2 If you know the book's **author**, look up the author's last name. (If the library has more than one book by that author, you will find a card for each book.)

3 If you don't know a title or an author, look up the **subject** to find books on that topic.

Sample Catalog Cards

Title Card

From Sheep to Sweater ———————— **Title heading**
———— **Call number**

J746.43 NEL   Nelson, Robin
From Sheep to Sweater

Minneapolis: Lerner, 2003
24 pp.: col. ill.

Author Card

J746.43 NEL   Nelson, Robin ———————— **Author heading**
From Sheep to Sweater ———— **Title**

Minneapolis: Lerner, 2003
24 pp.: col. ill.

Describes how a sheep grows wool, and how that wool is processed, spun into yarn, and knitted into a sweater.

Subject Card

Knitting ———————— **Subject heading**
J746.43 NEL   Nelson, Robin
From Sheep to Sweater

Minneapolis: Lerner, 2003
24 pp.: col. ill. ———— **Publisher and copyright date**

Describes how a sheep grows wool, and how that wool is processed, spun into yarn, and knitted into a sweater.

1. Wool 2. Knitting 3. Raising Sheep ———— **Related topics**

Finding Books

Nonfiction Books ● Nonfiction books are arranged on library shelves by call number.

- **Some call numbers contain decimals.**
  The call number 520.37 is a smaller number than 520.4 (which is really 520.40). So 520.37 would appear on the shelf before 520.4.

- **Some call numbers include letters.**
  The call number 520.37F would appear on the shelf before 520.37G. In the call number J520.37, the J means that the book is shelved in the children's section.

- **Most call numbers are based on the Dewey decimal system.**

THE TEN CLASSES OF THE DEWEY DECIMAL SYSTEM			
000	General Topics	500	Pure Science
100	Philosophy	600	Technology (Applied Science)
200	Religion	700	The Arts, Recreation
300	The Social Sciences	800	Literature
400	Language	900	Geography and History

Biographies ● Biographies (books that tell the history of a person's life) are all found under the call number 921. They are arranged on the shelves alphabetically by last name of the person written about. A biography about Samuel Morse would be found at **921 MORSE**. It would come before **921 NOBEL**.

Fiction Books ● Fiction books are arranged alphabetically by the first three letters of the author's last name. A book by Judith C. Greenburg would have the letters **GRE** on the spine.

Practice

Use the computer or card catalog in your library to find a book about inventions. Write down the title and the call number of the book and see if you can find it on the shelves.

Understanding the Parts of a Book

Knowing the common parts of nonfiction books can help you to find information quickly.

- The **title page** is usually the first printed page in the book. It gives the book's title, the author's name, the publisher, and the city where the book was published.

- The **copyright page** comes next. It gives the year the book was published.

- An **acknowledgement** or **preface** (if the book has one) comes before the table of contents and explains more about the book.

- The **table of contents** shows how the book is organized. It lists the names and page numbers of chapters and other divisions.

- The **body** is the main part of the book.

- A **cross-reference** sends the reader to another page for more information. *Example:* (See page 329.)

- An **appendix** is at the back of a book and has more information such as lists, tables, or maps. (Not every book has an appendix.)

- The **glossary** (if there is one) defines special words used in the book.

- The **bibliography** (if there is one) lists sources the author used when writing the book.

- The **index** is an alphabetical list of topics covered in the book. It shows the page numbers where you can find each topic.

Practice

Look in this textbook for the parts listed above. Write down the page numbers for each part you find.

Using Reference Materials

The reference section of your library holds resources such as dictionaries, encyclopedias, and thesauruses.

Using Encyclopedias

An **encyclopedia** is a set of books or a CD with articles on many topics.

- The topics are listed in alphabetical order. The part of the alphabet covered in each book is listed on the spine. (Example: Q-R)
- At the end of an article, you may find a list of related topics you can look up.
- The index volume lists all the places in the encyclopedia where you can find information about your topic.

Encyclopedia Index

This is a sample index entry for the topic *wool*.

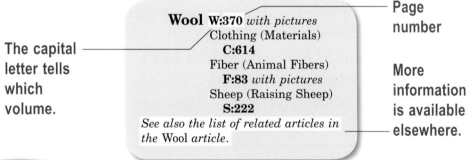

Page number

The capital letter tells which volume.

Wool W:370 *with pictures*
Clothing (Materials)
    C:614
Fiber (Animal Fibers)
    F:83 *with pictures*
Sheep (Raising Sheep)
    S:222
See also the list of related articles in the Wool *article.*

More information is available elsewhere.

Practice

Use the index entry above to find the volume and page for the following information.

1. A picture of wool fibers
2. How wool clothing is made
3. How wool is gathered

Checking a Dictionary

A **dictionary** defines words and provides other useful information. Dictionaries often include the following features.

- **Guide words** These words are listed at the top of each page. They tell the first and last words on that page.

- **Entry words** The entry words are defined on the dictionary page. The most commonly used meaning is usually listed first.

- **Stress marks** A stress (or accent) mark (´) shows which syllable should be stressed when you say a word.

- **Word history** Some words have stories about their origins or how their meanings have changed through the years.

- **Spelling and capital letters** If you don't know how to spell a word, try looking it up by how it sounds. If a word is capitalized in the dictionary, capitalize it in your writing.

- **Pronunciation** A dictionary respells each word phonetically (as it sounds). Special markings are found in the *pronunciation key*.

- **Synonyms** Synonyms (words with the same or similar meanings) are listed. Antonyms (words with opposite meanings) may also be listed.

- **Parts of speech** A dictionary tells how a word can be used (*noun, verb, adjective,* and so on).

- **Syllable division** A dictionary shows where to divide a word.

Practice

Open a dictionary and do the following three things:

1. Find a word you don't know. Write it with its first definition.

2. Find a word you can't pronounce. Use the pronunciation key to figure out how to say the word correctly.

3. Find an illustration that shows you something you didn't already know about a word.

Dictionary Page

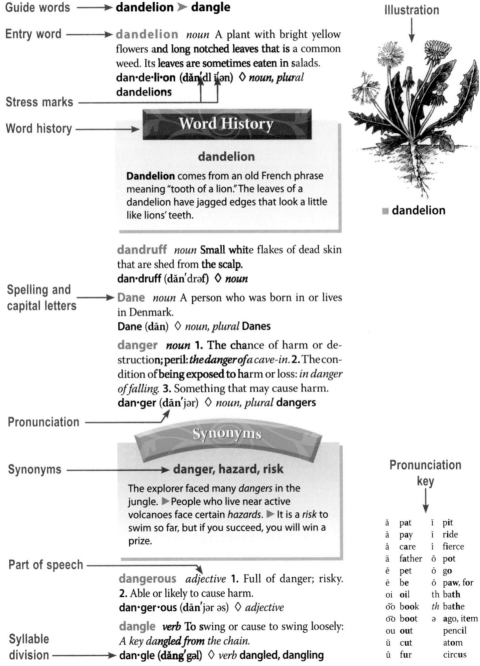

Guide words ⟶ **dandelion ➤ dangle**

Entry word ⟶ **dandelion** *noun* A plant with bright yellow flowers and long notched leaves that is a common weed. Its leaves are sometimes eaten in salads.
dan·de·li·on (dăn′dl ī′ən) ◊ *noun, plural* **dandelions**

Stress marks

Word history ⟶

Word History

dandelion

Dandelion comes from an old French phrase meaning "tooth of a lion." The leaves of a dandelion have jagged edges that look a little like lions' teeth.

Illustration

■ **dandelion**

dandruff *noun* Small white flakes of dead skin that are shed from the scalp.
dan·druff (dăn′drəf) ◊ *noun*

Spelling and capital letters ⟶ **Dane** *noun* A person who was born in or lives in Denmark.
Dane (dān) ◊ *noun, plural* **Danes**

danger *noun* **1.** The chance of harm or destruction; peril: *the danger of a cave-in.* **2.** The condition of being exposed to harm or loss: *in danger of falling.* **3.** Something that may cause harm.
dan·ger (dān′jər) ◊ *noun, plural* **dangers**

Pronunciation

Synonyms

Synonyms ⟶ **danger, hazard, risk**

The explorer faced many *dangers* in the jungle. ▶ People who live near active volcanoes face certain *hazards*. ▶ It is a *risk* to swim so far, but if you succeed, you will win a prize.

Part of speech ⟶ **dangerous** *adjective* **1.** Full of danger; risky. **2.** Able or likely to cause harm.
dan·ger·ous (dān′jər əs) ◊ *adjective*

dangle *verb* To swing or cause to swing loosely: *A key dangled from the chain.*
Syllable division ⟶ **dan·gle** (dăng′gəl) ◊ *verb* **dangled, dangling**

Pronunciation key

ă	pat	ĭ	pit
ā	pay	ī	ride
â	care	î	fierce
ä	father	ŏ	pot
ĕ	pet	ō	go
ē	be	ô	paw, for
oi	oil	th	bath
ŏŏ	book	*th*	bathe
ōō	boot	ə	ago, item
ou	out		pencil
ŭ	cut		atom
û	fur		circus

Using a Thesaurus

A **thesaurus** is a book that lists words with their synonyms. (Synonyms are words with similar meanings.) It may also list antonyms (words with opposite meanings). A thesaurus can help you . . .

- find the best word for a specific sentence and
- keep from using the same word again and again.

Thesaurus Entry

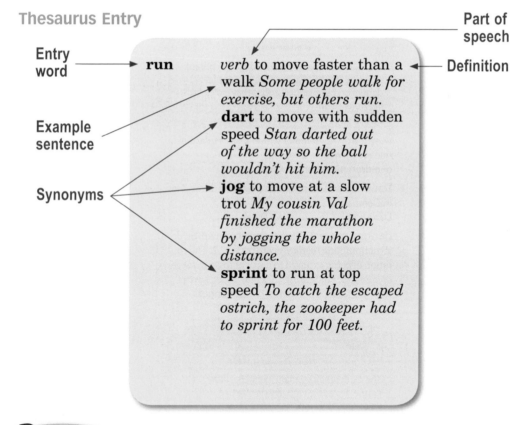

Part of speech

Entry word → **run**

verb to move faster than a walk *Some people walk for exercise, but others run.* — Definition

Example sentence

dart to move with sudden speed *Stan darted out of the way so the ball wouldn't hit him.*

Synonyms

jog to move at a slow trot *My cousin Val finished the marathon by jogging the whole distance.*

sprint to run at top speed *To catch the escaped ostrich, the zookeeper had to sprint for 100 feet.*

Practice

Use the thesaurus entry above to find the right synonym for the verb *runs* in the sentence below.

Our dog runs to the right and to the left because he knows we are trying to catch him for his bath.

Research Writing

Summary Paragraph

Writing a summary is like facing a big bowl of fruit salad with many kinds of fruit in it, everything from kiwi to blueberries. You only like the strawberries, bananas, watermelon, and cherries, so you carefully spoon your favorites into a bowl. In a similar way, when you write a summary, you read the whole article. Then you pick out only the main ideas and put them into a paragraph using your own words.

Summarizing is a useful research skill. It helps you to condense the information from a source so your reader gets only the main ideas.

Writing Guidelines

Subject: A research article

Form: Summary paragraph

Purpose: To express the main idea

Audience: Classmates

Summary Paragraph

The following article is summarized in the paragraph "Native American Inventions."

The New World of Native American Inventions

People have always invented objects to improve their lives. European settlers in the New World discovered Native American inventions and took them around the globe.

Eskimo tribes made kayaks–covered, watertight canoes. People still use them for fishing and sea travel. Now, kayaks are also used for recreation on rivers, lakes, and oceans. People even ride the surf in kayaks.

People of the American Northeast invented a long sled called a toboggan. People still use toboggans to haul gear across snow and ice. Now there are toboggan races in the Olympics.

Another Native American invention is the snowshoe. At first, people strapped pine boughs to their feet so they could walk on deep snow. Later, they made wooden frames with leather webbing. Modern snowshoes are worn by winter hikers and by adventurers who explore cold places like Antarctica.

The game of lacrosse is another Native American invention. French explorers found different versions of the game being played by the Cherokee and Iroquois. Today, lacrosse leagues have spread all the way to Australia!

Topic sentence (main idea)

Body

Closing sentence

Native American Inventions

Many early Native American inventions are still being used. The Eskimo kayak is still a hunting and fishing boat, but it's also used on rivers, lakes, and oceans for recreation. The toboggan still hauls gear, but it also is used for races in the Olympics. Snowshoes still help people get through deep snow wherever they are. Finally, like other Native American inventions, the game of lacrosse is now enjoyed around the world.

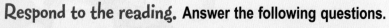

Respond to the reading. Answer the following questions.

- **Ideas** (1) What is the main idea of this summary?
- **Organization** (2) How is the paragraph organized?
- **Word Choice** (3) Compare the wording of the summary to the wording of the original. Which is simpler?

Prewriting **Selecting an Article**

When you practice summarizing, you must first find an article. Choose one that . . .

- relates to a subject you are studying,
- discusses an interesting topic, and
- is fairly short (three to five paragraphs).

 Choose an article. Look through magazines and newspapers for an article to summarize.

Reading the Article

If possible, make a photocopy of the article so that you can underline important facts, like the sample shown here. Otherwise, take brief notes.

Eskimo tribes made kayaks–covered, watertight canoes. People still use them for fishing and sea travel. Now, kayaks are also used for recreation on rivers, lakes, and oceans. People even ride the surf in kayaks.

 Read your article. Read through the article once to understand it. Then reread it to find the important ideas.

Finding the Main Idea

The topic sentence of a summary should contain the main idea of the article. By rereading the first paragraph of your article, along with the words you underlined throughout, you will find the main idea. Here's the topic sentence from the sample summary: "Many early Native American inventions are still being used."

 Write the main idea. Review the first paragraph of the article and the words you underlined. What main idea do they suggest? Include this idea in a topic sentence.

Writing **Developing the First Draft**

A summary paragraph contains three basic parts. The **topic sentence** states the main idea of the article. The **body** sentences put the most important information in your own words. And, the **closing sentence** shares a final important point.

Write the first draft of your summary paragraph. Write a topic sentence, support it with information from the article, and end with a closing sentence that relates to the main idea.

Revising **Reviewing Your Writing**

You can revise by checking your summary for the following traits.

- ■ **Ideas** Does the topic sentence give the main idea of the article? Does the body include important supporting details?
- ■ **Organization** Is all the information in logical order?
- ■ **Voice** Does my voice sound interested and informative?
- ■ **Word Choice** Do I explain things in my own words?
- ■ **Sentence Fluency** Do I vary sentence types and lengths?

Revise your paragraph. Reread the article and your summary. Using the questions above, make changes in your writing.

Editing **Checking for Conventions**

Editing means "correcting errors in conventions."

- ■ **Conventions** Are dates, names, or facts correct? Do I have any punctuation, spelling, or grammar errors?

Edit your work. Use the questions above as a guide to look for errors in your summary. Then make a clean final copy and proofread it again.

Research Writing

Research Report

The world is full of inventions. A book is an invention. So is the chair you're sitting on, the light above your head, the door to the classroom, and so on.

In this chapter, you will write a research report about an invention that interests you. Writing a research report gives you the chance to investigate a subject on your own and share what you have learned.

Writing Guidelines

Subject: An interesting invention

Form: Research report

Purpose: To find and share information about how something was invented

Audience: Classmates and parents

Research Report

In this report, Candra explains how the windshield wiper was invented. The side notes point out how ideas are arranged and other important features of the report.

1"

1/2"

Salazar 1 ← 1" →

The entire report is double-spaced.

Candra Salazar

Mr. Boege

← 1" → Social Studies

Oct. 1, 2005

A Vision of Safety

BEGINNING

The opening leads up to the thesis statement (underlined).

People say that necessity is the mother of invention. Someone sees a problem and invents something to solve it. That is just how windshield wipers were invented. A hundred years ago, rain and snow caused big problems for streetcar drivers. <u>Mary Anderson's invention helped drivers stay safe and dry in bad weather.</u>

The first body paragraph explains the problem.

Mary noticed the problem while visiting New York City in 1903. Because it was snowing, she rode a streetcar instead of walking. On the streetcar, she noticed that the driver had to squint to see through the icy windshield. Although the windshield could be opened in the middle to see, that let cold wind and

1"

Salazar 2

An information source is shown in parentheses.

snow inside. So the driver kept stopping the streetcar and getting out to scrape off the snow (Thimmish 11).

The next body paragraph tells how the invention came about.

Mary thought there should be some way to wipe the windshield from inside the streetcar. That way the driver could see clearly while staying warm and dry. She started sketching pictures of a wooden arm with rubber strips on the outside of the window. On the inside was a lever to move the arm. A weight held the arm against the glass, and a spring brought it back to its place. When Mary got back home to Atlanta, Georgia, she had a local shop make a model. Then she patented her invention (Thimmish 13).

The next body paragraph tells how people reacted to the invention.

Mary's idea didn't catch on at first. While she was sketching plans, people told her it was no use. They said that lots of solutions had been tried before, but nothing worked. Even after her invention was patented, "Many felt the movement of the windshield wipers would distract the drivers" ("Inventor"). Mary tried to sell her patent to a manufacturer, but no one was interested (Sillery).

Salazar 3

The ending reminds the reader of the thesis statement.

In the end, Mary's idea was accepted. Thirteen years after she invented the windshield wiper, Henry Ford put it on every Model T ("Inventor"). Now every car has windshield wipers. Mary's invention has helped to make driving safer for everyone.

The writer's name and page number go on every page.

Salazar 4

Works Cited

"Inventor of the Week: Windshield Wipers." Lemelson-MIT Program. Sept. 2001. 28 Sept. 2004 <http://web.mit.edu/invent/iow/anderson.html>.

Sillery, Bob. "FYI." Popular Science June 2002: 88.

Thimmish, Catherine. Girls Think of Everything. Boston: Houghton, 2000.

Sources are listed alphabetically.

Respond to the reading. After reading Candra's research report, answer the following questions about these traits of writing.

■ **Ideas** (1) List two things you learned from the report.

■ **Organization** (2) In your own words, what is the main point of each middle paragraph?

■ **Voice** (3) Find a sentence that shows the writer's feelings about the topic.

Prewriting

Writing a research report requires good planning. Here are five keys to help you get started.

Keys to Effective Prewriting

1. **Choose** an invention that interests you.

2. **Look** for answers to your research questions.

3. **Find** two or three details for each question.

4. **Use** a gathering grid and note cards to collect information.

5. **List** your sources so you can give them credit later.

Prewriting Selecting a Topic

In order to choose a topic, Candra listed inventions she was curious about.

Ideas Chart

Inventions I'm Curious About

At home	At school	In the car
CD players	computers	gasoline
reclining chairs	pencil sharpeners	tires
microwave ovens	pencils	windshield wipers
toasters	scissors	cup holders

Prewrite

Make an ideas chart. List inventions that interest you in a chart like the one above. Write three or four ideas under each heading.

Sizing Up Your Topic

Some topics are too small for a research report. Other topics are too big. To decide whether your topic is the right size for a report, look it up in an encyclopedia and think about the following questions:

1. What problem did the invention solve?
2. How did the invention happen? (Who invented it? When? How?)
3. How successful was the invention?

A good research paper should include one or two paragraphs about each of these research questions.

Too Big

Personal Computers

What was the problem?

- People had to take turns on expensive mainframes.
- They wanted more computer time.
- They needed cheaper computers.

How did the invention happen?

- March 1974, Scelbi Computer Consulting Company advertised a computer kit in QST.
- July 1974, Jonathan Titus advertised his Mark-8 kit in Radio Electronics.
- January 1975, the Altair kit by MITS (a calculator company) was in Popular Mechanics.
- 1977, Steven Jobs and Stephen Wozniak founded Apple Computer, Inc., and sold the first PC (Apple II).
- 1981, IBM started selling its own PC.

How successful was it?

- PC's were used in business and at home.
- The Internet made PC's useful for work and fun.

Too Small

Scissors

What was the problem?

- People wanted a better way to cut cloth.

How did the invention happen?

- Nobody knows.

How successful was it?

- All kinds of scissors exist.

Just Right

Windshield Wipers

What was the problem?

- People couldn't see through rain, ice, and snow on windshields.
- They had to get out to clear the windshield.

How did the invention happen?

- Mary Anderson felt sorry for a streetcar driver.
- She thought of a wiper with a lever inside the vehicle.
- She got her plans patented.

How successful was it?

- At first, her suggestion wasn't popular.
- Wipers became standard on Henry Ford's cars.

Prewriting Using a Gathering Grid

A gathering grid is one way to collect information for a report. Down the side, Candra listed her research questions, and across the top, she listed her sources. In the rest of the grid, she wrote answers to her questions.

Gathering Grid

Windshield wipers	Girls Think of Everything (book)	"FYI" (magazine article)	"Inventor of the Week" (Internet article)
What problem did the invention solve?	wiping rain and snow from windshields		
How did the invention come about?	See note card #1.		Mary Anderson got the idea while watching a streetcar operator in New York City.
How successful was the invention?	She patented it in 1903.	Friends teased Mary, but by 1913, wipers were standard.	See note card #2.
Other information		In 1917, Charlotte Bridgewood patented the first automatic wiper system.	

Creating Note Cards

When answers are too long to fit on your gathering grid, you can write them on note cards. Number each card and write your research question at the top. Then write your answer on the card. At the bottom, name the source of the information. If the source has page numbers, list the pages where you found the information.

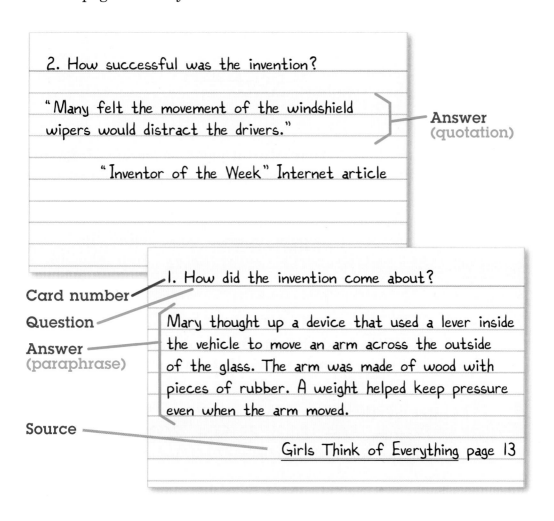

2. How successful was the invention?

"Many felt the movement of the windshield wipers would distract the drivers." — **Answer** (quotation)

"Inventor of the Week" Internet article

Card number

Question

1. How did the invention come about?

Answer (paraphrase)

Mary thought up a device that used a lever inside the vehicle to move an arm across the outside of the glass. The arm was made of wood with pieces of rubber. A weight helped keep pressure even when the arm moved.

Source

Girls Think of Everything page 13

Prewrite

Create note cards. Use note cards like those above to write answers that are too long for your gathering grid.

Prewriting Keeping Track of Your Sources

When you give credit to your sources and make a works-cited page, you will need the following information.

Books

Author (last name first). **Title** (underlined). **City** where the book was published: **Publisher, copyright date.**

> Thimmish, Catherine. Girls Think of Everything.
>   Boston: Houghton, 2000.

Magazines

Author (last name first). **Article title** (in quotation marks). **Magazine title** (underlined) **Date** (day, month, year): **Page numbers** of the article.

> Sillery, Bob. "FYI." Popular Science June 2002: 88.

Internet

Author (if available, last name first). **Page title** (if available, in quotation marks). **Site title** (underlined). **Date published** (if available). **Date visited (day, month, year)** <Internet address>.

> "Inventor of the Week: Windshield Wipers." Lemelson—MIT
>   Program. Sept. 2001. 28 Sept. 2004
>   <http://web.mit.edu/invent/iow/anderson.html>.

Note: If a source does not give all of the details shown above, just write down the ones it does give.

Prewrite

Keep track of your sources. As you read and take notes, record the publication information for each source.

Organizing Ideas

When your research is finished, you will need to organize your ideas. A thesis statement and an outline will help you to put the information in a good order.

Writing Your Thesis Statement

Your thesis statement tells what your report is about. A good thesis statement starts with an interesting topic and adds a special part to emphasize.

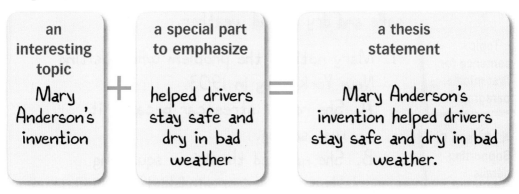

an interesting topic		a special part to emphasize		a thesis statement
Mary Anderson's invention	+	helped drivers stay safe and dry in bad weather	=	Mary Anderson's invention helped drivers stay safe and dry in bad weather.

Thesis Statements

The typewriter (an interesting topic) did not catch on for more than 70 years after it was patented (a special part to emphasize).

The idea for the microwave oven (an interesting topic) came when a scientist's chocolate bar melted in front of radar waves (a special part to emphasize).

Create your thesis statement. After reviewing your notes, use the formula above to write a thesis statement about your subject.

Prewriting **Making an Outline**

A sentence outline is a plan for putting your ideas in order. Below is the first part of Candra's sentence outline.

Sentence Outline

Thesis statement

I. Topic sentence for first middle paragraph

A., B., and C. Supporting details

II. Topic sentence for second middle paragraph

Continue . . .

THESIS STATEMENT:
Mary Anderson's invention helped drivers stay safe and dry in bad weather.

I. Mary noticed the problem while visiting New York City in 1903.
   A. She rode a streetcar because it was snowy.
   B. She noticed the driver squinting through the icy windshield.
   C. Driver kept stopping to clean windshield
II. Mary thought there should be some way to wipe the windshield from inside the streetcar.
   A. . . .
   B. . . .

Prewrite

Write your outline. Review your research notes (pages 344-345). Then write an outline for your report. Each topic sentence must relate to your thesis statement.

Writing

Once your planning is finished, it's time to write! The following key points will guide your work.

Keys to Writing

1. **Write** a strong first paragraph that gives your thesis statement.

2. **Start** each middle paragraph with an effective topic sentence.

3. **Organize** the supporting details in each middle paragraph.

4. **Write** a thoughtful ending paragraph that reminds the reader of your thesis.

5. **Cite** your sources on a works-cited page.

Writing **Starting Your Research Report**

Your opening paragraph should grab your reader's interest, introduce your topic, and lead to your thesis statement. Below are two possible ways to start a report about the invention of the windshield wiper.

> ▶ **Beginning**
> **Middle**
> **Ending**

Beginning Paragraph

This paragraph begins with an interesting idea and ends with the thesis statement.

> People say that necessity is the mother of invention. Someone sees a problem and invents something to solve it. That is just how windshield wipers were invented. A hundred years ago, rain and snow caused big problems for streetcar drivers. <u>Mary Anderson's invention helped drivers stay safe and dry in bad weather.</u>

This paragraph begins with a question and ends with the thesis statement.

> Have you ever thought about how important windshield wipers are? The earliest vehicles didn't have them. It was dangerous because drivers in those days had trouble seeing the road on rainy or snowy days. <u>Mary Anderson's invention helped drivers stay safe and dry in bad weather.</u>

Write your opening paragraph. Write a beginning paragraph for your report. Use one of the examples above as a guide, or try an idea of your own.

Developing the Middle Part

The middle of your report should support your thesis statement. Each middle paragraph should have a topic sentence that relates to the thesis. Other sentences in each paragraph should support the topic sentence.

Beginning

Middle

Ending

Middle Paragraphs

All the details support the topic sentence (underlined).

Mary noticed the problem while visiting New York City in 1903. Because it was snowing, she rode a streetcar instead of walking. On the streetcar, she noticed that the driver had to squint to see through the icy windshield. Although the windshield could be opened in the middle to see, that let cold wind and snow inside. So the driver kept stopping the streetcar and getting out to scrape off the snow (Thimmish 11).

Sentences lead naturally from one idea to the next.

Mary thought there should be some way to wipe the windshield from inside the streetcar. That way the driver could see clearly while staying warm and dry. She started sketching pictures of a wooden arm with rubber strips on the outside of the window. On the inside was a lever to move the arm. A weight held the arm against the glass, and a spring brought it back to its place. When Mary got back home to Atlanta, Georgia, she had a local shop make a model. Then she patented her invention (Thimmish 13).

Specific details are used to explain the invention.

A source is cited (in parentheses).

Final Middle Paragraph

Mary's idea didn't catch on at first. While she was sketching plans, people told her it was no use. They said that lots of solutions had been tried before, but nothing worked. Even after her invention was patented, "Many felt the movement of the windshield wipers would distract the drivers" ("Inventor"). Mary tried to sell her patent to a manufacturer, but no one was interested (Sillery).

A quotation adds authority to the report.

Write your middle paragraphs. Use your outline as a guide to write your middle paragraphs. A first draft doesn't need to be perfect. Just get your main ideas on paper.

Avoiding Plagiarism and Citing Sources

Plagiarism is using someone else's work without giving that person credit. Two examples of plagiarism are (1) using someone's exact words without quotation marks and (2) using ideas without giving their source. As you write your paper, do the following:

- **Use quotation marks for exact words.**
  (See final paragraph above.)

- **Show your sources in parentheses.**
  (See the author names and page numbers on page 351.)

- **List publication details on your works-cited page.**
  (See pages 340, 346, and 354.)

Writing **Ending Your Report**

Beginning

Middle

▶ Ending

The ending paragraph should close your report smoothly and remind your reader of the thesis. You can try one or more of the following ideas.

- **Explain what effect the invention has had on the world.**
- **Tell one last interesting fact about the invention or its inventor.**
- **Leave your reader with something to think about.**

Ending Paragraph

The ending sums up the invention's effect on the world.

> In the end, Mary's idea was accepted. Thirteen years after she invented the windshield wiper, Henry Ford put it on every Model T ("Inventor"). Now every car has windshield wipers. <u>Mary's invention has helped to make driving safer for everyone.</u>

The reader is reminded of the thesis (underlined).

Write

Write your final paragraph. Use one of the ideas listed above to write your ending paragraph. Also remind the reader of your thesis statement.

Look over your draft. Review your notes and outline. Then read through your first draft. Did you include all the necessary details? Do they lead naturally from one to the next? Make notes about possible changes and use them when you revise.

Writing Creating Your Works-Cited Page

Once you finish your report, you need to arrange the sources you used in alphabetical order on a works-cited page. Use the publication information you wrote down for each source (page 346). The works-cited page goes at the end of your report.

The title "Works Cited" is centered.

Sources are listed alphabetically.

Salazar 4

Works Cited

"Inventor of the Week: Windshield Wipers." <u>Lemelson–MIT Program.</u> Sept. 2001. 28 Sept. 2004 <http://web.mit.edu/invent/iow/anderson.html>.

Sillery, Bob. "FYI." <u>Popular Science</u> June 2002: 88.

Thimmish, Catherine. <u>Girls Think of Everything.</u> Boston: Houghton, 2000.

Create your works-cited page. List your sources in alphabetical order on a new page. (Put your last name and the page number in the upper right corner.) Center the title "Works Cited" and indent all lines after the first line of each entry.

Revising

Don't expect the first draft of your report to be perfect. Some ideas may be unclear or incomplete. Some sentences may be confusing or clumsy. The voice may sound dull in places. Use the keys to revising below to make changes to your report.

Keys to Revising

1. **Read** through your first draft to get an overall sense of your report.

2. **Review** each part carefully—the beginning, the middle, and the ending.

3. **Check** that your thesis statement emphasizes a special part of your topic.

4. **Be sure** the topic sentences of the middle paragraphs support your thesis.

5. **Check** that the ending reminds the reader of your thesis statement.

Revising **Improving Your** Ideas

Revising means cutting, adding, and changing (or moving). You may cut details that aren't needed, add details that are missing, or change the details in some way—all to make your ideas clear to the reader.

An unneeded sentence is cut.

Helpful details are added.

A weak sentence is replaced with a more interesting one.

> Mary noticed the problem while visiting
>
> New York City in 1903. ~~She was visiting from~~
>   Because it was snowing,
> ~~Atlanta, Georgia,~~ She rode a streetcar instead of
> On the streetcar,
> walking. She noticed that the driver had to squint
>
> to see through the icy windshield. Although the
>
> windshield could be opened in the middle to see,
>   So the driver kept stopping the streetcar and
> that let cold wind and snow inside. ~~The driver and~~
> getting out to scrape off the snow
> ~~passengers hated that~~ (Thimmish 11).

Revise

Check your report for weak or unclear sentences. Reread the first draft of your report. Are there details you should cut, add, or change? Make revisions to improve your paper.

Improving Your Organization

When revising your first draft, you may find that your ideas are not in the best order. A sentence, or even an entire paragraph, may need to be moved. For better organization, Candra moved a sentence in the middle paragraph below.

An idea is moved for better organization.

Mary thought there should be some way to wipe the windshield from inside the streetcar. She started sketching pictures of a wooden arm with rubber strips on the outside of the window. On the inside was a lever to move the arm. A weight held the arm against the glass, and a spring brought it back to its place. That way the driver could see clearly while staying warm and dry. When Mary got back home to Atlanta, Georgia, she had a local shop make a model. Then she patented her invention (Thimmish 13).

Revise

Check your organization. Read your report to see if any ideas or details need to be moved. Make changes to improve the organization.

Revising Using a Checklist

Check your revising. Number a piece of paper from 1 to 8. If you can answer "yes" to a question, put a check mark after that number. If not, continue to work on that part of your report.

Ideas

_____ **1.** Have I written a clear thesis statement?

_____ **2.** Do I have one main idea in each topic sentence?

Organization

_____ **3.** Do I have an effective beginning, middle, and ending?

_____ **4.** Are my sentences in the best order?

Voice & Word Choice

_____ **5.** Does my writing show my knowledge and interest?

_____ **6.** Do I define or explain any unfamiliar words?

Sentence Fluency

_____ **7.** Do I vary my sentence lengths?

_____ **8.** Do I vary my sentence beginnings?

Make a clean copy. When you have finished revising your report, make a clean copy for editing.

Editing

Prewrite • Revise • Publish • Write • Edit

After revising, it's time to edit. Editing is checking your writing for punctuation, capitalization, spelling, and grammar errors. The keys to editing below will guide your work.

Keys to Editing

1. **Use** a dictionary and the "Proofreader's Guide" in the back of this book for help.

2. **Make** corrections on a printed copy if you use a computer. Then enter your changes on the computer.

3. **Double-check** your punctuation, capitalization, spelling, and grammar.

4. **Use** the correct format for your report. (See pages 338–340.)

Editing **Using a Checklist**

Check your editing. Number a piece of paper from 1 to 9. If you can answer "yes" to a question below, put a check mark after that number. If not, continue to edit for that convention.

Conventions

PUNCTUATION

_____ **1.** Do I use the correct punctuation to end my sentences?

_____ **2.** Do I use quotation marks correctly?

_____ **3.** Have I correctly punctuated my works-cited page?

CAPITALIZATION

_____ **4.** Do I start all my sentences with capital letters?

_____ **5.** Do I capitalize proper nouns and titles?

SPELLING

_____ **6.** Do I spell all my words correctly?

_____ **7.** Have I double-checked the spelling of names in my report?

GRAMMAR

_____ **8.** Do I use the correct forms of verbs (*she rode,* not *she rided*)?

_____ **9.** Do my subjects and verbs agree in number (*every car has,* not *every car have*)?

Adding a Title

- ■ Describe the topic: **Inventing Windshield Wipers**
- ■ Be creative: **A Vision of Safety**
- ■ Borrow words from the report: **Windshield Wipers on Every Car**

Publishing

Prewrite • Write • Revise • Edit • Publish ✓

Using a Checklist

After finishing your report, it's time to share the results of your hard work. You may decide to turn your report into a multimedia persentation, add pictures or graphs, or publish your paper online.

Focus on Presentation

- Use black or blue ink and double-space the entire paper.
- Leave a one-inch margin on all four sides of your paper.
- Write your name, your teacher's name, the class, and the date in the upper left corner of page 1.
- Skip a line and center your title. Skip another line and start your report.
- Write your last name and the page number in the upper right corner of every page.

Prepare a Multimedia Presentation

Create a computer slide show of your report. (See pages 363–367 for more information.)

Develop an Illustrated Report

Draw pictures of the invention or make a time line that shows important dates in its development.

Publish Online

Visit the Write Source Web site **www.thewritesource.com** for information about publishing your writing online.

Make a final copy. Follow your teacher's instructions or use the guidelines above to make a clean final copy of your report. (If you are using a computer, see pages 44–46.)

Reflecting on Your Writing

Think about your research-report experience by completing the starter sentences below. This reflection will help you understand how you are growing as a writer.

My Research Report

1. The best part of my research report is . . .

2. The hardest part of writing the report was . . .

3. The main thing I learned about writing a report is . . .

4. Here is one question I still have about writing a research report:

Research Writing

Multimedia Presentations

A multimedia presentation is one special way to share your research report. Using a computer, you can prepare a slide show that presents your information—complete with moving text, illustrations, and sounds. This chapter will show you how.

Mini Index

- **Getting Started**
- **Presentation Checklist**

Getting Started

Your multimedia presentation begins with an essay, a speech, or a report you've already written. You list the main ideas from that writing and then use a computer program to make slides, add graphics, and include audio (sounds).

Prewrite

Get organized. Choose an essay, a speech, or a report to turn into a multimedia presentation. Make sure your computer has the needed slide-show software.

Creating the Slides

1 **Find the main ideas in your report.**

Each main idea in your report should have its own slide. To plan your slides, make a storyboard, as shown on page 366.

2 **Find pictures and sounds for each slide.**

You can find pictures and sounds in your software program, on the Internet, or on special CD's. Ask your teacher where to find these multimedia files.

Write

Gather your thoughts. Make a cluster like the one below for each slide. Write the main idea for the slide in the middle of the cluster. Then add picture and sound ideas around it.

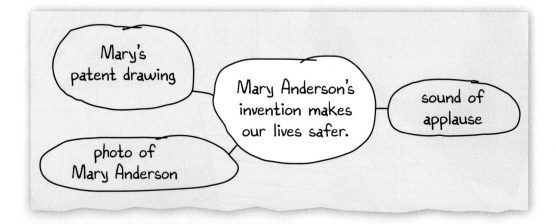

3 Design your slides.

Use similar colors and the same easy-to-read fonts on all your slides.

4 Build your slides one by one.

Make your slides attractive and easy to read. Put them in order so the ideas make sense.

Improving Your Presentation

A multimedia presentation should be given smoothly. Your goal is to make the information clear and interesting. You must practice running the slide show and speaking at the same time.

 Rehearse your presentation. Practice your presentation in front of friends and family. Ask for comments and suggestions. Change any parts that are not clear.

It is also important that your slides be free of any errors. So check your slides carefully and ask a friend or an adult to check them, too.

 Make corrections. Check each slide for punctuation, capitalization, spelling, and grammar errors.

Giving a Multimedia Presentation

Giving your presentation is a lot like giving a speech. See the chapter "Giving Speeches" (pages 373–378) for help.

 Present your report. Take a deep breath, relax, and have fun giving your presentation. This is a chance to show how hard you have worked and to share some good information.

Multimedia Presentation Storyboard

This storyboard is based on the report "A Vision of Safety" on pages 338–340. Each box represents one slide in the report.

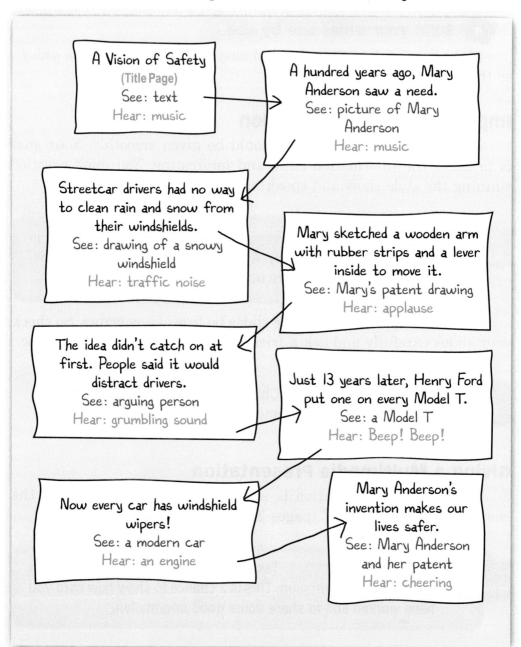

A Vision of Safety
(Title Page)
See: text
Hear: music

A hundred years ago, Mary Anderson saw a need.
See: picture of Mary Anderson
Hear: music

Streetcar drivers had no way to clean rain and snow from their windshields.
See: drawing of a snowy windshield
Hear: traffic noise

Mary sketched a wooden arm with rubber strips and a lever inside to move it.
See: Mary's patent drawing
Hear: applause

The idea didn't catch on at first. People said it would distract drivers.
See: arguing person
Hear: grumbling sound

Just 13 years later, Henry Ford put one on every Model T.
See: a Model T
Hear: Beep! Beep!

Now every car has windshield wipers!
See: a modern car
Hear: an engine

Mary Anderson's invention makes our lives safer.
See: Mary Anderson and her patent
Hear: cheering

Presentation Checklist

Use this checklist to make sure your presentation is the best you can make it. When you can answer all 10 questions with a "yes," your presentation is ready!

Ideas

_____ 1. Have I chosen an interesting speech or report for my presentation?

Organization

_____ 2. Does the beginning clearly introduce my topic?
_____ 3. Does the middle include all the main points?
_____ 4. Does the end summarize or give a final thought?

Voice

_____ 5. Do I show interest in my topic?
_____ 6. Does my voice fit my audience and topic?

Word and Multimedia Choices

_____ 7. Is the text on each slide clear and interesting?
_____ 8. Do I include interesting pictures and sounds?

Presentation Fluency

_____ 9. Do the ideas flow smoothly from one slide to the next?

Conventions

_____ 10. Have I corrected all errors in punctuation, capitalization, spelling, and grammar?

Speaking and Writing to Learn

Listening and Speaking

Speaking is more than talking. Parrots are famous for talking without saying anything worth hearing. When *you* talk, however, you need to deliver a clear message to listeners.

Likewise, listening is more than hearing. Sometimes people say, "I can hear you, but I'm not listening . . . la, la, la, la!" When you actually listen, you think about what you hear.

This chapter will help you improve your speaking and listening skills—and it may even open your mind!

Mini Index

- Listening in Class
- Participating in a Group
- Speaking in Class

Listening in Class

When your teacher asks you to listen, you know that means thinking about what is being said. In fact, listening is one of the best ways to learn. Follow these tips to become a better listener:

1. **Know your purpose for listening.** Are you learning something new, getting directions, or reviewing for a test?

2. **Take notes.** Think about what's being said. Write the main points in your notebook. Write down questions about things you don't understand.

3. **Ask questions.** Ask specific questions about the things you don't understand. Wait until the speaker is finished and then ask your questions.

Note Taking in Action

When you take notes, write down the main ideas in your own words, as in the following example:

Sample Notes

Electricity and Magnets   Mar. 9

Magnets can be used to make electricity.
Electricity can be used to make magnets.

Electricity and magnets in our house
   —motor in refrigerator
   —doorbell

        Question: Are there electromagnets in cars?

Participating in a Group

Participating in a group means cooperating with others. Two important parts of cooperation are respecting yourself and respecting others.

Skills for Cooperating

In a group, you respect yourself when you . . .

- know that your own ideas are important.
- share your ideas with the group.
- ask questions when you don't understand something.

In a group, you respect others when you . . .

- listen politely.
- wait your turn before speaking or asking a question.
- make helpful comments.
- encourage everyone to participate.

> Don't be afraid to ask questions.

Practice

Read the following situations. For each one, decide which of the skills listed above would help the group work together more effectively.

Situation 1

You have an idea that no one else has talked about. You're afraid to speak up because you're not sure it's a good idea.

Situation 2

One member of the group keeps interrupting while others are speaking. He has just interrupted you to ask a question.

Speaking in Class

Speaking in class is an important part of learning. The guidelines below will help you and your classmates become better speakers.

- **Pay attention.** Listen to what others are saying and stay on the topic being discussed.

- **Think ahead.** Think before you speak. Be sure that you have something important to say.

- **Make eye contact.** Look at your classmates as you speak to them.

- **Wait your turn.** Show respect for others by not interrupting.

- **Get to the point.** State your ideas briefly and clearly.

> Respond politely to what others say.

Work on your speaking skills. The whole class can play the following game. Everyone should take a turn being the speaker.

1 The speaker pulls a topic from a hat (prepared by your teacher).

2 He or she talks for one minute about the topic. The speaker's turn ends if he or she jumps to a different topic, stops for more than five seconds, or does not keep eye contact with the audience.

3 After everyone is finished, the class votes for the best one-minute speech.

Giving Speeches

Sometimes, you just can't wait to tell your friends what you're up to, like taking tae kwon do, learning to play a saxophone, or building a model submarine. Your latest hobbies or new skills are good topics for speeches.

In this chapter, you will learn to give a how-to speech. You will find tips on planning your speech, using visual aids, and helping your listeners experience what you are explaining.

Mini Index

- **Preparing Your Speech**
- **Organizing a How-To Speech**
- **Giving Your Speech**

Preparing Your Speech

If you want your audience to enjoy your speech, choose a topic that you find interesting. One of your completed how-to essays may be a good place to begin. Here's how to get started.

Rewriting in Action

In the opening of the original essay below ("Pinching for Fun," page 17), Fumi was excited about making a pinch pot. Notice how the rewritten speech beginning adds a new twist to grab the audience's attention.

Original Essay

Did you ever think pinching was fun? I did when I learned how to make a small bowl called a pinch pot. There are four steps to making a pinch pot: preparing, shaping, firing, and glazing.

Speech

"It's a snap. Just use your thumb and fingers to do this project." My art teacher surprised our class by telling us the tools we needed for our next project. We tried to guess what the project would be, but no one did. Then she told us the four steps: preparing, shaping, firing, and glazing. I remembered that my older sister had made a clay pinch pot, so I guessed right. I could hardly wait to start.

Rework your beginning. Choose an essay that you would like to present as a how-to speech. Rewrite your opening and add some drama to grab your audience's attention.

Using Visual Aids

After you write the beginning of your how-to speech, read through your essay and choose the main details for your speech. (Either list these separately or highlight them in your essay.) Next, decide what visual aids would help your listeners "see" and understand the details of your speech. Here are some possibilities:

Charts	compare ideas or explain main points.
Maps	show specific places being discussed.
Objects	allow your audience to see the real thing.
Photographs	help your audience see what you are talking about.
Posters	show words, pictures, or both.
Transparencies	highlight key words, ideas, or graphics.

The following tips will help you prepare your visual aids.

1 Make your visual aids big enough for classmates in the back of the room to see.

2 Use pictures and graphs with short, easy-to-read labels.

3 Make your visual aids colorful.

List ideas for visual aids. After you make your list, select two.

* Clay models of each stage of the project
  Pictures of the stages from start to finish
  Chart listing the steps
* Picture of the kiln

Organizing a How-To Speech

Next, you must organize the main details of your speech on note cards or pieces of paper. Except for the beginning and ending cards, which are written out word for word, short phrases will remind you what to say and what to do.

Sample Note Cards

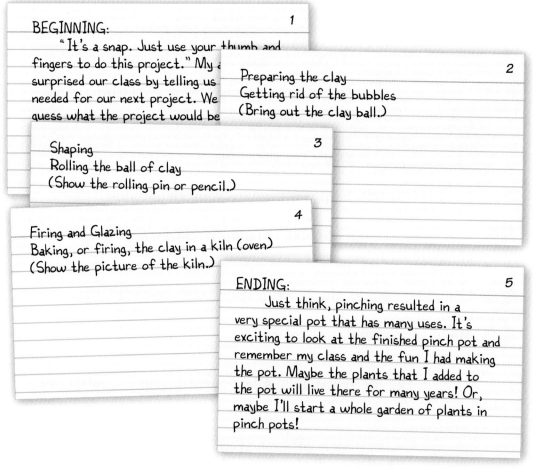

BEGINNING: 1
   "It's a snap. Just use your thumb and
fingers to do this project." My ___
surprised our class by telling us ___
needed for our next project. We ___
guess what the project would be ___

Preparing the clay   2
Getting rid of the bubbles
(Bring out the clay ball.)

Shaping   3
Rolling the ball of clay
(Show the rolling pin or pencil.)

Firing and Glazing   4
Baking, or firing, the clay in a kiln (oven)
(Show the picture of the kiln.)

ENDING: 5
   Just think, pinching resulted in a
very special pot that has many uses. It's
exciting to look at the finished pinch pot and
remember my class and the fun I had making
the pot. Maybe the plants that I added to
the pot will live there for many years! Or,
maybe I'll start a whole garden of plants in
pinch pots!

Create your note cards. Read the note cards on this page. Then create a note card for each step in your how-to speech. Write out your beginning and ending word for word.

Giving Your Speech

After completing your note cards, you are ready to practice and present your speech.

Practicing Your Speech

Practice your speech several times. Use the following tips and the checklist at the bottom of the page.

- Practice in a quiet place, in front of a mirror, if possible.
- Practice in front of friends or parents. Listen to their suggestions.
- If possible, videotape or tape-record yourself.

Giving Your Speech

When you give your speech, remember the following guidelines.

- Look at your audience.
- Stand up straight.
- Speak loudly, clearly, and slowly.

Practicing Checklist

Number a piece of paper from 1 to 7. Practice your speech until you can answer "yes" to every question.

_____ **1.** Do I have good posture and look relaxed?

_____ **2.** Do I look at my audience as I speak?

_____ **3.** Can my voice be heard at the back of the room?

_____ **4.** Do I sound interested in my topic?

_____ **5.** Am I speaking slowly and clearly?

_____ **6.** Are my visual aids large and easy to understand?

_____ **7.** Do I point to information on my visual aids?

SPEAKING TIPS

Before your speech . . .

- **Get everything organized.**
  Put the main points of your speech on note cards and make your visual aids.
- **Time your speech.**
  Read and talk through your note cards out loud. If your speech is too short or too long, add or remove details to adjust the length.
- **Practice.**
  The more you remember without looking at your notes, the easier it will be to give your speech.

During your speech . . .

- **Speak loudly.** Be sure that everyone can hear you.
- **Speak clearly and slowly.**
  Don't hurry through your speech.
- **Look at your audience.** Connect with your listeners.
- **Put visual aids where everyone can see them.**
  Point out the things that you are talking about.

After your speech . . .

- **Answer questions.**
  Ask if anyone has questions about your topic.
- **Collect materials.**
  Gather your visual aids and note cards and return to your seat.

Practice and present. Practice your speech one more time with a friend or family member. After you present your speech in the classroom, listen for suggestions from your teacher or classmates.

Keeping Journals and Learning Logs

What is a learning log? Is it a piece of wood that goes to school? Is it a "board of education"? Of course not. A learning log is a notebook where you can write about the things you are learning . . . and become a better student.

What is a journal? A journal is a notebook where you write about your life. Can writing in a journal be a valuable experience? Well, some of the greatest people in history kept journals, so the answer is yes! The following chapter will show you how to start a journal and a learning log.

Mini Index

- Keeping a Personal Journal
- Writing in Other Journals
- Writing in a Learning Log
- Writing-to-Learn Activities

Keeping a Personal Journal

A personal journal is a special place to explore ideas, feelings, and experiences. You can write about people, events, ups and downs, and anything else in your life.

Getting Started

Follow these steps to begin your personal journal.

1 Gather the right tools.

All you need is a notebook and a pen or pencil. Some people buy a special book with blank pages. You could also use a computer and print or save your pages.

2 Find a special time and place to write.

Find a quiet place where you can write every day. Try to write freely for 5 to 10 minutes. As you continue to keep a journal, writing for this amount of time will become easier for you.

3 Write about what is important to you.

Here are some suggestions:

- Special events or memories
- Big things and little things
- What you see and what you hear
- Thoughts and feelings you want to capture or work through

4 Keep it organized.

Write the date at the beginning of each entry. Whenever you read your journal, underline ideas that you would like to write more about later.

Start your journal writing. Write in a personal journal for two weeks for at least 5 to 10 minutes a day. At the end of that time, put a star next to your favorite entry.

Journal Entries

In the journal entry below, a student writes about why she especially likes one season of the year.

Oct. 12

The leaves crackled under my feet when I walked home from school today. I walked slower because it was warm, and I liked the crunching sounds. A blanket of yellow leaves covered the ground. The trees were yellow, too.

The air smelled damp and moldy this morning. By this afternoon, it was dry and fresh.

Mom taped orange, red, and yellow leaves in the front windows. Our front steps are piled with pumpkins. Cornstalks and a bale of straw guard the front door.

It's getting colder outside, but I feel warm inside. For me, fall (Grandma calls it autumn) is the best time of year.

The following questions can help you focus on things that you might like to write about:

What experience have you had lately? How do you feel about it?

Writing in Other Journals

Personal journals can help you keep track of your thoughts and experiences. Here are three more journals you can try.

Diary

A diary is a personal journal that focuses on day-to-day events in your life. You usually make entries in a diary every day.

Reader-Response Journal

A reader-response journal will help you better understand whatever you read. As you read a book or a story, you can write your thoughts and answer questions like these:

1 Is this book funny? Sad? Surprising?

2 Are there any connections between my life and the story?

3 Would I recommend this book to others? Why or why not?

Travel Journal

In a travel journal, you write about a trip. Whether you take a bus downtown or travel for weeks, you can write about your experience.

July 5

We drove up Going to the Sun Highway. Glacier Park was cool but sunny at Logan Pass. We had on shorts, but there was snow everywhere. We hiked along the wooden walkways. Suddenly, I saw a furry animal. It looked like a woodchuck. Someone yelled, "There's a marmot!" Next I heard a roar like thunder. People were shouting and pointing. A cloud of snow exploded as an avalanche roared down a nearby mountain. Wow!

Write in a travel journal. The next time you take a long or short trip, record your thoughts and feelings in a travel journal.

Writing in a Learning Log

In a learning log, you write about a subject you are studying. It's a place to explore how new information connects to your own experiences. Here are some tips.

1 Set up a learning log for any subject.
Learning logs can help you understand new ideas and information in all your classes.

2 Keep your logs organized.
Use a separate notebook for each subject or divide a notebook into sections. Date each entry and leave room to answer questions you jot down . . . or to ask new questions later.

3 Make drawings and charts.
Diagrams and pictures can help you understand and remember new ideas.

4 Write freely about . . .
- thoughts or feelings about a subject or an assignment.
- questions you have.
- new ideas or information.

Science Class   Oct. 18
                              Sounds

Sounds are caused by vibrations.

- Put your hand on your throat.
- Say the word "sound."
- Feel the vibrations.
- The same thing happens when you play a guitar.
- The strings vibrate.

Social Studies Log

You can use learning logs for any subject. In the sample below, a student writes about an upcoming test. She figures out a way to remember the map of her state.

Social Studies   Oct. 1

            Map of Wisconsin

     On Friday's test I have to draw the outline of Wisconsin and name the capital, marked with a star. Then I have to label the boundaries all the way around.

     I'll remember the state's shape by thinking of a left-hand mitten with the palm down. The capital's star goes above the middle of the wrist. Here are the boundaries:

–Illinois across the bottom

–Lake Michigan up the right side

–the state of Michigan and Lake Superior on the top

–the St. Croix River and the Mississippi River down the left side

Lake Superior

Michigan

St. Croix River

Lake Michigan

Mississippi River

Madison

Illinois

Log on in math or social studies. On your own paper, write about something you are studying in math or social studies. Use your own words and make a drawing.

Writing-to-Learn Activities

There are many ways to write and learn in your learning logs. The next two pages cover six writing ideas.

The Basic Three

Clustering A cluster shows you a picture of how your ideas fit together. Write the subject in the middle of a page and circle it. Around the subject, write words and phrases about it. (See page 454.)

Listing This activity can give you a long list of ideas, feelings, and questions. Write words and phrases that come to mind about your subject.

Freewriting Freewriting is fast writing. Your ideas flow from your mind onto the paper until you run out of them. See the example below.

Health Class   February 18

The Skeletal System

All the systems of the body help each other. A good example is the skeletal system. I used to think that bones just help people stand up. But, they do something else. They protect us. The bones of the skull protect our brains. A soft spot on a baby's head is where the bones haven't come together yet. Bones also protect the circulatory system. The ribs make a cage for the heart and lungs. Bones sure do a lot more than I thought.

Freewriting Try freewriting about something you are learning in one of your classes. First, write the subject and the date at the top of the page. Then, write until you run out of ideas.

386

More Writing-to-Learn Activities

Here are three more ways to write and learn.

First Thoughts Make a list of key words that come to mind before you begin to study a new topic. In a Know-Want-Learn (KWL) chart, these words would be what you already know. Thinking about what you already know helps you begin to ask what you want or need to know. Writing down your first thoughts prepares you to learn new information.

KWL Reading Strategy		
Know	Want to know	Learned
–West Nile virus kills birds.	How is it affecting birds in my state?	

Notes to the Teacher Write down questions you have about the subject. Ask your teacher to respond to your questions in writing or in a class discussion.

> Dear Mrs. Johnson,
>
> Would you please explain the difference between "lend" and "borrow" again?
>
> Thanks,
> Charlie

Drawing Add pictures and charts to your learning log to show what you have learned or thought about.

Practice

Think about a subject or topic that is hard for you. Then write a question about it. Ask your teacher to respond.

Taking Notes

Musicians play beautiful notes, people write polite thank-you notes, and students take class notes. But they should never *pass* notes. How confusing! Just what should you do with notes?

The answer is simple. Always take notes to remember important ideas from class. Then read your notes when you do assignments or study for tests. Take note! This chapter will help you improve your note-taking skills.

Mini Index

- **Taking Classroom Notes**
- **Taking Reading Notes**

Taking Classroom Notes

Taking notes during class can help you remember information. Writing down important facts and ideas helps you . . .

- listen carefully,
- pay attention,
- remember what you hear, and
- review and study what you have learned.

Guidelines for Taking Good Notes

These guidelines will help you improve your note-taking skills.

Listen carefully!
1. Pay close attention.
2. Write down information that the teacher puts on the board or on an overhead projector.

Summarize!
1. Write down only the important ideas.
2. Draw pictures if they help you understand the ideas.

Get organized!
1. Write the subject and date at the top of each page of notes.
2. Use numbers to organize your notes (1, 2, 3).
3. Check your notes and recopy anything that is hard to read.

Take class notes. The next time you take notes, use these guidelines. Also look over the sample set of notes on the next page.

Setting Up Two-Column Notes

Two-column notes help you organize information. Fold your paper or draw a line that makes the left column narrower than the right column. Write key ideas on the left and related details on the right. You can also add drawings, questions, or comments.

Science   Sept. 15
              Sound, Heat, and Light

sound | —form of energy
       | —moves by vibration

heat | —form of energy
       | —moves by conduction (touch)
       | —moves by convection (circulation)

light | —form of energy
       | —moves in a straight line

Attic ——————— Warmest

                                    Hot air
Second Floor——Warmer   rises by
                                    convection.

First Floor——Warm

Review your notes. After you take notes, read them over. Are they clear and complete? Add comments or drawings like the diagram shown above to help you understand the material.

Taking Reading Notes

Taking notes will help you understand and remember what you read. Whenever you read an assignment, keep your notebook handy to write down key ideas and details. Here are some tips to follow.

Preview the Assignment

Skim the assigned reading to see what it is about. You can get clues from . . .

- **titles,**
- **headings,** and
- **photos, illustrations, and graphs.**

Take Notes

As you read, write down . . .

- **headings** and subheadings,
- **details** about the main ideas,
- **information** shown on charts and other graphics,
- **new vocabulary words** often in bold print, and
- **questions** about things that you don't understand.

Organize Your Thoughts

Add to your notes by drawing . . .

- **diagrams,**
- **charts,** or
- **graphic organizers** (see pages 456–457).

Practice

With a partner, preview a chapter that you haven't read in science or social studies. Use the preview guidelines above and predict what the chapter will be about.

Using a Time Line

Many reading assignments are about important events in history. You can organize history notes by making a **time line**, which lists events in the order in which they happened.

Read the following paragraph. Then study the time line to see how the information is listed in time order.

America's Earliest Colony Settled by Europeans

Columbus, sent by Spain, landed in the West Indies (North America) in 1492. However, many people think that America's first European colony was established more than 100 years later, in 1607. That year, England founded Jamestown, Virginia. Still, long before that, in 1513, Ponce de Leon explored Florida for Spain. By 1565, Spain had settled St. Augustine, Florida—the first permanent European colony in America.

Time Line

1492	Columbus lands in the West Indies.
1513	Ponce de Leon explores Florida.
1565	Spain settles St. Augustine, Florida.
1607	English settlers establish Jamestown, Virginia.

Practice

Create a time line for the information in the paragraph below.

By 1700, the European population of the American colonies was 250,000. The first settlers came slowly, though. The English sent 110 settlers to Jamestown in 1608 to help replace the original settlers. Of the 105 sent in 1607, only 32 were alive after the first winter. Slowly, the number of colonists grew. In 1620, 101 more English came on the *Mayflower.* Later, 30 Dutch families settled in New York in 1624.

Using a T-Chart

Writing is often organized around main ideas. Each main idea is supported by details. A **T-chart** will help you take notes when you have two types of information. The chart label names the main idea, and each column lists one type of details. (See page 204.)

Read the following paragraph. Then look at the T-chart to see how the information is organized.

> ### The Euro
> In 2002, the currency in many European countries changed to euros. The euro has seven different bills and eight coins. The bills are available in 5, 10, 20, 50, 100, 200, and 500 euro values. There are 1 euro and 2 euros coins, also. In addition, there are coins available for 1, 2, 5, 10, 20, and 50 euro cents.

T-Chart

The Euro in European Countries

Euro Bills	Euro Coins
5	1 euro
10	2 euros
20	1 cent
50	2 cents
100	5 cents
200	10 cents
500	20 cents
	50 cents

Create a T-chart. After you read the following paragraph, create a T-chart for the information it contains.

Writing can be divided between fiction and nonfiction. Some examples of fiction are tall tales, novels, folklore, and science fiction. Nonfiction includes autobiographies, biographies, histories, and diaries. Science books are also nonfiction.

Improving Viewing Skills

Do you know how to watch TV? That sounds silly, doesn't it? After all, it's simple to plop down and turn on the TV. What isn't easy, however, is to turn on your brain while you watch TV.

Always use your eyes *and* your brain when viewing TV or surfing the Internet. This is important because the information you get from those sources is sometimes incomplete or incorrect. This chapter will help you use your brain to improve your viewing skills.

Mini Index

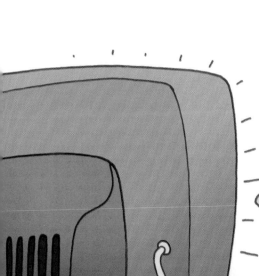

Watching the News

Remember that the people who put together news programs decide what you will hear and see. When you watch the news, ask yourself whether the information is complete, correct, and fair.

1 Complete: Are you getting enough information?

A news story should answer the 5 W's and H about an event.

How?   *Who?*   *What?*
Using climate records, scientists have been studying weather patterns

When?   *Why?*
for the last 10 years to discover the cause of a serious drought

Where?
in the American Southwest.

2 Correct: Are you sure of the facts?

When reporters are unsure of their facts, they use special words like those in blue in the following sentence:

There are reports **that everyone in the United States will own an airplane by 2012,** according to sources in Washington.

3 Fair: Are both sides of the story presented fairly?

A newscast should tell the whole story, not just one side of it. Think about the facts and pictures included in the news story.

The city council says that more parking spaces are needed downtown. (The camera shows a street where all the spaces are filled.)

Think about it: Are the parking spaces filled on *all* the streets downtown? Are the spaces filled *all* the time?

Respond to a newscast. The next time you watch a news story, answer the 5W and H questions about it to see if it is complete. (See number 1 above.)

Watching Television Specials

You may be assigned to watch a TV special, a program about one topic. Here are some tips to help you learn from this kind of program:

1 **Before viewing . . .**
- Write down facts you already know about the topic.
- Write down questions you have about the subject.

2 **During viewing . . .**
- Watch and listen for the answers to your questions.
- Take a few notes. Write down main ideas and details.
- Ask yourself whether the information is complete, correct, and fair. (See page 394.)

3 **After viewing . . .**
- Compare notes with someone else who saw the special.
- Write about the program in your learning log.

Notes from TV special about whales   Feb. 15

    I already knew that whales are mammals before I watched the special. Some people think that whales are fish. But I didn't know that whales are the biggest creatures that have ever lived. They're even bigger than the biggest dinosaurs!

    I also didn't know that some whales can live as long as humans. Too much hunting and pollution are killing the whales. Some kinds of whales are endangered.

Respond to a TV special. In a learning-log entry, write what you learned from a television special.

Checking What You Watch

It's fun to watch television, but it's also important to think about what you're watching. Do the following three checks.

Reality Check ● Some shows made for entertainment look real, but they aren't. Medical emergencies, car chases, and other scenes may be exaggerated to create excitement.

Fact-based programs (documentaries) often act out events that have actually happened, like the landing of the *Mayflower*. If the event is more recent, the program may use real movie footage along with scenes performed by actors. Try to tell the difference between what is real and what is staged.

Fact Check ● An athlete or a movie star on TV may give an opinion like "Everyone should become a vegetarian." Remember that famous people are not necessarily experts on what you should eat, wear, or do.

Prejudice Check ● A prejudice is a strong feeling held without a good reason. One type of prejudice, called a stereotype, unfairly says that all members of a group are a certain way. Here is an example of a stereotype:

> Old people live in the past. They don't want anything to change.

Some old people may not want change, but many do want it. Watch for prejudice on television. Don't judge an entire group by the actions of one member.

Log your viewing. Make entries in your learning log the next time you watch TV. Try to record one example of each of the following:

1 A program that looks like reality, but is not real

2 A reporter, an actor, or other personality who states an opinion

3 A character or statement that shows prejudice

Being Aware of Commercials

Television commercials have only one purpose—to get you to buy things. Here are five common selling methods:

Selling Methods	On Television	In Real Life
1 Slice of Life looks like everyday life.	A happy family is eating Cheesy Chicken Bits for lunch.	Actors are being paid to look happy. They may never eat Cheesy Chicken Bits.
2 Famous Faces shows a celebrity using a product.	Your favorite athlete drinks Power Juice during a game.	Celebrities are paid to appear in commercials. No law says they must use the product.
3 Just the Facts focuses on a fact about the product.	Health Watch Bacon is low in carbohydrates.	All bacon is low in carbohydrates. But bacon is high in fat.
4 Problem-Solution shows a product solving a problem.	A boy is bored until his parents buy him the latest video game.	Most problems have a number of solutions, not just one.
5 Infomercial looks like a TV show.	One kitchen machine fixes a whole meal for you.	People are being paid to sell the product.

Respond to a commercial. **Watch several commercials on television. Try to find an example of each selling method listed above.**

Viewing Web Sites

Like watching television, looking at Web sites on the Internet requires you to think. The following questions will help you become a smart viewer of what's on your computer screen.

Is the information fair or one-sided?

Let's say that you want to compare margarine to butter. You could get fair information from government and university Web sites. However, margarine companies or dairy organizations may present just one side of the issue.

Is the information from a reliable source?

If you're writing a report on tornadoes, the National Weather Service Web site will have information that you can trust. A personal Web site with a story about a tornado would not be as dependable.

Is the site up-to-date?

Information changes. Some Web sites are updated every day. Other sites have information that is too old to be useful. Look for sites that tell you when they were updated.

How does the information compare to other sources?

When you search the Web for information, look at several sites and at books or magazines. Do all the sources agree on the facts? Comparing sources helps you check for accuracy. Give credit to the sources you use for a report. (See page 346.)

Check out the Web. On the Internet, look up a current topic or event. List Web sites that look like good sources of information. Also, list a few sites that do not look helpful.

Taking Classroom Tests

Have you ever helped make spaghetti sauce or chili? If you have, you know that preparing ahead of time makes the job much easier. Good cooks start with a recipe. Then they make sure they have everything else they need. The same thing is true for taking a classroom test. Having a plan is the best way to succeed.

The first step in preparing for a test is to keep up with your daily class work. Then, if you follow a few simple steps, you'll be ready for test day!

Mini Index

- Preparing for a Test
- Taking Objective Tests
- Responding to Writing Prompts

Preparing for a Test

When your teacher announces a test, prepare for it by using the guidelines below:

Ask questions. Ask your teacher . . .
- What will be on the test?
- What kind of test will it be? (Multiple choice? True/false? Writing prompts?)

Review. Use your time wisely . . .
- Begin reviewing as soon as your teacher announces the test.
- Look over your notes and your textbook. List the things that you think are the most difficult.
- Be sure that you understand everything. Get help with anything that is still unclear.

3

Study. Use several ways to study . . .
- Write the main ideas and important vocabulary words on note cards.
- Say the information out loud and explain it to a partner in your own words.
- Study with an adult and explain the information to him or her.

Practice

Review the information under the three headings above. List two or three suggestions that you think would help you prepare for your next test.

TEST-TAKING TIPS

Before you start . . .

- **Read** all of the directions. Can you use notes, a dictionary, or your textbook?
- **Have a couple of sharpened pencils** and an eraser ready.
- **Write your full name** on the test.
- **Look over the entire test** so that you can plan your time.

During the test . . .

- **Read the directions** and follow them carefully. Ask the teacher about any questions that confuse you.
- **Study each question** by looking for key words like *always, only, all,* and *never.*
- **Answer the questions** you are sure of first. Don't spend too much time on any one question.
- **Go back to any questions** that you skipped.

After the test . . .

- **Be sure** you answered all the questions.
- **Read over your answers,** if you have time, to make sure they sound correct.

Taking Objective Tests

The four basic kinds of questions on objective tests are *multiple-choice, true/false, matching,* and *fill-in-the-blanks.*

Multiple-Choice Test

■ **READ** all the choices before marking an answer. There may be more than one correct answer. If there is, look for a choice like "all of the above" or "both a and b."

Question: A fish, a dog, and a bird all have_____.

    a. backbones   **b.** eyes   **c.** legs   **d.** both a and b

■ **BE AWARE** that a question may ask you to find a mistake in one of the choices. Check for the choice "no mistake."

Question: Circle the letter for the sentence that needs to be corrected.

    a. Gills and lungs are similar.

    b. Feathers and fur are similar.

    c. Arms and wings are similar.

    d. No mistake.

■ **PAY ATTENTION** to negative words like *not, never, except,* and *unless.* Also notice any numbers.

Question: Which two choices do not describe mammals?

    a. cold blooded   **b.** warm blooded   **c.** egg laying

■ **FOLLOW DIRECTIONS** carefully. A question may ask you to mark the choice that matches a sample sentence.

Question: Which sentence below uses the word <u>control</u> in the same way as the following sentence? Circle the correct letter.

Some mammals keep the insect population under <u>control</u>.

    a. Our TV's remote <u>control</u> is broken.

    b. The pilot adjusted the fuel <u>control</u>.

    c. The Salk vaccine helped to <u>control</u> polio outbreaks.

Answers: d., d., a. and c., c.

True/False Test

■ **READ** the whole question before you answer. For a statement to be true, the entire statement must be true.

■ **WATCH** for words like *all, every, always, never.* Statements with these words in them are often false.

   Directions: Mark each statement "T" for true or "F" for false.

   _____ **1.** All titles should be underlined.
   _____ **2.** Never capitalize *a, an,* or *the* in a title.
   _____ **3.** Use apostrophes to show possession and to end sentences.

   Answers: All three are false. 1. Not *all* titles should be underlined. 2. *A, an,* and *the* should be capitalized if they are the first word in a title. 3. The first part of the statement is true, but the last part is false.

Matching Test

■ **REVIEW** both lists before you make any matches.

■ **CHECK OFF** each answer you use.

   Directions: Match the definitions on the right to the terms on the left.

   _____ nocturnal   **a.** kind of sonar sounds
   _____ roosts   **b.** active during the night
   _____ echolocation   **c.** bats' homesites

   Answers: b. nocturnal, c. roosts, a. echolocation

Fill-in-the-Blanks Test

■ **READ** each sentence completely before filling in the blank.

   Directions: Fill in the blanks below with the correct answers.

   1. The prefix *anti* means _____.
   2. Words with the same or similar meanings are _____.

   Answers: 1. against 2. synonyms

Responding to Writing Prompts

Sometimes test questions ask you to write about topics that you've been studying. To answer this type of question, you must first understand the prompt. Here are two sample prompts:

- List the conditions needed to start a thunderstorm.
- Describe a thunderstorm.

Both prompts have the same topic: thunderstorms. But each prompt asks you to write about the topic in a different way. The first asks you to *list,* and the second asks you to *describe*.

1 Find the key word in the writing prompt.

It is important to understand the key words used in writing prompts. Here are some common ones:

Compare/Contrast ● To **compare**, tell how two things are alike. To **contrast**, tell how things are different. A prompt may ask you to compare, contrast, or both.

Example: Compare a hurricane and a tornado.

Define ● To **define** something, tell what it means, what it is, or what it does. Example: Define erosion.

Describe ● To **describe** something, tell how it looks, sounds, smells, tastes, and/or feels. Example: Describe a blizzard.

Explain ● To **explain** something, tell how it works, how it happens, or how to do it. Example: Explain how a lightbulb works.

List ● To **list**, give a number of facts, ideas, reasons, or other details about the topic.

Example: List three products that are made in your state.

Persuade ● To **persuade**, give facts and reasons that would convince someone to agree with your opinion.

Example: Do you think all bicyclists should wear helmets? Write a paragraph to persuade someone else of your opinion.

2 **Plan your answer.**

Here are the steps to answering a writing prompt:

1 **Listen** carefully to all directions.

2 **Find out** how much time you have for the test.

3 **Pay attention** to the key word.

4 **Think** about the prompt before you begin writing.

5 **List** your main points in a simple graphic organizer.

6 **Write** your response and check it for errors.

Sample Responses

The two answers below are different, even though they are about the same topic. The first *lists,* and the second *describes.*

List the conditions needed to start a thunderstorm.
(The answer lists three conditions.)

A thunderstorm needs at least three conditions to get started. First, there must be moisture for clouds and rain. Second, warm air must be able to rise. Finally, something (like a mountain or cold air) must lift the warm, moist air. When these three things come together, a thunderstorm forms.

Describe a thunderstorm.
(The answer tells about a thunderstorm using several senses.)

A thunderstorm begins with a huge, dark cloud. The air changes from warm to cool, and bright bolts of lightning flash in the sky. Booming thunder rumbles all around. Howling wind splatters rain against roofs and windows. After it stops, the air is fresh and clean again. The warm sun comes out, and a rainbow may appear in the sky.

Practice

For each prompt below, write the key word and tell what you need to do.

1. Explain how hail forms. **3.** Define *antonym.*

2. Persuade people to support a lake cleanup project.

The Basic Elements of Writing

Working with Words

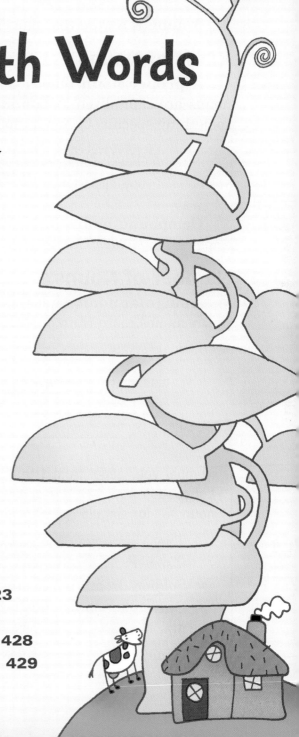

The English language just keeps growing bigger and stronger. Some people estimate that there are nearly 800,000 words in our language! But only about 200,000 of those words are used regularly. How many of them you actually use depends on your level of reading and learning.

There are eight different types of words called **the parts of speech.** They are *nouns, pronouns, verbs, adjectives, adverbs, prepositions, conjunctions,* and *interjections.* You will learn about the parts of speech in this chapter.

Mini Index

Using Nouns

A **noun** is a word that names a person, a place, a thing, or an idea.

Kinds of Nouns

A **proper noun** names someone or something specific. Proper nouns are capitalized. A **common noun** does not name someone or something specific. Common nouns are not capitalized.

COMMON NOUNS	PROPER NOUNS
boy, airport, holiday	Sergio, O'Hare Field, Kwanzaa

Compound nouns are made up of two or more words: *firefighter, watermelon, Golden Gate Bridge, General Pershing.*

Number of Nouns

A **singular noun** names one person, place, thing, or idea. A **plural noun** names more than one person, place, thing, or idea.

SINGULAR NOUNS	PLURAL NOUNS
teacher, woman, basketball	teachers, women, basketballs

Practice

Number your paper from 1 to 4 and copy the nouns in each sentence. Label each noun "C" for common or "P" for proper. Also label each noun "S" for singular or "PL" for plural.

■ The <u>Alamo</u> was the <u>site</u> of a famous <u>battle</u>.
Alamo–P, S   site–C, S   battle–C, S

1. <u>Soldiers</u> from <u>Mexico</u> stormed the <u>Alamo</u>.
2. Only 189 <u>men</u> defended the <u>mission</u>.
3. <u>Jim Bowie</u> and <u>Davy Crockett</u> were <u>heroes</u>.
4. None of the <u>fighters</u> inside the <u>mission</u> survived.

Gender of Nouns

Nouns can be *feminine*, *masculine*, *neuter*, or *indefinite*.

Feminine (female) nouns: mother, woman, hen, cow
. . . .
Masculine (male) nouns: father, man, rooster, bull
. . . .
Neuter (neither male nor female) nouns: foot, closet, trampoline, park
. . . .
Indefinite (either male or female) nouns: parent, doctor, child, birds

Practice

List three feminine nouns, three masculine nouns, three neuter nouns, and three indefinite nouns.

Possessive Nouns

A **possessive** noun shows ownership. Singular nouns are usually made possessive by adding an apostrophe and the letter *s* to the end of the word. In most cases, plural nouns ending in the letter *s* just need an apostrophe to make them possessive. (See page 492.)

SINGULAR POSSESSIVE	PLURAL POSSESSIVE
my *mother's* briefcase	two *mothers'* briefcases
the *dog's* collar	the three *dogs'* collars

Practice

Write a sentence for each of the following nouns. Have each of these nouns show possession.

Example: My <u>friend's</u> house is up for sale.

friend   teachers   park   dogs   pirates   car

How can I improve my writing with nouns?

Include Specific Nouns

Some nouns are **general nouns** and do not give the reader a clear picture. Other nouns are **specific nouns.** They name particular people, places, or things. Specific nouns make your writing more clear and interesting.

GENERAL NOUNS	fruit	building	coat	country	food
SPECIFIC NOUNS	apricot	Eiffel Tower	parka	Italy	tacos

 tip How can you tell if a noun is specific enough? Ask yourself this question: Does the noun create a clear picture in my mind? A specific noun like *poodle* creates a clearer picture than the general noun *dog*.

Practice

Number your paper from 1 to 5. Rewrite the following sentences using specific nouns in place of the underlined general nouns. The questions in parentheses will help you change the nouns.

■ I turned quickly when I heard <u>the sound</u>. (*What sound?*)
   barking

1. Grandma is cooking <u>vegetables</u>. (*Which vegetables?*)
2. My mom bought me some <u>clothes</u>. (*What type of clothes?*)
3. Marta took a <u>boat</u> out on the lake. (*What kind of boat?*)
4. Teena spilled the <u>snack</u> on the carpet. (*What kind of snack?*)
5. Franco enjoys fixing <u>things</u>. (*What things?*)

 Write **NOW** Write at least five sentences about an activity you like. Try to use specific nouns in your explanation.

Make Comparisons

Sometimes you can make an idea clearer and more colorful by creating a figure of speech. When you create a **simile** or **metaphor,** you compare two nouns.

Simile: **A simile compares two nouns using the word** like **or** as.

Those butterflies **look** like **flying** flowers.

Metaphor: **A metaphor compares two nouns without using** like **or** as.

In our city, high school football **is** king.

> At first, making comparisons may not be easy. But they can make your writing fun to read, so keep trying.

Practice

Number your paper from 1 to 5. Then, in each sentence below, list the two nouns being compared. Also tell if the comparison is a simile or a metaphor.

■ The racing cars hung together like fish.
  cars and fish–simile

1. This book is a door to the galaxies.

2. The dog danced around like loose litter blowing in the wind.

3. The hot soup was the best medicine for my cold.

4. The snowplow blasted through the snow like a stallion.

5. A beautiful sunrise is a gift of peace.

Write NOW Create at least one simile and one metaphor to share. Ask your classmates to identify the two nouns being compared.

Special Challenge: On your own paper, list four comparisons from books, stories, or articles that you have read. Tell these three things about each comparison: (1) where you found it, (2) what two nouns are being compared, and (3) whether the comparison is a simile or a metaphor.

Using Pronouns

A **pronoun** is a word used in place of a noun. An **antecedent** is the word the pronoun refers to or replaces. (See 576.1.)

Jamal **yelled that** he **was ready.**

(*Jamal* is the antecedent of the pronoun *he*.)

Hanna **went bowling.** She **had three strikes.**

(*Hanna* is the antecedent of the pronoun *she*.)

Personal Pronouns

Personal pronouns are the most common type of pronoun.

PERSONAL PRONOUNS	I	you	he	she	we	they
	me	it	him	her	us	them

Person and Number of a Pronoun

Pronouns can vary in **person** and in **number**.

PERSON	NUMBER: SINGULAR	PLURAL
First person (*the person speaking*)	I eat.	We eat.
Second person (*the person spoken to*)	You eat.	You eat.
Third person (*the person spoken about*)	He/She/It eats.	They eat.

Practice

Number your paper from 1 to 4. Write a sentence using each pronoun described below as the subject. Underline the subject in each sentence.

■ third-person plural <u>They</u> should make a snow fort.

1. first-person singular
2. first-person plural
3. second-person singular
4. third-person singular

Subject and Object Pronouns

A **subject pronoun** is used as the subject of a sentence.

She **told me funny stories.**   They **made me laugh.**

SUBJECT PRONOUNS CAN BE SINGULAR OR PLURAL.

Singular: I, you, he, she, it   *Plural:* we, you, they

An **object pronoun** is used as a direct object, as an indirect object, or as an object of preposition in a prepositional phrase.

Mr. Jacobs helped her. (*direct object*)

Todd gave me **the present.** (*indirect object*)

We planned a surprise party for him. (*object of the preposition*)

OBJECT PRONOUNS CAN BE SINGULAR OR PLURAL.

Singular: me, you, him, her, it   *Plural:* us, you, them

Some pronouns like *my, your, his, her, mine,* and *yours* show ownership. They are called **possessive pronouns.**

Practice

Number your paper from 1 to 6. Write a sentence using an example of each pronoun described below. Underline the pronoun.

■ singular subject pronoun
  She saw the band arrive.

1. plural subject pronoun   4. plural object pronoun

2. singular object pronoun   5. plural subject pronoun

3. singular subject pronoun   6. singular object pronoun

How can I use pronouns properly?

Check the Number of Your Pronouns

The pronouns in your sentence must agree in number with their antecedents. If the antecedent is singular, the pronoun also must be singular. If the antecedent is plural, the pronoun must be plural.

The girl took her cat to the veterinarian clinic.
(The pronoun *her* and its antecedent *girl* are both singular, so they agree in number.)

The clinic assistants said that they were surprised by the size of the cat.
(The pronoun *they* and its antecedent *assistants* are both plural, so they agree in number.)

Dr. Stephanie said she had never seen such a big cat.
(The pronoun *she* and its antecedent *Dr. Stephanie* are both singular, so they agree in number.)

Practice

> A pronoun can be either singular or plural in number.

Number your paper from 1 to 5 and write the correct pronoun for each sentence below. Then write the antecedent that each pronoun refers to.

■ Luis and Orlando brought (*his, their*) dog in for a checkup.
their, Luis and Orlando

1. An assistant said that (*he, they*) would take the dog to the examining room.

2. Then Dr. Stephanie used (*her, their*) stethoscope to check the dog's heart.

3. The dog received (*its, their*) yearly shots, too.

4. Afterward, the doctor told the boys to give (*his, their*) dog more exercise.

5. The boys like Dr. Stephanie and really trust (*her, they*).

Check the Gender of Your Pronouns

The singular pronouns in your sentences must also agree in gender with their antecedents. Singular pronouns can be masculine (male), feminine (female), or neuter (neither male nor female).

Pedro **found** his **skateboard in the basement.**
(The masculine pronoun *his* and its antecedent *Pedro* agree.)

Lisa **said that** she **wrote a poem.**
(The feminine pronoun *she* and its antecedent *Lisa* agree.)

My new shirt **has an ink stain on** it.
(The neuter pronoun *it* and its antecedent *shirt* agree.)

Practice

Number your paper from 1 to 5. Then write the correct pronoun for each sentence below and the antecedent that the pronoun refers to. (Make sure that the pronoun and its antecedent agree in gender.)

■ Mari Sandoz has written a book about Crazy Horse, and _____ got her information through interviews.
she, Mari Sandoz

1. Crazy Horse was a member of the Sioux tribe, and _____ was born about 1840.

2. Crazy Horse gained _____ greatest fame in two battles—the Rosebud and the Little Bighorn.

3. Crazy Horse was greatly admired because _____ helped the needy people in his tribe.

4. Crazy Horse's first wife was Black Shawl, but _____ died very young. His second wife was Nellie Larrabee.

5. A monument to Crazy Horse is being carved from a mountain in South Dakota, but _____ has a long way to go.

Choosing Verbs

A **verb** shows action or links the subject to another word in the sentence. There are three types of verbs: action verbs, linking verbs, and helping verbs. (See page 582.)

Action Verbs

Action verbs tell what the subject is doing. Use specific action verbs in your sentences to make them interesting and fun to read.

General Action Verbs

> A snowstorm came through. The wind made noise, and snow fell around the house. We got under quilts and drank hot cider.

Specific Action Verbs

> A snowstorm roared outside. The wind howled, and snow drifted around the house. We burrowed under quilts and sipped hot cider.

Practice

Number your paper from 1 to 5. Skip two or three lines between each number. Study the pairs of actions verbs below. List the more specific one on your paper. Then write a sentence for each verb that you have listed.

■ laugh   giggle

    giggle   Samantha and Josie giggled in the lunchroom.

1. whisper   talk
2. run   sprint
3. smash   hit
4. drink   gulp
5. stare   look

 Write NOW Write three or four sentences about something fun that you have done with a friend. Use specific actions verbs in your sentences.

Linking and Helping Verbs

A **linking verb** connects a subject to a noun or an adjective in the predicate part of a sentence.

Linking Verbs: *is, are, was, being, been,* and *am;* also *smell, look taste, feel,* and *seem.* (See page 582 for a complete list.)

> **Spaghetti is my favorite meal.** (The linking verb *is* connects the subject *spaghetti* to the noun *meal.)*

> **The sauce tastes spicy.** (The linking verb *tastes* connects the subject *sauce* to the adjective *spicy.)*

A **helping verb** comes before the main verb and gives it a more specific meaning.

Helping Verbs: *has, have, had, do, did, should, would,* and *could;* also *is, are, was, were,* and *been.* (See page 582 for a complete list.)

> **Lana will make the banners for the club.**
> (The helping verb *will* helps state a future action, *will make.)*

> **Thomas did help last year.**
> (The helping verb *did* helps state a past action, *did help.)*

 Practice

> Words like *is, are, was,* and *were* can be linking verbs or helping verbs.

Number your paper from 1 to 4. Then identify the underlined verb as either a linking verb or a helping verb.

- Farley Mowat <u>has</u> written wildlife books. helping verb
1. *Never Cry Wolf* <u>is</u> his most famous book.
2. Mowat <u>had</u> lived among wolves before he wrote this book.
3. He saw that the wolves <u>were</u> eating mice.
4. So the author <u>would</u> eat mice, just like the wolves!

 Write **NOW**   **Write a sentence for each of these helping verbs: *had, did,* and *should.***

Tenses of Verbs

A verb's **tense** tells when the action takes place. **Simple** tenses include *present*, *past*, and *future*. (Also see page 584.)

Simple Tenses

The present tense of a verb shows action that is *happening now* or that *happens regularly*.

I collect models of cars, planes, and boats.

The past tense of a verb states an action that *happened in the past*. It is usually formed by adding *-ed* to the present tense verb.

Yesterday, I finished a model of a submarine.

The future tense of a verb states an action that *will take place in the future*. It is formed by using *will* or *shall* before the main verb.

Next week, I will start a new model.

I shall finish it in two days.

Practice

Number your paper from 1 to 6. Identify the tense of each underlined verb below.

■ My grandfather <u>grows</u> his own vegetables.
  Present

1. He <u>started</u> gardening many years ago.
2. Last year, he <u>planted</u> 12 different vegetables.
3. We <u>picked</u> tons of tomatoes and green peppers!
4. To help my grandfather, I <u>weed</u> the garden.
5. I <u>water</u> the garden, too.
6. Next year, we <u>will add</u> more corn, my favorite vegetable.

How can I use verbs correctly?
Number of a Verb

The subjects and verbs in your sentences must agree in number. If you use a singular subject, use a singular verb. If you use a plural subject, use a plural verb.

Subject-Verb Agreement

The chart below shows how subject-verb agreement works.

SINGULAR SUBJECT	SINGULAR VERBS	PLURAL SUBJECT	PLURAL VERBS
Mr. King	swims	exercisers	swim
Mr. King	runs	exercisers	run

Mr. King swims laps in the pool. (The subject *Mr. King* and the verb *swims* are both singular. They agree in number.)

The exercisers run laps on the track. (The subject *exercisers* and the verb *run* are both plural. They agree in number.)

Practice

Write a sentence for each pair of subjects and verbs below. Supply your own verbs for the last three subjects.

■ Kerry   plays

Kerry plays volleyball on Saturday mornings.

1. brother   eats   **4.** girls   _____

2. firefighters   practice   **5.** cat   _____

3. Max   asks   **6.** balloons   _____

Write NOW Write a paragraph (at least four sentences) about your favorite class. Make sure your verbs agree in number with their subjects.

Irregular Verbs

Most verbs in the English language are **regular**. That means you add -ed to the verb to form the past tense. (See regular verbs on page 418.) Other verbs are **irregular.** That means you do not add -ed to form the past tense.

Past Tense Form

To state the past action of an **irregular** verb, the word changes. (You do not add -ed to the verb.)

Sam made many of her own birthday cards.
(*Made* is the past tense form of the irregular verb *make.*)

Devon wrote an e-mail message to his aunt.
(*Wrote* is the past tense form of the irregular verb *write.*)

Past Participle Form

The form of a verb used with certain helping verbs (such as *has, had,* or *have)* is called the past participle. Regular verbs add -ed to make this form. Irregular verbs change to make this form.

Sam has made many of her own birthday cards.
(*Made* is the past participle form of the irregular verb *make.*)

Devon has written an e-mail message to his aunt.
(*Written* is the past participle form of the irregular verb *write.*)

Practice

Write a sentence using each verb form indicated below. Remember that the past participle needs a helping verb (*had, has,* or *have*).

■ think *(past participle)* I had thought about many things.

1. swim *(past tense)*

2. shake *(past tense)*

3. take *(past participle)*

4. break *(past tense)*

5. catch *(past participle)*

6. write *(past participle)*

Subject-Verb Agreement in Sentences with Compound Subjects

A **compound subject** has two or more simple subjects joined by a conjunction *(and, or)*. Listed below are the two main rules for subject-verb agreement in sentences with compound subjects.

Rule 1: When a sentence has a compound subject connected by *and,* the verb should be plural.

> Soccer **and** tennis **are** my favorite sports.
> (*Soccer* and *tennis* is a compound subject connected by *and.* The subject **agrees** in number with the plural verb *are.)*

> Alan **and** I **play** tennis on the park courts.
> (*Alan* and *I* is a compound subject connected by *and.* The subject agrees in number with the plural verb *play.)*

Rule 2: When a sentence has a compound subject connected by *or,* the verb should agree with the subject closest to it.

> **Either the** park directors **or** Alan supplies **the tennis balls.**
> (The subject *Alan* is nearer to the verb *supplies.* They are both singular and agree in number.)

> Josh **or my other** friends **usually** shoot **hoops in the park.**
> (The subject *friends* is nearer to the verb *shoot.* They are both plural and agree in number.)

> See page 419 for more information about subject-verb agreement.

Practice

Write a sentence for each pair of subjects below.

■ Josie and I Josie and I make fruit smoothies.

1. backpack and books
2. my brothers or I
3. teachers or the PTO
4. cars and trucks
5. Mandi and Matt
6. a cat or dogs

How can I improve my writing with verbs?

Avoid Too Many *Be* Verbs

Try not to use the *be* verbs *(is, are, was, were)* too often. Many times, a stronger action verb can be made from another word in the same sentence.

A *be* verb: **Rosa is a forceful speaker.**
A stronger action verb: **Rosa speaks forcefully.**

Practice

The sentences below contain *be* verbs (underlined). Rewrite each sentence by making another word in the sentence an action verb.

■ Our dog Henry is a loud barker.
  Our dog Henry barks loudly.

1. You are a wonderful singer.

2. My cousins are constant whiners.

3. My dad is a skilled cook.

4. Our car was a rough ride.

Share the Right Feeling

Different verbs create different feelings. Make sure that the verbs you use fit the feeling that you want to share.

Leon tiptoed into the room. *(moved slowly and quietly)*
Leon strutted into the room. *(moved proudly)*
Leon stumbled into the room. *(moved in a clumsy way)*

The connotation of a word is the feeling that the word expresses.

Practice

Write a sentence using the verb *talk*. Then rewrite the sentence twice, using two different synonyms for *talk*. Each synonym should have a different connotation.

Describing with Adjectives

An **adjective** is a word that describes a noun or a pronoun. Adjectives answer four main questions: *what kind? how many? how much?* or *which one?*

EXAMPLE ADJECTIVES			
What kind?	narrow **path**	green **hat**	small **dog**
How much?	some **salt**	small **amount**	enough **rain**
How many?	several **boats**	four **miles**	no **animals**
Which one?	this **cup**	that **train**	those **people**

Placement of Adjectives

Adjectives often come right before the noun they describe.

> The golden **leaves fell.**

Adjectives can also come after the word they describe, as they do when they appear after a *be* verb.

> **The leaves are** golden. **Soon the leaves will be** brown.

Practice

Number your paper from 1 to 5. Write each underlined adjective and tell whether it answers *what kind*? *how many*? *how much*? or *which one*?

■ There are *many* places I would like to visit.
   many, how many

1. I would like to take a *long* trip to the Mojave Desert.
2. *Desert* sunsets are beautiful.
3. Deserts have deep *blue* skies.
4. This desert gets *little* rain but supports *gorgeous* life-forms.
5. We have an *amazing* climate, *unusual* plants, and *fantastic* animals.

Forms of Adjectives

Adjectives have three forms: the positive, the comparative, and the superlative. For most one-syllable adjectives, add *-er* or *-est* to form the comparative and superlative. Place *more* or *most* in front of most multisyllable adjectives to form the comparative and superlative.

POSITIVE	COMPARATIVE	SUPERLATIVE
small	smaller	smallest
beautiful	more beautiful	most beautiful

The **positive** form describes a noun without comparing it to another noun.

> My cat, Tasha, is a smart animal. She is a curious cat.

The **comparative** form compares a noun with another noun.

> She is smarter than my dog, Rip. She is also more curious than he is.

The **superlative** form compares a noun with several other nouns.

> Tasha is the smartest animal I have ever known.
> She is the most curious animal in town.

Practice

Number your paper from 1 to 6. Skip one or two lines between each number. Then write a sentence using the form of the adjective given in parentheses.

■ beautiful *(superlative)*
St. Mary's Church is the most beautiful building in town.

1. large *(comparative)*

2. exciting *(positive)*

3. clean *(superlative)*

4. amazing *(comparative)*

5. surprising *(superlative)*

6. hungry *(positive)*

How can I improve my writing with adjectives?

Combine Short Sentences

Sometimes ideas included in short sentences can be combined into one longer sentence using one or more adjectives. Longer sentences can connect your ideas and make your writing flow.

Combining with One Adjective

The two short sentences below can be combined by moving the adjective *old* to the first sentence.

Short Sentences: I saw my uncle's barn yesterday. The barn was old.

Combined Sentence: I saw my uncle's old barn yesterday.

Combining with a Series of Adjectives

The string of short sentences below can be combined by using a series of adjectives. (A *series* is three items or more in a row: *red, white,* and *blue.*)

Short Sentences: The barn was smelly. It was dusty. It was creepy.

Combined Sentence: The barn was smelly, dusty, and creepy.

Practice

Combine each set of short sentences into one longer sentence. Combine the sentences using one adjective or a series of adjectives.

■ Farm machinery cluttered the yard. It was rusty.
  Rusty farm machinery cluttered the yard.

1. A path led to the barnyard. The path was overgrown.
2. Once the farm was active. It was well kept. It was clean.
3. A fence circles a nearby field. The fence is useless.
4. My uncle raised cows. He raised chickens. He raised pigs.

Describing with Adverbs

An **adverb** is a word that describes a verb, an adjective, or another adverb. An adverb answers four main questions: *how? when? where?* or *how often?*

> Tomorrow, **we are going to make clay pots.** *(when?)*
> **We will have to work** carefully. *(how?)*
> **Our art class meets** weekly. *(how often?)*
> **We meet** downstairs **in the old art room.** *(where?)*

Forms of Adverbs

Adverbs come in three different forms: positive, comparative, and superlative. For most one-syllable adverbs, add *-er* or *-est* to form the comparative and superlative.

POSITIVE	COMPARATIVE	SUPERLATIVE
fast	faster	fastest

Comparative: **Geoff works** faster **than I do.**
Superlative: **Geoff works the** fastest **of all my friends.**

Place *more* or *most* in front of most multisyllable adverbs to form the comparative and superlative.

POSITIVE	COMPARATIVE	SUPERLATIVE
slowly	more slowly	most slowly

Comparative: **Grandpa walks** more slowly **than before.**
Superlative: **Of all the times I've seen him, Grandpa walked** most slowly **after his surgery.**

Write NOW On your own paper, write a paragraph of at least four sentences about your typical lunch hour in school. Try to use at least one comparative form of an adverb and one superlative form.

How can I improve my writing with adverbs?

Combine Short Sentences

Sometimes ideas included in short sentences can be combined into one longer sentence by moving an adverb from one sentence to another. The two sentences that follow can be combined by moving the adverb *quickly* to the first sentence.

Short Sentences: **The deer ran through the woods. It ran quickly.**
Combined Sentence: **The deer ran quickly through the woods.**

Practice

Number your paper from 1 to 3. Combine each pair of sentences by moving the adverb from one to the other.

◼ I followed the trail. I moved quietly.
I quietly followed the trail. *or* I followed the trail quietly.

1. The breeze rustled the leaves. It rustled them softly.
2. The deer looked ahead. It looked nervously.
3. Then it stopped. It stopped suddenly.

Tell About the Verb

Using specific adverbs to modify verbs can make your writing more colorful.

The deer moved.   The deer moved cautiously.

Practice

Rewrite each of the following sentences two times. Each time, use a different adverb to modify the verb.

◼ Kelly coughed.
Kelly coughed loudly. Kelly coughed constantly.

1. Bev entered the room.   3. Sam waved.
2. Reggie turned around.   4. The man snored.

Connecting with Prepositions

Prepositions are words that introduce prepositional phrases. A preposition can show direction or position.

Cory hid behind the couch. (The preposition *behind* introduces the prepositional phrase *behind the couch.*)

Saul tiptoed into the kitchen. (The preposition *into* introduces the prepositional phrase *into the kitchen.*)

Identify Prepositional Phrases

A **prepositional phrase** includes a preposition, the object of the preposition (a noun or pronoun), and any words that modify the object.

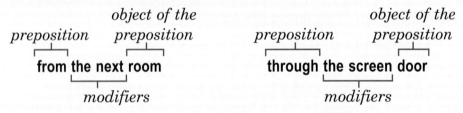

tip See page 598 for a complete list of prepositions.

Practice

Number your paper from 1 to 5. Then identify the prepositional phrases in the sentences below. There may be more than one prepositional phrase in some of the sentences.

■ Jayden played soccer during recess.
   during recess

1. I live around the corner from the grocery store.
2. The gopher burrowed underneath the front porch.
3. Ty jumped off the raft and into the water.
4. With the help of my teacher, I raised my math grade.
5. After a few days, the clay on the shelf will be dry.

Connecting with Conjunctions

Conjunctions connect individual words or groups of words.

The road is long and narrow.
We play ball after school or
on Saturday.

Kinds of Conjunctions

COORDINATING

Coordinating conjunctions (and, but, or, for, nor, so, yet) connect equal words, phrases, or clauses.

Mimi and Leann played a saxophone duet. *(words)*

We had a picnic after the game but before the rain. *(phrases)*

Jessica walked to school, and Luis rode the bus. *(clauses)*

CORRELATIVE

Correlative conjunctions are used in pairs (either/or, neither/nor) to connect words or groups of words.

Either Linda or Ashley will take care of your dog.

SUBORDINATING

Subordinating conjunctions (after, because, when, until) introduce the dependent clauses in complex sentences. (Dependent clauses cannot stand alone as a sentence.)

Angel likes Tuesdays because he has photography club.

(For a more complete list of conjunctions, see page 600.)

Write NOW Write four sentences about your typical Saturday morning. Use at least two different types of conjunctions in your writing.

How can I use prepositions and conjunctions?

Add Information

Prepositional phrases are useful for adding information to sentences.

Sentence without prepositional phrases:
Kelli's mom made a fruit salad.
Sentence with prepositional phrases:
In the morning, **Kelli's mom made a fruit salad** for the banquet.

Practice

Expand the following sentences by adding one or more prepositional phrases.

1. Kara brought a sleeping bag.
2. Tyler saw a black bear.
3. The stars twinkled.
4. We slept in cabins.

Connect Short Sentences

Conjunctions can connect short, choppy sentences. Combining sentences makes your writing sound smoother.

Two short sentences:
Ben's brother went to the movies. Ben stayed home.
The two sentences combined:
Ben's brother went to the movies, but **Ben stayed home.**

Practice

Combine each pair of sentences using the conjunction in parentheses.

1. We can't go swimming. The lifeguard's not on duty. *(because)*
2. Vicki read a book. Molly watched a movie. *(but)*
3. Hector plays baseball. He plays basketball. *(and)*

Building Effective Sentences

Look around. Do you see walls and windows? Do you see desks and chairs? Most things around you were built by someone. Now, look at the sentences you are reading. They were built, too! Word by word, writers and editors built every sentence in this book.

Good writing begins with strong sentences. Sentences of different types and lengths all work together to build ideas. Whether you want to create a little clubhouse of memories or a huge castle of dreams, this chapter can help you build the sentences you need.

Mini Index

Writing Complete Sentences

How can I write complete sentences?

A **complete sentence** is a group of words that expresses a complete thought. A sentence needs a **subject** and a **predicate**. Without a subject and a predicate, a sentence is incomplete.

INCOMPLETE THOUGHT	COMPLETE SENTENCE
My best friend Lupe *(A predicate is missing.)*	My best friend Lupe *plays* the piano.
plays very well *(A subject is missing.)*	*She* plays very well.
in a concert *(Both the subject and predicate are missing.)*	Last week, *she played* in a concert.

Practice

Number your paper from 1 to 5. Then study each group of words below. If the words form a complete sentence, write the sentence with correct capitalization and punctuation on your paper. If the thought is incomplete, add words to make it a complete sentence.

■ after the concert We will have pizza after the concert.

1. the front-row seat
2. Raji asked us to sit with him
3. wore special hats for one song
4. the band director
5. the band played my favorite song

Write NOW Write five complete sentences about a time you went to a concert, a play, or a movie. Be sure each sentence has a subject and a predicate.

Simple Subjects and Predicates

A **simple subject** (shown in orange) is the subject without the words that modify or describe it. A **simple predicate** (shown in blue) is the predicate without the words that modify it.

SIMPLE SUBJECT	SIMPLE PREDICATE
My friend Amber	came to the party.
A new student	introduces herself to the class.
All the club members	welcome Mrs. Greene.
We	talked.

The simple predicate can also be called the verb.

Practice

Number your paper from 1 to 5. List the simple subject and simple predicate for each sentence below.

◼ Our fourth-grade class visited the state capitol building.
class, visited

1. Our teacher planned a meeting with our senator.
2. Senator O'Reilly showed us the senate chamber.
3. We saw Governor Sanchez!
4. He said hello to our class.
5. Our chaperone took pictures of us with the governor.

Write NOW Write four or five sentences about an important building you have visited. In each sentence, underline the simple subject with one line and the simple predicate with two lines.

Compound Subjects and Predicates

A **compound subject** includes two or more simple subjects.

> **COMPOUND SUBJECT**
>
> Mr. Clark and Mrs. Stewart plan our field trips.
> ....
> Bubbles and smoke formed in the bottle.

A **compound predicate** includes two or more simple predicates.

> **COMPOUND PREDICATE**
>
> Our class wrote and illustrated a book about pets.
> ....
> The students measure and mix the materials.

> *A simple sentence can have both a compound subject and a compound predicate.*

Practice

Copy sentences 1 to 5 on your paper. For each sentence, underline the simple subject with one line and the simple predicate with two lines.

■ The teacher and students looked at the overflowing liquid.
The <u>teacher</u> and <u>students</u> <u>looked</u> at the overflowing liquid.

1. Mr. Huan gathered paper towels and mopped up the mess.
2. Then another bottle tipped over and spilled onto the floor.
3. Marah and Paul collected more paper towels.
4. Other students and teachers entered the classroom and asked about the hubbub.
5. Mr. Huan laughed and pointed at the messy experiment.

Write NOW Write three or four sentences about a class project. Use at least one compound subject and one compound predicate in your writing.

Complete Subjects and Predicates

The **complete subject** is the simple subject with all the words that modify it. The **complete predicate** is the simple predicate with all the words that modify it.

COMPLETE SUBJECT	COMPLETE PREDICATE
Who or what is doing something?	*What is being done?*
Our teacher	brought two gerbils to school.
Grandpa's loud snoring	keeps me awake.
The giant oak tree	fell over during the storm.
Our principal and music teacher	act in the community theater.

See pages 560 and 562 for more information about subjects and predicates.

Practice

Copy sentences 1 through 5 on your own paper. Then draw a line between the complete subject and the complete predicate in each sentence.

■ I had a funny dream.

I | had a funny dream.

1. Jennie and I were exploring Antarctica.
2. Both of us stood on an iceberg.
3. Cute little penguins swam all around us.
4. Some laughing seals pushed us into the water.
5. My mother woke me up.

Write NOW Write four sentences about a funny dream you've had. Then draw a line between the complete subject and the complete predicate in each sentence.

Fixing Sentence Problems

How can I make sure my sentences are correct?

Check your writing for sentence fragments. A **fragment** is an incomplete sentence that is missing a subject, a predicate, or both.

FRAGMENT	SENTENCE
Collects stuffed animals. *(Missing a subject)*	My sister collects stuffed animals.
Family members. *(Missing a predicate)*	Family members give her stuffed animals for presents.
All around her room. *(Missing a subject and a predicate)*	They are all around her room.

Practice

Number your paper from 1 to 5. Write "C" if a group of words is a complete sentence. Write "F" if it is a fragment. Rewrite each fragment to make it a complete sentence.

■ Started many years ago.

   F | Her collection started many years ago.

1. Aunt Susan bought her the first stuffed animal.
2. A small stuffed giraffe.
3. Her favorites.
4. My father made shelves for the animals.
5. Sit on her bed.

> Reading your sentences aloud will help you check for fragments.

Write NOW Write four sentences about something you collect or would like to collect. Make sure your sentences are complete.

Check for Run-On Sentences

A **run-on sentence** happens when two sentences run together without punctuation or a connecting word. You can correct a run-on sentence by forming two sentences or by adding a comma and a conjunction *(and, but, or)* between the two sentences.

RUN-ON SENTENCE	CORRECTED
The sky turned dark lightning flashed in the distance.	The sky turned dark. Lightning flashed in the distance. *(Form two sentences.)*
The wind picked up a few sprinkles started to fall.	The wind picked up, and a few sprinkles started to fall. *(Add a comma and a conjunction.)*

Practice

On your own paper, correct the run-on sentences below. Correct each one according to the directions in parentheses. Use the conjunctions *and* and *but*.

■ My horse started to trot I bounced up and down. *(Add a comma and a conjunction.)*

My horse started to trot, and I bounced up and down.

1. My friend Marti rode up next to me then my horse slowed down. *(Form two sentences.)*

2. We tried to turn our horses around they wanted to go in a different direction. *(Add a comma and a conjunction.)*

3. Finally, the horses headed back to the stable they were probably hungry and thirsty. *(Form two sentences.)*

4. A stable worker was waiting for us we were glad to see him. *(Add a comma and a conjunction.)*

Watch for Subject-Verb Agreement

Subjects and verbs should always agree in number in your sentences. That means that whenever you use a singular subject, you need to use a singular verb; and whenever you use a plural subject, you need to use a plural verb.

SINGULAR AGREEMENT	PLURAL AGREEMENT
Brad builds birdhouses.	Brad and Paul build birdhouses.
My dog barks all night.	Our dogs bark all night.
I bake bread.	Lan and I bake bread.

Practice

> Most nouns ending in "s" or "es" are plural, but most verbs ending in "s" are singular.

Number your paper from 1 to 5. For each sentence below, write the correct form of the verb in parentheses.

■ My <u>mother</u> (*decorate, decorates*) the house for every holiday.
   decorates

1. <u>She</u> (*set, sets*) candles and flowers on the tables.

2. My <u>brother</u> and <u>I</u> (*hang, hangs*) strings of colorful lights around the windows.

3. My <u>father</u> (*say, says*) that it always looks like we're having a party.

4. My <u>friends</u> (*think, thinks*) that it's great.

5. <u>They</u> (*like, likes*) to see what we've done.

Write NOW   **Write four sentences about your favorite celebration or holiday. Try to use some singular and some plural subjects. Make sure the verbs agree with the subjects.**

Subject-Verb Agreement with Compound Subjects

Subject-verb agreement is trickier when there is a compound subject. Look carefully at the compound subject and the conjunction to decide whether to use a singular or a plural verb.

COMPOUND SUBJECT	PREDICATE
Metal and **glass**	form **pieces of art.**
Welders and **artists**	work **with these materials.**

If the conjunction *and* is used, the verb must be plural.

Glass beads or **links**	decorate **a necklace.**
Either the artists or **the welder**	locks **the studio door.**

If the conjunction *or* is used, the verb must agree with the subject closest to it.

Practice

Number your paper from 1 to 5. For each sentence below, write the correct form of the verb in parentheses.

◼ Allie and Susan (*like, likes*) the artwork at Pigs and Pots.
like

1. The girls and their mothers (*visit, visits*) the shop often.
2. Statues and a row of pots (*line, lines*) the shelves.
3. That necklace or those earrings (*look, looks*) pretty.
4. Susan and her mom (*buy, buys*) it for Grandma's birthday.
5. Thursday or Friday (*is, are*) her birthday.

Improving Sentence Style

How can I add variety to my sentences?

Here are five ideas for improving your writing by adding variety to your sentences.

1 Try different kinds of sentences.

2 Use different types of sentences.

3 Combine short sentences.

4 Expand sentences with prepositional phrases.

5 Model sentences other writers have created.

SENTENCES LACKING VARIETY

I went go-kart racing for the first time. I went on Saturday. I was a little nervous when I got into my go-kart. It was bright orange. The attendant showed me how to drive my machine. Before I knew it, I was on my way. I had a blast!

SENTENCE VARIETY IMPROVED

On Saturday, I went go-kart racing for the first time. I was a little nervous when I got into my go-kart, a bright orange one. Then the attendant showed me how to drive my machine, and before I knew it, I was on my way. I had a blast!

Your stories will be fun to read if you use a variety of sentences.

Try Different Kinds of Sentences

You can add variety to your writing by using the four different kinds of sentences.

KINDS OF SENTENCES			
Declarative .	Makes a statement	My cousin is always late.	This is the most common kind of sentence.
Interrogative ?	Asks a question	Are you ready?	A question gets the reader's attention.
Imperative . or !	Gives a command	Drink your milk. Hurry up!	Commands often appear in dialogue or directions.
Exclamatory !	Shows strong emotion or feeling	Wow, we're late!	These sentences emphasize a point.

Practice

Number your paper from 1 to 5. Label each sentence as "DEC" for declarative, "INT" for interrogative, "IMP" for imperative, or "EX" for exclamatory.

■ Stop tapping your pencil. IMP

1. It's so annoying!

2. Put your pencil down.

3. Did you realize you were doing it?

4. You must be thinking very hard.

5. What is your story about?

Write a paragraph about going to the dentist or the doctor. Use at least three different kinds of sentences.

Use Different Types of Sentences

You can add style to your writing by using different types of sentences. There are three types of sentences: **simple, compound,** and **complex.**

Use Effective Simple Sentences

A **simple sentence** states one complete thought.

SIMPLE SENTENCES	
Single subject with single predicate	Lisha wrote **a report on marsupials.**
Single subject with compound predicate	Marsupials carry **and** nurse **their young in pouches.**
Compound subject with compound predicate	Kangaroos **and** koalas amuse **and** astound **people.**

Practice

Copy sentences 1 through 5 on your own paper. In each sentence, underline the simple subject once and the simple predicate twice.

▪ Gray kangaroos and red kangaroos are taller than wallaroos.

  Gray <u>kangaroos</u> and red <u>kangaroos</u> <u><u>are</u></u> taller than wallaroos.

1. Some kangaroos weigh more than 150 pounds.
2. These marsupials walk and hop very quickly.
3. Most kangaroos roam the plains or live in woodlands.
4. Potoroos and wallabies are small kangaroos.
5. Australian law protects them.

Write NOW Write four simple sentences about an animal that you find interesting.

Write Compound Sentences

A **compound sentence** is made up of two or more simple sentences joined together. One way to join simple sentences is by using a comma and a coordinating conjunction. (See **482.3**.)

COMPOUND SENTENCES		
My brother Joe went hiking	**, and**	he asked me to go.
Our hike was exhausting	**, but**	we learned a lot about nature.
I asked Joe about a bird	**, or**	I looked in my bird book.

Practice

On your paper, combine the pairs of sentences in numbers 1 to 5 below. Use a comma and the coordinating conjunction given in parentheses.

■ I want to be a Scout. I want to be in my brother's troop. *(and)*

   I want to be a Scout, and I want to be in my brother's troop.

1. Scouts do volunteer work. They also have fun. *(but)*

2. I could work on a cleanup project. I could volunteer at a nursing home. *(or)*

3. I like helping people. It's a good way to make friends. *(and)*

4. My brother's troop meets every Tuesday. Everybody works on projects at other times. *(but)*

5. Our troop will go on a campout. We will go to the nature center. *(or)*

Write NOW Write two compound sentences about volunteer activities you could do in your community. Punctuate your sentences correctly.

Write Complex Sentences

You can join simple sentences by forming a **complex sentence.** A complex sentence has one independent clause and one or more dependent clauses.

An **independent clause** expresses a complete thought and can stand alone as a sentence. A **dependent clause** does not express a complete thought and cannot stand alone as a sentence. It often begins with a subordinating conjunction such as **when, because,** or **as.** (See page 600 for a list of subordinating conjunctions.)

COMPLEX SENTENCE		
AN INDEPENDENT CLAUSE	**+**	**A DEPENDENT CLAUSE**
I take the bus to school		when my mom can't drive me.
A DEPENDENT CLAUSE	**+**	**AN INDEPENDENT CLAUSE**
As the marching band went by,		we cheered and yelled.

Practice

Copy each complex sentence below. Underline the dependent clause in each sentence.

■ When Abe Lincoln was a flatboat pilot, he settled in Illinois.
<u>When Abe Lincoln was a flatboat pilot</u>, he settled in Illinois.

1. The future president liked the town of New Salem because it was built along the Sangamon River.

2. As the town developed, Lincoln became a merchant.

3. While Lincoln lived in New Salem, he also studied law.

4. Lincoln became a militia captain before he moved on.

5. After Lincoln left New Salem, he moved to Springfield.

Write NOW Write a paragraph about a person or place from history. Use at least two complex sentences.

Combine Short Sentences

Use Key Words and Phrases

You can combine short sentences by moving a key word or phrase from one sentence to another.

SHORT SENTENCES	COMBINED SENTENCES
Karly writes letters. They are <u>crazy</u>. *(The key word is underlined.)*	Karly writes crazy letters. *(The adjective* crazy *has been moved to the first sentence.)*
Grant draws cartoons. He draws them <u>for the newspaper</u>. *(The prepositional phrase is underlined.)*	Grant draws cartoons for the newspaper. *(The prepositional phrase has been moved to the first sentence.)*

Practice

On your own paper, combine the pairs of short sentences below. Move a key word or phrase from one sentence to the other.

■ Stephanie wrote a play. She wrote it for her friends.
  Stephanie wrote a play for her friends.

1. Her play starts in a snowstorm. The snowstorm is blinding.
2. The girls are trapped. They are trapped in an old barn.
3. They search everywhere in the barn. They search for tools.
4. One of the girls finds a ball of twine. The ball is huge.
5. The twine gives them an idea. It gives them an idea for their escape.

 Write NOW **Write a paragraph describing how the girls in the sentences above escape from the barn. Try not to use any short, choppy sentences.**

Use a Series of Words or Phrases

Ideas in short sentences can be combined using a **series of words or phrases**. All of the words or phrases in a series should be parallel. That means they are stated in the same way. (See **482.1**.)

SHORT SENTENCES	COMBINED SENTENCES
The cabin is dusty. The cabin is musty. It is also messy.	The cabin is dusty, musty, and messy.
We watch games on TV. We watch games in the park. We also watch games at the high school.	We watch games on TV, in the park, and at the high school.

Practice

Combine each group of sentences using a series of words or phrases. (Some words may need to be changed to make the sentences work.)

■ In the winter, I go sledding. I go downhill skiing. I also go ice-skating.

   In the winter, I go sledding, downhill skiing, and ice-skating.

1. While ice-skating, I can spin. I can go backward. I can stop suddenly.

2. Angie likes to do tricks. Mora likes to do tricks. Kala likes to do tricks, too.

3. I always feel the cold on my face. I feel it on my fingertips. I also feel it on my toes.

4. To get warm, I go to the skating shelter. To rest, I go to the shelter. To have a snack, I go to the shelter.

 Write NOW Write three sentences for a classmate to combine. Make sure your sentences can be combined using a series of words or phrases.

Combine Sentences with Compound Subjects and Predicates

Sometimes you can combine two sentences by moving a subject or a predicate from one sentence to another. This makes a compound subject or a compound predicate. (See page 434.)

SHORT SENTENCES	COMBINED SENTENCES
Maria makes posters for the school carnival. Brandi also makes posters.	Maria and Brandi make posters for the school carnival. *(A compound subject is formed.)*
The girls finished five posters. Then they hung them up.	The girls finished five posters and hung them up. *(A compound predicate is formed.)*

Practice

Combine the following sets of short sentences using a compound subject or a compound predicate. (Some words may need to be changed.)

■ The PTO organized the carnival. The Booster Club did, too.
  The PTO and the Booster Club organized the carnival.

1. The students designed the booths. They also built them.

2. Ling sold tickets for each activity. Bette sold tickets, too.

3. Bowling was a popular activity. Shooting baskets was popular. Tossing rings was popular, too.

4. Devon fished for prizes. He threw beanbags for popcorn.

5. Mr. Harris dressed as a clown. Ms. Butler did, too.

Write NOW Write two sets of short sentences for a classmate to combine. Make sure that the sentences can be combined using a compound subject or a compound predicate.

Expand Sentences with Prepositional Phrases

A prepositional phrase can add information to a sentence. Prepositional phrases begin with words like *on, in, to, about, at, of, with, down, through, for, until,* and *under.* (See page 598 for more prepositions.)

> Prepositional phrases add details to your sentences.

PREPOSITIONAL PHRASES

Crystal flew down the waterslide.

We went to lunch with my grandma.

I found my backpack on a shelf in the library.

Practice

Number your paper from 1 to 5. Write the prepositional phrases you find in each of the following sentences.

■ Every day the sun moves across the sky.

across the sky

1. In ancient Greece, people believed it was a golden chariot.
2. Apollo drove the chariot of heat and light.
3. His son, Phaeton, tried steering the chariot through the sky.
4. Apollo warned his son about the danger.
5. Phaeton dropped the reins and fell to the earth.

Write NOW Think of one or two prepositional phrases to add information to each of the sentences below. Write the new sentences on your own paper.

1. Casey plays softball.
2. She catches and pitches.
3. Casey won the last game.
4. Her team practices.

Model Sentences

You can learn a lot about sentences by studying and modeling the work of your favorite writers. Modeling is following a writer's pattern of words and punctuation in sentences of your own.

PROFESSIONAL MODEL	STUDENT SENTENCE
In the clearing, I saw a deer, slim and silent, staring at me.	Under the steps, I noticed a kitten, small and frightened, meowing for food.

Guidelines for Modeling

- **Varying Sentence Beginnings**

  Try starting sentences with a dependent clause or phrase, set apart by a comma.

  No matter how hard he tries, **Walnut doesn't see as well as others do.**
  —*Sees Behind Trees* by Michael Dorris

- **Moving Adjectives**

  Sometimes you can vary a sentence by placing an adjective or two after the noun it modifies.

  Ramona Quimby, brave **and** fearless, **was half running, half skipping to keep up with her big sister Beatrice on their way home from the park.**
  —*Ramona the Brave* by Beverly Cleary

- **Repeating a Word**

  You can repeat a word to emphasize a particular idea or feeling.

  Pigs enjoy eating, **and they also** enjoy **lying around most of the day thinking about** eating **again.**
  —*Babe the Gallant Pig* by Dick King-Smith

Practice

Write three of your own sentences modeled after the examples given above. Try to follow the pattern of the original sentence as closely as you can.

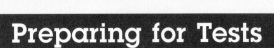

Preparing for Tests

How can I check my sentence knowledge?

Read the paragraph below. Then answer the questions that follow it.

1. Skijoring is an interesting winter sport. **2.** It started in Scandinavia and has spread to many other countries. **3.** The word is Norwegian and means "ski driving." **4.** To skijor, you need cross-country skis, a harness, a tow line, and a dog. **5.** Yes, I said a dog! **6.** Skijoring is a form of dogsled running. **7.** The dog doesn't tow a sled. **8.** But tows a skier. **9.** A skier can use any dog more than a year and a half old and weighing more than 35 pounds. **10.** Sometimes the skier uses just one dog, and sometimes two or three dogs make up a team. **11.** Can you imagine being towed by three dogs, yelping and racing? **12.** Skijorers even takes part in races. **13.** Some races are sprints of five miles, but distance racers can go a lot farther. **14.** Although it doesn't seem possible, some dogs often average speeds as high as 20 miles per hour!

1. Which of the sentences is a fragment?
   a. Sentence 5
   b. Sentence 8
   c. Sentence 12
   d. Sentence 14

2. Which of the sentences is an interrogatory sentence?
   a. Sentence 2
   b. Sentence 3
   c. Sentence 11
   d. Sentence 12

3. Which of the sentences contains an error in subject-verb agreement?
   a. Sentence 7
   b. Sentence 10
   c. Sentence 12
   d. Sentence 14

4. Which sentence is an exclamatory sentence?
   a. Sentence 3
   b. Sentence 5
   c. Sentence 11
   d. Sentence 13

5. Which of the sentences is a complex sentence?
   a. Sentence 9
   b. Sentence 10
   c. Sentence 13
   d. Sentence 14

6. Which of the sentences are compound sentences?
   a. Sentences 2 and 3
   b. Sentences 9 and 11
   c. Sentences 4 and 12
   d. Sentences 10 and 13

7. Which of the sentences contain adjectives or modifying phrases after the noun they modify?
   a. Sentence 1
   b. Sentence 2
   c. Sentence 7
   d. Sentence 11

A Writer's Resource

A Writer's Resource

When a frog needs help with his writing, what can he do? He can't attend a school of fish, but he can flip to the "A Writer's Resource."

This chapter can help you find topics, organize details, create a strong voice, improve vocabulary, and write better sentences—just to name a few things. Whenever you have questions, check these pages for answers.

Mini Index

You will learn how to . . .

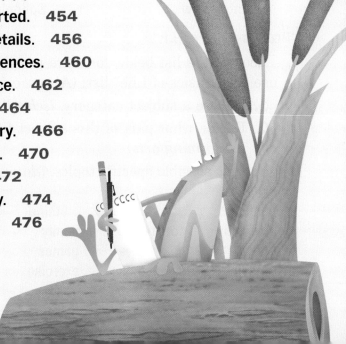

How can I find a good topic to write about?

Try a Topic-Selecting Strategy

The following strategies will help you select specific topics that you truly want to write about.

Clustering Begin a cluster by writing the topic or main idea of your assignment in the center of your paper. Then list, circle, and connect related words and ideas around it. (See the cluster on page 456.)

Freewriting With your general subject in mind, write freely for 3 to 5 minutes. Do not stop to make corrections or look up facts—just write. As you freewrite, you may find one or two specific topics you could use.

Sentence Completion Another way to find a topic is to complete a sentence starter in as many ways as you can. Make sure that your sentence starter has something to do with your assignment. Here are some samples:

I remember when . . .   I really get excited when . . .
One thing I know about . . .   I just learned . . .
I wonder how . . .   School is . . .

"Basics-of-Life" List

Look at the list below for more possible topic areas. Here's how to use the "Basics-of-Life" list: (Also see page 148.)

1. Choose a subject category. *(school)*
2. Decide what part of this subject fits your assignment. *(performing arts)*
3. List possible specific topics. *(dance and drama)*

animals	school	clothing	sports	food
friends	community	family	faith	environment
health	computers	games	rules	books
movies	science	exercise	money	television

What else can I do to get started?

Use a List of Writing Topics

The following topics are organized according to the four basic forms of writing. Look through these lists to find ideas that relate to your assignment.

Descriptive Writing

People: a clerk, a teacher, a friend, a neighbor, yourself, a family member, someone you admire, someone from history

Places: a room, a garage, a cave, a canyon, a rooftop, the alley, the gym, a store, an art gallery, a river, the jungle, a farm, a circus

Things: a pet, a painting, a video game, a junk drawer, a photograph, a special object, a Web site, a stuffed animal, a car, a tree

Narrative Writing

Tell about . . . getting in trouble, getting lost, making a memory, helping someone, being surprised, being scared, learning to do something

Expository Writing

How to . . . make a sub sandwich, care for a pet, juggle, earn money, get in shape, be a good friend, eat a balanced diet, saddle a horse

The causes of . . . pollution, rust, hurricanes, infections, success in school, happiness, accidents, tornadoes, erosion, tooth decay

Kinds of . . . music, commercials, clouds, heroes, clothes, restaurants, fun, books, games, animals, houses, vehicles, art, governments

The definition of . . . friendship, courage, a hero, geology, freedom, love, a team, family, compassion, failure, peace

Persuasive Writing

Issues: school rules, recycling, helmets (bicycle, skateboard), things that need to be changed, causes to support, pet peeves, something to avoid, a need for more or less of something

How can I collect details for my writing?

Try Graphic Organizers

You can use graphic organizers to gather details for different types of writing.

Web Organizer A web or cluster will help you gather facts and ideas for reports, narratives, and poems. Begin by writing the subject in the middle of the page. Then list, circle, and connect related words around it.

Personal Narrative: My first train trip to the city

- got up early Saturday
- train late
- train stopped often
- My Train Trip
- stood in line to get tickets
- missed the train home
- Dad drove to get us

Sensory Details Chart This organizer will help you collect descriptive details for observation reports and other types of expository writing. At the tops of the columns, write the names of the five senses. In each column, list sensory details related to your topic.

Expository Essay: Kinds of transportation

Sight	Sound	Smell	Taste	Touch
– gleaming jet – yellow school bus	– rumbling truck – squeal of train wheels	– city bus exhaust	– salty spray on an oceangoing ship	– floating in hot-air balloon

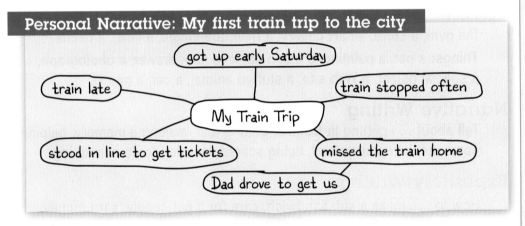

Time Line Time lines help you organize events in chronological (time) order. Personal narratives and how-to essays are often arranged this way. Start your time line by writing the topic at the top. Then list the events or steps in order, the earliest ones first.

How-To Essay: Making a papier-mâché piñata

1. Mix two cups each of flour and water in a big bowl.
2. Dip newspaper strips in flour and water mixture.
3. Lay the coated newspaper on the form.
4. When the papier-mâché is dry, decorate it with paint.

Venn Diagram A Venn diagram can be used to organize your thoughts when you need to compare and contrast two subjects. List the specific details that only one of your subjects has in area 1. List the specific details that only the second subject has in area 2. In area 3, list the details the two things have in common.

Expository Writing: Apples versus oranges

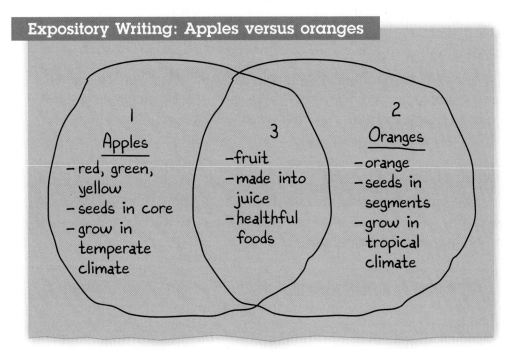

1
Apples
– red, green, yellow
– seeds in core
– grow in temperate climate

3
– fruit
– made into juice
– healthful foods

2
Oranges
– orange
– seeds in segments
– grow in tropical climate

How can I organize my details effectively?

Put Ideas in Order

After you choose your topic and collect details, you should organize your information. First, decide on an order and then make an outline. Here are three ways to put your information in order.

Time Order

The details are explained in the order in which they happen (*after, before, during,* and so on). Time order works well in narrative or expository writing.

> The **first** step in planning a bug hunt is to call your friends and set up a time. **Next**, everyone should find a pencil and a notebook. If someone has a bug identification book, that would also be helpful. **Finally**, go outside and see how many bugs you can find!

Order of Location

Details are described in the order in which they are located (*above, behind, beneath,* and so on). Order of location works well in descriptive or expository writing.

> Bugs are all **around** you **in** your backyard. When you look **under** rocks or logs, bugs scurry away. **Above** the ground **on** a tree trunk, bugs run **up and down**. Flying insects buzz **over** your head. Bugs are everywhere.

Order of Importance

The most important detail comes either first or last (*most important, best, funniest,* and so on). Persuasive and expository writing can be organized in this way.

> **For one thing**, a bug hunt gets you outside. You can **also** have fun with your friends and enjoy nature. **Best of all**, you can learn something about the hundreds of interesting insects that are all around you every day.

Build a Topic Outline

After you have decided what kind of order to use, you can write an outline. Choose several main points that support your topic. Under each main point, list the details that explain it. A **topic outline** contains only words and phrases, and a **sentence outline** contains complete thoughts.

Topic Outline

I. Problem of icy streetcar windshields seen by Mary Anderson in New York City in 1903
   A. Streetcar ride on snowy day
   B. Driver squinting and stopping to clean windshield
II. Plan to clean windshield from inside streetcar
   A. Sketches of wooden arm with rubber strips
   B. Arm on outside connected to lever inside
   C. Weight to hold arm and spring to return it
III. Idea doesn't catch on
   A. Failure of other solutions
   B. Distraction for drivers

Sentence Outline

I. Mary Anderson saw a windshield problem in New York City in 1903.
   A. She rode a streetcar on a snowy day.
   B. She saw the driver squinting and stopping to clean off snow.
II. Mary thought there should be some way to wipe the windshield from inside the streetcar.

How can I write strong topic sentences?

Try a Special Strategy

A good paragraph starts with a strong topic sentence. A topic sentence should (1) name the topic and (2) state a detail or feeling about it. The strategies below will help you write great topic sentences.

Use a Number

Use number words to tell what the paragraph will be about.

Four forces shape and reshape the earth's surface.

Create a List

Create a list of the things that the paragraph will include.

We didn't think our puppy would get out of its crate, chew up a shoe, and break a lamp **before we got home.**

Join Two Ideas

Combine two ideas by using a comma and a coordinating conjunction: *and, but, or, for, so, nor, yet.*

Jamie wanted to get up early, but **we wanted to sleep late.**

Explorers never found a city of gold, yet **their adventures led them to new lands.**

Quote an Expert

To get your paragraph off to a strong start, quote someone who knows something about your topic.

My Dad tells me that professional carpenters always say, "Measure twice, cut once."

"You have to love dolphins to be a good trainer," **says dolphin expert Sue Stanson.**

"If you want to be a good musician," **my piano teacher, Mrs. Wright, always says,** "you must practice, practice, practice."

What forms can I use for my writing?

Try These Forms of Writing

Finding the right form for your writing is very important. When you choose a form, think about *who* you're writing for (your *audience*) and *why* you're writing (your *purpose*). Listed below are a few different forms of descriptive, narrative, expository, and persuasive writing.

Anecdote	A little story used to make a point
Autobiography	The story of the writer's own life (See pages 83–124.)
Biography	The story of someone else's life
Book Review	Writing that shares your thoughts and feelings about a book (See pages 257–272.)
Cartoon	A simple drawing with a funny message
Character Sketch	A description of one character in a story
Editorial	Newspaper letter or article that gives opinions
Fable	A short story that often uses talking animals as characters to teach a lesson
News Release	An explanation of a newsworthy event using the 5 W's *(who, what, where, when,* and *why)*
Pet Peeve	A personal feeling about something that bugs someone
Proposal	Writing that asks for approval of an idea, a report, or a schedule
Tall Tale	A funny, exaggerated story about a character that does impossible things (See pages 292–297.)
Travelogue	Writing that describes a trip or travel pictures

How can I create an effective voice?

Make Your Voice Fit Your Purpose

Your writing should sound like it fits your purpose. The four basic purposes of writing are to describe, to narrate, to explain, and to persuade.

Descriptive Voice

A good descriptive voice sounds *interested*. One way to improve your descriptive voice is to follow this rule: "*show,* don't *tell.*"

- **Telling:** (The writer tells about a mouse.)

    The little mouse came into the room.

- **Showing:** (The writer shows us the mouse.)

    Everyone at the table was eating and talking. In a quiet moment, I heard a scratching sound coming from across the room. No else seemed to notice. Then I saw Tasha our cat lift her head and look toward the noise. Then she got into pounce position. That's when I spotted a little mouse in the corner.

Narrative Voice

A good narrative voice sounds *natural* and *personal*. Your narrative writing should sound like you're telling a story to a friend.

- **Not Natural and Personal:**

    Uncle Ned came from Texas. He came to visit us last week. He always surprises me. He makes me laugh.

- **Natural and Personal:**

    When I came home last Wednesday, the front door was open. I called for Mom. She answered from the kitchen. Then the closet door squeaked and flew open! I jumped back before I saw a huge handlebar mustache. My uncle Ned from Texas jumped out. I couldn't stop laughing. He had surprised me again.

Expository Voice

An effective expository voice uses interesting (specific) *details*.

- **Without Interesting Details:**

    The Rocky Mountains stretch through most of North America. The Rockies include many mountain ranges. The highest point is in Colorado.

- **With Interesting (Specific) Details:**

    The Rocky Mountains stretch almost 2,000 miles from northern Mexico through the western part of the United States and Canada into eastern Alaska. The Rockies include more than 100 mountain ranges. At 14,433 feet, Mt. Elbert near Leadville, Colorado, is the highest point in the Rocky Mountain chain.

Persuasive Voice

A persuasive voice sounds *positive,* not negative.

- **Negative:**

    Our Bloomfield Youth Club meetings are boring. We have to sit still and be quiet, and that's not fun. Somebody should do something about it.

- **Positive:**

    We should have more activities at our Bloomfield Youth Club meetings. We could practice our camp and map skills to get ready for our summer outing. After that, we could play some games. Youth club meetings would be a good time to get things done and have some fun.

How can I spice up my writing style?

Use Some Writing Techniques

You can develop a lively writing style by using some special effects. For example, you can add dialogue to your stories to make them more personal and natural (see page 96). Experiment with some of the following techniques in your own writing.

Exaggeration Stating something that goes beyond the truth to make a point (works well in descriptive and narrative writing)

> **The giraffe** peeked over the clouds **and spotted the missing balloon.**

Idiom Using a word to mean something different from its usual or dictionary meaning

> **Julian got up and said,** "I'm cutting out."
> (Here, *cutting out* means "leaving.")
> **Ray said he'd buy the bike** sight unseen.
> (Here, *sight unseen* means "without seeing it first.")

Metaphor Comparing two things without using the word *like* or *as*

> **Dad's** temper **was** a pot boiling over.
> **The cruise** ship **was** a floating hotel.

Personification Giving human qualities to nonhuman things

> **The wind** whispers **through the trees.**
> (The verb *whispers* describes a human activity.)

Sensory Details Details that help the reader hear, see, smell, taste, or touch what is being described

> **The** soft black **kitten** purred quietly **as I** cuddled **her** in my arms.

Simile Comparing two things using the word *like* or *as*

> **A cold** lemonade **refreshes me just** as a dip in the pool does.
> **In track meets,** Sophie **runs** like a deer.

How can I learn to talk about my writing?

Study Some Writing Terms

This glossary includes terms that name important parts of the writing process.

Audience	The people who read or hear your writing
Dialogue	Written conversation between two or more people
Focus Statement	A sentence telling the specific part of a topic the writer will concentrate or "focus" on (See page 151.)
Point of View	The angle or viewpoint from which a story is told (See page 310.)
Purpose	The main reason for writing a certain piece
	to describe to narrate to explain to persuade
Style	The way a writer puts words, phrases, and sentences together
Supporting Details	Specific details used to develop a topic or bring a story to life
Theme	A main idea or message in a piece of writing
Topic	The specific subject of a piece of writing
Topic Sentence	The sentence that expresses the main idea of a paragraph (See page 460.)
Transition	A word or phrase that ties ideas together in essays, paragraphs, and sentences (See pages 472–473.)
Voice	The tone or feeling a writer uses to express ideas

How can I increase my vocabulary skills?

Try Vocabulary-Building Techniques

Use context.

When you are reading, you may come to a word you don't know. Check the words around it to see if you can figure out its meaning. (See the next page.)

Everyone thought that Jason was making a frivolous **comment, but he was being** serious. (The word *but* suggests that *serious* is the opposite of *frivolous*. So *frivolous* means "not serious, or of little importance.")

Look up words in the dictionary.

When you come to a word you don't know, look it up in the dictionary. (See page 331.)

My cousin Clare likes mush **for breakfast.**

> **mush**[1] (mŭsh) *n.* **1.** A porridge made of cornmeal boiled in water or milk.

Learn about word parts.

You can figure out the meanings of new words by learning about prefixes, suffixes, and roots. (See pages 468–469.) The following sentence contains three examples:

During revising, **you make sure your para**graph **flows smooth**ly.
(*Re-* is a prefix meaning "again"; *graph* is a root meaning "write"; *-ly* is a suffix meaning "in some manner.")

Use Context

You can often figure out a challenging word by looking at the words around it. Here are some ways to do this:

- Study the sentence containing the word, as well as the sentences that come before and after it.

    Chuck Yeager broke the sound barrier in 1947. That year he flew the first successful supersonic flight. No one had ever flown faster than the speed of sound before.
    (*Supersonic* means "faster than the speed of sound.")

- Look for **word parts.** In the example above, *super* is a prefix that means "over and above," and *sonic* is a root word meaning "sound."

- Search for **synonyms** (words with the same meaning).

    Mom calls me an aviator because I want to be a pilot.
    (An *aviator* is a "pilot.")

- Search for **antonyms** (words with the opposite meaning).

    Sandy thought the bug was repulsive, but I thought it was beautiful. (The word *but* suggests that *repulsive* is the opposite of *beautiful.* So *repulsive* means "ugly.")

- Search for a **definition** of the word.

    My friend Mark has a hedgehog, a small porcupine-like animal.
    (A *hedgehog* is a porcupine-like animal.)

- Search for **familiar words in a series** with the new word.

    Is that a Lhasa apso, a poodle, or a terrier?
    (A *Lhasa apso* is a small dog.)

Learn About Word Parts

Beginning with Prefixes

Prefixes are word parts that come before the root or base word (*pre-* means "before"). Prefixes can change the meaning of a word. For example, *kind* means "gentle." When you add the prefix *un-*, meaning "not," the resulting word, *unkind*, means "not gentle." Here are some other common prefixes:

equi *(equal)*
    equinox (a day and night of equal length)

ex *(out)*
    expel (to drive out)

inter *(among, between)*
    international (between two or more nations)

mal *(bad, poor)*
    malnutrition (poor nutrition)

multi *(many, much)*
    multicultural (including many cultures)

non *(absence of, not)*
    nonfat (without fat)

pre *(before)*
    preview (to show something before the regular time)

re *(again, back)*
    rewrite (to write again)

Ending with Suffixes

Suffixes are word parts that come at the end of a word. Sometimes a suffix will tell you what part of speech a word is. For example, many adverbs end in the suffix *-ly*. Add the suffix *-able*, which means "able to," to the word *agree*, and the resulting word, *agreeable*, means "able or willing to agree." Here are some other suffixes:

ion *(state of)*
    infection (state of being infected)

less *(without)*
    careless (without care)

ly *(in some manner)*
    bashfully (in a bashful manner)

ness *(state of)*
    carelessness (state of being careless)

logy *(study, science)*
    biology (study of living things)

y *(tending to)*
    itchy (tending to itch)

Knowing Your Roots

A **root** is the main part of a word. If you know the root of a difficult word, you may be able to figure out the word's meaning.

Suppose that you hear your teacher say, "I couldn't understand what the speaker said because his voice was *inaudible.*" If you know that the prefix *in-* means "not" and the root *aud* means "hear or listen," you will know that your teacher couldn't hear the speaker's voice. Here are some other roots:

alter *(other)*
   alternate (another choice)

bio *(life)*
   biography (book about a person's life)

chron *(time)*
   chronological (in time order)

cise *(cut)*
   incision (a thin, clean cut)

cycl, cyclo *(wheel, circular)*
   bicycle (a cycle with two wheels)
   cyclone (a circular wind)

dem *(people)*
   democracy (ruled by the people)

fin *(end)*
   final (the last or end of something)

flex *(bend)*
   flexible (able to bend)

fract, frag *(break)*
   fracture (to break)
   fragment (a small piece)

geo *(earth)*
   geography (the description of the earth's surface)

graph *(write)*
   autograph (writing one's name)

mit, miss *(send)*
   emit (send out, give off)
   missile (an object sent flying)

port *(carry)*
   export (to carry out)

scope *(see, watch)*
   microscope (an instrument used for viewing objects too small to be seen with the naked eye)

spir *(breath)*
   expire (breathe out, die)
   inspire (breathe in, give life to)

therm *(heat)*
   thermostat (a device for controlling heat)

voc *(call)*
   vocalize (to use the voice; sing)

How can I write better sentences?

Study Sentence Patterns

Use a variety of sentence patterns to create better sentence fluency. Some basic sentence patterns are shown below.

1 Subject + Action Verb

S   AV
Sally walked. (Some action verbs, like *walked,* do not need a direct object to make a complete thought.)

2 Subject + Action Verb + Direct Object

S   AV DO
Thad collects coins. (Some action verbs, like *collects,* need a direct object, like *coins,* to make a complete thought.)

3 Subject + Action Verb + Indirect Object + Direct Object

S AV IO   DO
Mom gave Allison an apple.

4 Subject + Action Verb + Direct Object + Object Complement

S   AV DO OC
Miss Dyer named Alexis treasurer.

5 Subject + Linking Verb + Predicate Noun

S   LV PN
Palominos are horses.

6 Subject + Linking Verb + Predicate Adjective

S   LV PA
Clydesdales are huge.

In the patterns above, the subject comes before the verb. In the patterns below, the subject (called a *delayed subject*) comes after the verb.

LV S PA
7 **Are you sleepy?** (A question)

LV   S
8 **There are five ants.** (A sentence beginning with *there* or *here*)

Practice Sentence Diagramming

Diagramming a sentence can help you see the purpose of each word in the sentence. Below you can see diagrams of the sentences on page 470.

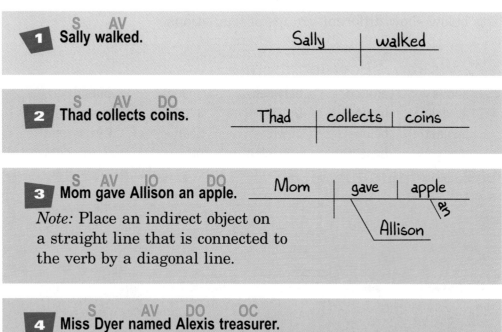

1 S   AV
Sally walked.

Sally | walked

2 S   AV   DO
Thad collects coins.

Thad | collects | coins

3 S   AV   IO   DO
Mom gave Allison an apple.

Mom | gave | apple
Allison   an

Note: Place an indirect object on a straight line that is connected to the verb by a diagonal line.

4 S   AV   DO   OC
Miss Dyer named Alexis treasurer.

Miss Dyer | named | Alexis \ treasurer

Note: Place a vertical line between a verb and its direct object. Use a diagonal line before the object complement.

5 S   LV   PN
Palominos are horses.

Palominos | are \ horses

Note: Place a diagonal line between a linking verb and the predicate noun or adjective.

6 S   LV   PA
Clydesdales are huge.

Clydesdales | are \ huge

How can I connect my ideas?

Use Transitions

Transitions can be used to connect sentences and paragraphs. The lists below show different groups of transitions.

Words that show location:

above	around	between	inside	outside
across	behind	by	into	over
against	below	down	near	throughout
along	beneath	in back of	off	to the right
among	beside	in front of	on top of	under

My favorite bakery is near our apartment. Around the corner, there's a coffee shop that Mom likes.

Words that show time:

about	during	until	yesterday	finally
after	first	meanwhile	next	then
at	second	today	soon	as soon as
before	third	tomorrow	later	when

Today I saw frost on the lawn. Yesterday it was warm when I walked to school.

Words that compare (show similarities):

in the same way	likewise	as	while
similarly	like	also	

The summer clouds looked like giant balloons floating across the sky.

Words that contrast (show differences):

on the other hand	otherwise	but	although
even though	however	still	yet

Be sure to eat a balanced diet. Otherwise, you won't get enough vitamins and minerals.

Words that emphasize a point:

again	truly	especially	for this reason
to repeat	in fact	to emphasize	

In fact, of all the ways you can protect yourself while skateboarding, the most important way is wearing a helmet.

Words that add information:

again	for instance	and	as well
also	besides	next	along with
another	for example	finally	in addition

The principal could tell the tree was dead and would have to be cut down.

Words that summarize:

as a result	finally	in conclusion
therefore	lastly	because

Finally, write your name at the bottom of the page and turn in your paper.

How can I make my final copy look better?

Add Diagrams and Graphs

Diagrams are simple drawings that include labels.

■ **Line diagrams** help you see how or where someone or something fits into a situation (like in a family tree). A line diagram can also show how things are organized into groups.

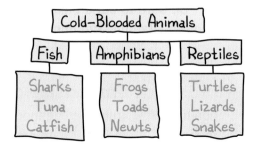

Graphs show information about how things change over time or about how things compare to each other. They show information that includes a range of numbers.

■ A **bar graph** compares two or more things at one point in time—like a snapshot. The bars on a graph can be shown horizontally in rows or vertically in columns.

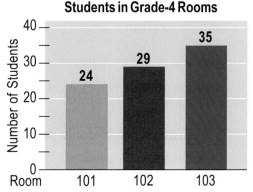

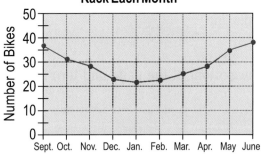

■ A **line graph** is plotted on a grid. The information at the bottom shows equal amounts of time. The vertical side refers to the subject of the graph. The plotted line shows how the subject increased and decreased within the time frame shown.

Add Pictures

Pictures will help make your final copy clear and interesting. Use photos from magazines or newspapers, or download pictures from the Internet (if you have permission). Consider making your own drawings or taking your own photographs for a more personal touch.

■ **To Inform** . . . Pictures can help the reader understand your topic. They add color and interesting details in the body of a report or an essay. They can also be used to decorate a report cover. The picture below is part of an essay about how to search the Internet.

If you don't know how to search the Internet, here's how you do it. Turn on your computer, grab the mouse, and open your browser. Find a search engine like Yahoo.com or Google.com, and you will have plenty of information to research.

■ **To Set the Tone** . . . Pictures can show the reader how you feel about your topic. The picture below could be included in a report on pets. The reader would see what the writer thinks about cats. Notice how the words and picture work together.

Many people think that cats make the best pets. They are clean and quiet. It's possible to leave them alone for several days with their food, water, and litter box. Cats often like to curl up in a lap or stay close to people. A soft, purring cat can make a very good pet.

How should I set up my practical writing?

Follow Guidelines for Letters

Friendly letters and **business letters** have the same basic parts—*heading, salutation, body, closing,* and *signature.* In addition, a business letter has an *inside address.*

Friendly Letter

In a friendly letter, the paragraphs are indented. The side notes below explain the parts.

Heading
Sender's address and date

Salutation
A greeting followed by a comma

Body
Paragraphs indented; no space between them

Closing
First word capitalized; a comma at the end

Signature
Written signature

712 Main Street
Salina, KS 67402
November 15, 2005

Dear Aunt Min,

Thank you very much for sending me the birthday gift. I am already halfway through the book. You got me interested in the author, and now I want to read all of her books.

I love horse stories. Dad says that maybe we can get a pony next spring. Sarah, Danny, and I are very excited about that. We're lucky to have a small barn. Maybe we'll get more than one pony!

I'm sorry that you won't be coming to our house for Thanksgiving. Your trip to Florida should be interesting, but we will miss the stories you always tell as we sit around the dinner table. Send me a postcard when you go to the Everglades.

Your niece,
Julie

Business Letter

The parts of a business letter all start at the left margin. Check the side notes below for more details.

Heading
Sender's address and date

Inside Address
Name and address of person or company

Salutation
A greeting followed by a colon

Body
No indentations and double-spaced between paragraphs

Closing
First word capitalized; a comma at the end
Signature
Written signature above the typed or printed name

401 Horace Street
Burlington, CO 80807
January 21, 2005

Mr. Darjeeling, Manager
Pets and More
1017 Tomike Avenue
Burlington, CO 80807

Dear Mr. Darjeeling:

We are studying mammals in Mr. Leonard's fourth-grade class. The class chose me to organize the supplies for our study. I would like to order two hamsters, one male and one female. We also need a bag of sawdust and a box of hamster food.

If you have a small book about raising hamsters, we need one copy. Please call Burlington Elementary School office to find out who should get the bill for our project.

Sincerely,

Sandy Delaney
Sandy Delaney

Envelope

Address envelopes for business and friendly letters the same way: Use all capital letters and no punctuation.

SANDY DELANEY
401 HORACE ST
BURLINGTON CO 80807

MR DARJEELING MANAGER
PETS AND MORE
1017 TOMIKE AVE
BURLINGTON CO 80807

Proofreader's Guide

Marking Punctuation

Periods

A **period** is used to end a sentence. It is also used after initials, after abbreviations, and as a decimal point.

479.1

At the End of a Sentence

Use a period to end a sentence that is a statement, a command, or a request.

> **Taro won the pitching contest.** (statement)
>
> **Take his picture.** (command)
>
> **Please loan me your baseball cap.** (request)

479.2

After an Initial

Use a period after an initial in a person's name. (An initial is the first letter of a name.)

> **B. B. King** (blues musician)
>
> **A. A. Milne** (writer)

479.3

As a Decimal Point

Use a period as a decimal point and to separate dollars and cents.

> **Robert is 99.9 percent sure that the bus pass costs $2.50.**

479.4

In Abbreviations

Use a period after an abbreviation. (See page 520 for more about abbreviations.)

> **Mr. Mrs. Jr. Dr. B.C.E. U.S.A.**

Use only one period when an abbreviation is the last word in a sentence.

> **A library has books, CD's, DVD's, magazines, etc.**

Question Marks

A **question mark** is used after a direct question (an interrogative sentence). Sometimes it is used to show doubt (uncertainty) about the correctness of a detail.

480.1
In Direct Questions

Place a question mark at the end of a direct question.

Do air bags make cars safer?

No question mark is used after an indirect question. (In an indirect question, you tell about the question you or someone else asked.)

I asked if air bags make cars safer.

480.2
In Tag Questions

A question mark is used when you add a short question to the end of a statement. (This type of statement is called a *tag question*.)

The end of this century is the year 2099, isn't it?

480.3
To Show Doubt

Place a question mark in parentheses to show that you aren't sure a fact is correct.

The ship arrived in Boston on July 23(?), 1652.

Exclamation Points

An **exclamation point** is used to express strong feeling. It may be placed after a word, a phrase, or a sentence.

480.4
To Show Strong Feeling

Surprise! (word)

Happy birthday! (phrase)

Wait for me! (sentence)

TIP: Never use extra exclamation points (Hooray!!!) in school writing assignments or in business letters.

End Punctuation

For each of the following sentences, write the correct end-punctuation mark (a period, a question mark, or an exclamation point).

Example: My gosh, look at that!

1. Is that what I think it is

2. There are many kinds of flying fish

3. Can a fish really fly

4. Some flying fish can glide more than 300 feet.

5. They spread out their large fins

6. Of course, their fins look like wings

7. Why do they jump out of the water

8. They are trying to escape other fish that want to eat them

9. How far can they go

10. Flying fish actually jump out of the water and glide through the air

Next Step: Write an exclamatory sentence about an unusual creature. Make sure you use the correct end punctuation.

Commas

Commas keep words and ideas from running together. They tell your reader where to pause, which makes your writing easier to read.

482.1
Between Items in a Series

Place commas between words, phrases, or clauses in a series. (A series is three or more items in a row.)

> **Hanae likes pepperoni, pineapple, and olives on her pizza.** (words)

> **During the summer I read mysteries, ride my bike, and play basketball.** (phrases)

482.2
To Set Off Dialogue

Use a comma to set off the words of the speaker from the rest of the sentence.

> **The stranded frog replied, "I'm just waiting for the toad truck."**

If you are telling what someone has said but are not using the person's exact words, do *not* use commas or quotation marks.

> **The stranded frog told me that he was just waiting for the toad truck.**

482.3
In Compound Sentences

Use a comma between two independent clauses that are joined by the coordinating conjunction *and, but, or, nor, for, so,* or *yet.*

> **Aunt Carrie offered to pay my way, so I am going to the amusement park with her.**

> **We'll try to get on all the rides, and we'll see one of the stage shows.**

TIP: Do not connect two independent clauses with a comma only. That is called a comma splice. (See 564.2 for more information about independent clauses.)

Commas 1

- **In Compound Sentences**
- **To Set Off Dialogue**

▶ **For each sentence below, write the word or words that should be followed by a comma. Write the comma, too.**

Example: A bunch of cows came to Chicago in 1999 and we went to see them.

1999,

1. My little sister yelled "Look at the cows, Daddy!"

2. I saw the cows, too but they weren't what I expected.

3. "They're not real cows" I said. "They're statues!"

4. Artists had decorated the cows and local businesses displayed them all around the city.

5. "People worked very hard to make these" Dad noted.

6. "They're really beautiful" my sister said.

7. We walked around the city all day but we didn't see every cow.

8. Dad told us "There are 300 cows in the exhibit."

Next Step: In two sentences, explain what the cows thought about their visit to Chicago. (Write as though the cows were alive and could talk.) Write one compound sentence and one sentence with dialogue.

Commas . . .

484.1
To Separate Introductory Phrases and Clauses

Use a comma to separate a long phrase or clause that comes before the main part of the sentence.

After checking my knee pads, I started off. (phrase)

If you practice often, skating is easy. (clause)

You usually do not need a comma when the phrase or the clause comes after the main part of the sentence.

Skating is easy if you practice often.

Also, a comma is usually unnecessary after a short opening phrase.

In time you'll find yourself looking forward to practice.
(No comma is needed after *In time*.)

484.2
In Dates and Addresses

Commas are used to set off the different parts in addresses and dates. (Do *not* use a comma between the state and ZIP code.)

My family's address is 2463 Bell Street, Atlanta, Georgia 30200.

I will be 21 years old on January 15, 2015.

Do not use a comma if only the month and year are written (January 2015).

484.3
To Keep Numbers Clear

Place commas between hundreds, thousands, millions, and billions.

Junji's car has 200,000 miles on it. He's trying to sell it for $1,000.

When a number refers to a year, street address, or ZIP code, no comma is used. Also, write numbers in the millions and billions this way: 7.5 million, 16 billion. (See **524.2**.)

Brazil is a country of 184 million people.

Commas 2

■ To Separate Introductory Phrases and Clauses
■ To Keep Numbers Clear

For each sentence below, write the number that needs a comma or the word that should be followed by a comma. Write the comma, too.

Example: There are lots of mountain peaks above 10000 feet in the Alps.

10,000

1. When people lived there long ago there were no phones.

2. To communicate neighbors yodeled at each other.

3. Yodeling probably began more than 1500 years ago.

4. With no words to sing a true yodeler simply calls out different notes.

5. Imagine calling out to a neighbor on 15771-foot-high Mont Blanc!

6. Echoing off the mountains a yodel makes an amazing sound.

Next Step: Write a sentence about an amazing sound you have heard. Begin with an introductory phrase or clause and use commas correctly.

Commas . . .

Use commas to set off a word, phrase, or clause that interrupts the main thought of a sentence.

> **You could, for example, take the dog for a walk instead of watching TV.**

Here is a list of words and phrases that you can use to interrupt main thoughts.

for example	to be sure	moreover
however	as a matter of fact	in fact

TESTS: Try one of these tests to see if a word or phrase interrupts a main thought:

1. Take out the word or phrase. The meaning of the sentence should not change.
2. Move the word or phrase to another place in the sentence. The meaning should not change.

Use a comma to separate an interjection or a weak exclamation from the rest of the sentence.

> **Wow, look at that sunrise!**
>
> **Hey, we're up early!**

If an interjection shows strong feeling, an exclamation point (!) may be used after it.

> **Whoa! Let's slow down.**

The following words are often used as interjections.

Hello	Hey	Ah
Oh my	No kidding	Hmm
Really	Wow	Well

Use commas to separate a noun of direct address (the person being spoken to) from the rest of the sentence.

> **Yuri, some computers do not need keyboards.**
>
> **I know that, Maria. They respond to voice commands.**

Commas 3

- ■ In Direct Address
- ■ To Set Off Interruptions

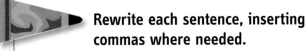

Rewrite each sentence, inserting commas where needed.

Example: "Ken do you think we should go to a movie today?" Aunt Mabel asked.

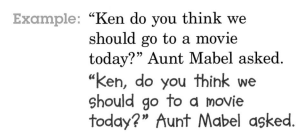

"Ken, do you think we should go to a movie today?" Aunt Mabel asked.

1. "We could for example go see the outer-space movie," she added.

2. "Is that the one in the big museum theater Aunt Mabel?" asked Ken.

3. "I was as a matter of fact just thinking about going there," he said.

4. "Oh Ken I meant the one in the multiplex," said Aunt Mabel.

5. "Auntie do you know if they have popcorn at those theaters?" Ken asked.

6. "The last time we went if you remember they did have popcorn," she answered.

Next Step: Write two sentences about going to the movies. Use an interruption in one and direct address in the other. Use commas correctly.

Commas . . .

488.1
To Separate Equal Adjectives

Use commas to separate two or more adjectives that equally modify a noun.

There are plenty of nutritious, edible plants in the world. (*Nutritious* and *edible* are separated by a comma because they modify *plants* equally.)

We may eat many unusual plants in the years to come. (*Many* and *unusual* do *not* modify *plants* equally. No comma is needed.)

TESTS: Use one of the tests below to help you decide if adjectives modify equally:

1. Switch the order of the adjectives. If the sentence is still clear, the adjectives modify equally.

2. Put the word *and* between the adjectives. If the sentence sounds clear, the adjectives modify equally.

   TIP: Do not use a comma between the last adjective and the noun.

488.2
To Set Off Explanatory Phrases and Appositives

Use a comma to set off an explanatory phrase from the rest of the sentence. (*Explanatory* means "helping to explain.")

Sonja, back from a visit to Florida, showed us some seashells.

Use commas to set off appositives. An appositive is a word or phrase that is another way of saying the noun or pronoun before it. (See 566.5.)

Mrs. Chinn, our science teacher, says that the sun is an important source of energy.

Solar power and wind power, two very clean sources of energy, should be used more.

488.3
In Letter Writing

Place a comma after the salutation, or greeting, in a friendly letter and after the closing in all letters.

Dear Uncle Jim, (greeting)   **Love,** (closing)

Commas 4

■ To Set Off Appositives
■ In Letter Writing

Write the line number where you find a word that should be followed by a comma. Write the word or words along with the commas.

Example: 1 I wrote to Uncle Ted
2 my mother's brother to tell
3 him about my new pet.

1. Uncle Ted,

2. my mother's brother,

October 11, 2005

1 Dear Uncle Ted

2   I got an iguana a kind of lizard as a present. Ramona

3 a good friend of mine gave it to me. I named him Rocky. I

4 like him very much.

5   Rocky's dewlap the flap of skin under his throat sticks

6 out whenever he sees me. That is normal for iguanas. He

7 is an herbivore a plant eater. We feed him mostly greens

8 and vegetables.

9   I hope you can meet Rocky soon.

10   Love

11   Jolene

Next Step: Pretend you are Uncle Ted. Write a short letter
back to Jolene.

Apostrophes

An **apostrophe** is used to form contractions, to show possession, to form some plurals, or to show that letters have been left out of a word.

490.1

In Contractions

Use an apostrophe to show that one or more letters have been left out of a word, forming a contraction. The list below shows some common contractions.

Common Contractions

couldn't (could not)	**it's** (it is; it has)
didn't (did not)	**I've** (I have)
doesn't (does not)	**she's** (she is)
don't (do not)	**they'll** (they will)
hasn't (has not)	**they're** (they are)
haven't (have not)	**we've** (we have)
I'll (I will)	**wouldn't** (would not)
isn't (is not)	**you'd** (you would)

490.2

To Form Singular Possessives

Form the possessive of most singular nouns by adding an apostrophe and -s.

My sister's hobby is jazz dancing.

When a singular noun ends with an s or a z sound, the possessive may be formed by adding just an apostrophe.

Carlos' weather chart is very detailed.
(or) **Carlos's chart**

If the singular noun is a one-syllable word, form the possessive by adding both an apostrophe and -s.

Chris's lab report is incomplete.

TIP: An apostrophe is never used with a possessive pronoun (*its, hers, yours*).

The horse had its hooves trimmed.

Apostrophes 1

■ In Contractions
■ To Form Singular Possessives

Find the words in the following sentences that should have apostrophes but don't. Write these words correctly.

Example: Jacks uncle brought him a gift.
         Jack's

1. "Its not my birthday," Jack said.

2. "It doesnt have to be your birthday to get a little something from me," Uncle James said.

3. The packages wrapping was simply a bag tied with a bow.

4. As Jack opened it, Uncle Jamess smile got bigger.

5. Jack didnt have a clue about the bags contents.

6. Then he exclaimed, "Theyre goldfish!"

7. The fish, in a bag of water inside a fishbowl, werent very big.

8. Jack couldnt wait to pour the two goldfish and the water into the bowl.

9. "Ill take good care of them," Jack promised.

10. "Get your moms help," his uncle suggested.

Apostrophes . . .

492.1
To Form Plural Possessives

Add just an apostrophe to make the possessive form of plural nouns ending in *s*.

> **The visitors' ideas were helpful.**
>
> **The girls' washroom should be expanded.**

For plural nouns not ending in *s*, add an apostrophe and an *-s*.

> **The children's team practices today, and the men's league starts this weekend.**

Remember: The word before the apostrophe is the owner.

> **Justin's CD** (The CD belongs to Justin.)
>
> **the boys' shoes** (The shoes belong to the boys.)

492.2
To Form Possessives with Indefinite Pronouns

Form the possessive of an indefinite pronoun (*someone, everyone, no one, anyone*) by adding an apostrophe and *-s*.

> **everyone's idea**   **no one's fault**
>
> **somebody's book**   **another's suggestion**

492.3
To Form Shared Possessives

When possession is shared by more than one noun, add an apostrophe and *-s* to the last noun only.

> **Danetta, Sasha, and Olga's science project deals with electricity.**

492.4
To Form Some Plurals

An apostrophe and *s* are used to form the plural of a letter, a number, or a sign.

> **A's   B's   3's   10's   +'s   &'s**

492.5
In Place of Omitted Letters or Numbers

Use an apostrophe to show that one or more letters or numbers have been left out.

> **class of '15** (*20* is left out)
>
> **fixin' to go** (*g* is left out)

Apostrophes 2

■ **To Form Plural Possessives**
■ **To Form Some Plurals**

Find the words in the sentences below that should have apostrophes but don't. Write these words correctly.

Example: Every year the Millers cows waited for the first snowfall.
Millers'

1. When it came, the cows snowmobiles came out of the shed.

2. They checked both of the snowmobiles engines.

3. Carla, Bessie, and Daisy hopped onto the snowmobile with three 3s painted on it.

4. The cows hats and scarves were ready.

5. Two of the friends mittens were missing.

6. All their boots buckles had gotten rusty since last winter.

7. A stiff brush with bristles shaped like upside-down Js took care of the rust.

8. Soon the cows were zooming across the local ranchers pastures.

Next Step: Write two sentences about animals that act and speak like humans. Use two plural possessives.

Quotation Marks

Quotation marks are used to enclose the exact words of the speaker, to show that words are used in a special way, and to punctuate some titles.

494.1

To Set Off Dialogue

Place quotation marks before and after the spoken words in dialogue.

> Martha asked, **"How long did you live in Mexico?"**

494.2

Placement of Punctuation

Put periods and commas *inside* quotation marks.

> Trev said, **"Let's make tuna sandwiches."**
>
> **"Sounds good,"** said Rich.

Place question marks or exclamation points *inside* the quotation marks when they punctuate the quotation.

> **"Do we have any apples?"** asked Trev.
>
> **"Yes!"** replied Mom.

Place them *outside* the quotation marks when they punctuate the main sentence.

> Did you hear Rich say, **"We're out of pickles"**?

494.3

To Punctuate Titles

Place quotation marks around titles of songs, poems, short stories, book chapters, and titles of articles in encyclopedias, magazines, or electronic sources. (See 502.1 for information on other kinds of titles.)

> **"Oh! Susanna"** (song)   **"Casey at the Bat"** (poem)
>
> **"McBroom Tells the Truth"** (short story)
>
> **"Local Boy Wins Competition"** (newspaper article)

(See 514.2 for information on capitalization of titles.)

494.4

For Special Words

Quotation marks may be used to set apart a word that is used in a special way.

> The queen wanted to sell the royal chairs rather than see them **"throne"** away.

Quotation Marks

■ To Set Off Dialogue
■ To Punctuate Titles

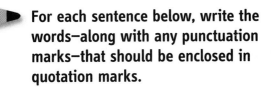

For each sentence below, write the words—along with any punctuation marks—that should be enclosed in quotation marks.

Example: What chapter are you
reading? Lea's dad asked.
"What chapter are you
reading?"

1. The title of the chapter was Castles in the Air.

2. It's a good book, Lea said.

3. She had learned about the book *Little Women* in a magazine article called Great Books for Kids.

4. Lea's favorite song, Bongo Bop, played loudly on the radio.

5. Can you read with the music on? her father asked.

6. I'm doing research for a poem I'm writing, Dad, she said.

7. He said, I'd like to see it.

8. Lea gave him her poem called Read to the Beat.

Next Step: Write two sentences. Use quotation marks to set off dialogue and to punctuate a title.

Hyphens

A **hyphen** is used to divide a word at the end of a line. Hyphens are also used to join or create new words.

496.1

To Divide a Word

Use a hyphen to divide a word when you run out of room at the end of a line. A word may be divided only between syllables (*ex-plor-er*). Always refer to a dictionary if you're not sure how to divide a word. Here are some guidelines for hyphenating words:

- Never divide a one-syllable word (*act, large, school*).
- Try not to divide a word of five or fewer letters (*older, habit, loyal*).
- Never divide a one-letter syllable from the rest of the word (*apart-ment*, not *a-partment*).
- Never divide abbreviations or contractions (*Mrs., Dr., don't, haven't*).

496.2

In Compound Words

Use a hyphen in certain compound words.

> **the two-year-old**   **sister-in-law**

496.3

In Fractions

Use a hyphen between the numbers in a fraction.

> **one-half (1/2)**   **five-tenths (5/10)**

496.4

To Create New Words

Use a hyphen to form new words beginning with the prefixes *all-*, *self-*, *ex-*, or *great-*. A hyphen is also used with suffixes such as *-elect* and *-free*.

> **all-star team**   **self-respect**   **president-elect**
> **great-grandmother**   **ex-hero**   **smoke-free**

Use a hyphen to join two or more words that work together to form a single adjective *before* a noun.

> **school-age children**   **lightning-fast skating**

496.5

To Join Letters and Words

A hyphen is often used to join a letter to a word.

> **T-shirt**   **X-ray**   **e-mail**   **U-turn**

Hyphens

■ **To Divide a Word**
■ **To Join Letters and Words**

If a word at the end of a line is hyphenated incorrectly, or if a hyphen is needed to join a letter to a word, write the word correctly on your paper.

Example: Della loves trying to do tricks on her ska-teboard and bike.

skate—board

1. When she's riding her board, she likes to wear a special T shirt.

2. "This is my lucky shirt," Della tells almost anyone who will listen.

3. The art on the back of her shirt is by the famous skateboarder Davy Downhill.

4. Della likes doing U turns and other fancy moves.

5. "Every week I try to do something more complex than I did the week before," she says.

6. She knows she has to be careful if she wants to avoid an X ray.

Next Step: Pretend that the words *doctor, Thanksgiving,* and *connect* come at the end of a line in some sentences. Write each word with a hyphen in the correct place.

Colons

A **colon** may be used to introduce a list or a quotation. Colons are also used in business letters and between the numbers expressing time.

498.1

To Introduce a List

Use a colon to introduce a list that follows a complete sentence.

> **The following materials can be used to build houses: plants, shells, sod, and sand.**

When introducing a list, the colon often comes after summary words like *the following* or *these things.*

> **On cleaning day, I do these things: sweep the floor, clean the bathroom mirror, and take out the garbage.**

> **TIP:** It is incorrect to use a colon after a verb or after a preposition.

498.2

As a Formal Introduction

Use a colon to introduce an important quotation in a serious report, essay, or news story.

> **President Lincoln concluded the Gettysburg Address with these famous words: " . . . government of the people, by the people, for the people, shall not perish from the earth."**

498.3

In Business Letters

A colon is used after the greeting in a business letter.

> **Dear Ms. Kununga:**
> **Dear Sir:**
> **Dear Dr. Watts:**

498.4

Between Numbers in Time

Place a colon between the parts of a number that shows time.

> **7:30 a.m.   1:00 p.m.   12:00 noon**

Colons

- Between Numbers in Time
- In Business Letters

Write the line number where you find a number that needs a colon or a word that should be followed by a colon. Write the number or word along with the colon.

Example: 1 Mr. Ugh set out his
2 recycling bin at 1000 a.m.
3 on Thursday.

2. 10:00

1 Dear Sabertooth Recycling

2   I put my recycling bin out before 1000 a.m.

3 on Thursday, but you never picked it up. If the

4 pick-up time has changed, please let me know.

5 Sincerely,

6 Ig Ugh

7 Dear Mr. Ugh

8   We changed your pick-up time to 800 a.m.

9 We're sorry you missed our letter about this

10 change! We sent it at 900 a.m. last Monday.

11 Sincerely,

12 Sabertooth Recycling

Next Step: Write a short business letter setting up a time to meet someone. Correctly use colons after the greeting and in the time.

Semicolons

A **semicolon** sometimes works in the same way that a comma does. At other times, it works like a period and indicates a stronger pause.

500.1 **To Join Two Independent Clauses**	You can join two independent clauses with a semicolon when there is no coordinating conjunction (like *and* or *but*) between them. (See **564.2** for more information about independent clauses.) **In the future, some cities may rest on the ocean floor; other cities may float like islands.** **Floating cities sound great; however, I get seasick.** **TIP:** Independent clauses can stand alone as separate sentences.
500.2 **To Separate Groups in a Series with Commas**	Use a semicolon to separate a series of phrases that already contain commas. **We crossed the stream; unpacked our lunches, cameras, and journals; and finally took time to rest.** (The second phrase contains commas.)

Ellipses

An **ellipsis** (three periods with a space before, between, and after) is used to show omitted words or sentences and to show a pause in dialogue.

500.3 **To Show Omitted Words**	Use an ellipsis to show that one or more words have been left out of a quotation. **"Give me liberty or give me death."** **"Give me liberty or . . . death."**
500.4 **To Show a Pause**	Use an ellipsis to indicate a pause in dialogue. **"That's . . . incredible!" I cried.**

Semicolons

For each sentence below, write the word or words that should be followed by a semicolon. Write the semicolons, too.

Example: Our family drove from Omaha to New York City the trip was very long.

City;

1. We locked up the house packed our luggage, toys, and extra food in the trunk and then got on the road.

2. My mom checked a map to find the best route Dad drove the car.

3. We drove through some midwestern states the middle Atlantic states of Ohio, Pennsylvania, and New Jersey and finally crossed the bridge into New York City.

4. We could see the skyscrapers of New York long before we got there the buildings were really tall!

5. We were all very tired on our first night in the city we checked into our hotel and went to bed.

6. The next day we were ready to see the sights our first stop was Central Park.

Next Step: Write a compound sentence about something that might happen on a family trip. Use a semicolon to join the independent clauses.

Italics and Underlining

Italics is a style of type that is slightly slanted, like this: *girl*. It is used for some titles and special words. If you use a computer, you should use italics. In handwritten material, underline words that should be in italics.

502.1
In Titles

Use italics (or underlining) for the titles of books, plays, very long poems, magazines, and newspapers; the titles of television programs, movies (videos and DVD's), and albums of music (cassettes and CD's); and the names of ships and aircraft. (See **494.3** for information on other kinds of titles.)

> *The Giver* . . . The Giver (book)
> *National Geographic* . . . National Geographic (magazine)
> *Air Bud* . . . Air Bud (movie)
> *Dance on a Moonbeam* . . . Dance on a Moonbeam (CD)
> *Los Angeles Times* . . . Los Angeles Times (newspaper)
> *Titanic* . . . Titanic (ship)
> *Discovery* . . . Discovery (spacecraft)

502.2
For Special Words

Use italics (or underlining) for scientific names and for words or letters being discussed or used in a special way.

> The marigold's scientific name is *Tagetes*.
>
> The word *friend* has different meanings to different people.

Punctuation Marks

'	Apostrophe	. . .	Ellipsis	.	Period
:	Colon	!	Exclamation point	?	Question mark
,	Comma	-	Hyphen	" "	Quotation marks
–	Dash	( )	Parentheses	;	Semicolon

Italics and Underlining

- In Titles
- For Special Words

For each sentence, write the words that should be italicized and underline them.

Example: First Men in the Moon, a book by H. G. Wells, was also made into a movie.
<u>First Men in the Moon</u>

1. The film The Ugly Duckling was based on a short story by Hans Christian Anderson.

2. The movie The Raven came from a poem by Edgar Allan Poe.

3. The magazine All the Year Round first printed some of Charles Dickens' work.

4. My dad reviews movies for our town's newspaper, the Smithville Call.

5. Jarrett liked the sound track from a movie he just saw and bought the CD Shark Tale.

6. I hope to see the book Olive's Ocean as a movie someday.

Next Step: Write a sentence that includes the title of your favorite book or movie.

Dashes

A **dash** is used to show a break in a sentence, to emphasize certain words, or to show that a speaker has been interrupted.

504.1
To Show a Sentence Break

A dash can show a sudden break in a sentence.

Because of computers, our world—and the way we describe it—has changed greatly.

With a computer—or a cell phone—people can connect to the Internet.

504.2
For Emphasis

Use a dash to emphasize a word, a series of words, a phrase, or a clause.

You can learn about customs, careers, sports, weather—just about anything—on the Internet.

504.3
To Show Interrupted Speech

Use a dash to show that someone's speech is being interrupted by another person.

Well, hello—yes, I—that's right—yes, I—sure, I'd love—I'll be there!

Parentheses

Parentheses are used around words that add extra information to a sentence or make an idea clearer.

504.4
To Add Information

Use parentheses when adding information or making an idea clearer.

I accidentally left the keys to Mom's car (a blue Osprey) on the front seat.

Five of the students provided background music (very quiet humming) for the singer.

Dashes and Parentheses

For each sentence, write whether you would use parentheses or a dash (or dashes) to set off the underlined words.

Example: A big group of fire ants <u>major pests in the South</u> went to Chicago.

parentheses

1. A big ant said, "I want to climb the Sears Tower <u>all 1,725 feet of it.</u>"

2. "But <u>let me speak, please</u> I want to see Navy Pier," a second ant spoke up.

3. The ants went to both Navy Pier <u>named in honor of Navy veterans</u> and the Sears Tower.

4. At Navy Pier, they shopped for gifts <u>very tiny ones, of course</u> and ate lunch.

5. They also saw the big Ferris wheel, which <u>imagine this</u> is 150 feet tall.

6. Later, they went to the Field Museum <u>home of the T. rex Sue.</u>

Next Step: Suppose you hear only one side of a telephone conversation. Write a sentence telling what you hear, using dashes to show interrupted speech.

Test Prep

Number your paper from 1 to 10. For each underlined part of the paragraphs below, write the letter (from the answer choices on the next page) of the best way to punctuate it.

Have you ever been to a natural history <u>museum</u> When I
₁
took a trip to New York City with my <u>family we</u> went to the
₂
American Museum of Natural History.

<u>Look at those dinosaurs!</u> Mom exclaimed.
₃

After learning about <u>dinosaurs we</u> saw the Hall of North
₄
American Forests. I liked the Butterfly Conservatory.

"There are about <u>18000</u> species of butterflies in the world,"
₅
a guide said.

My two <u>sisters</u> gasps were easy to hear. "I <u>cant</u> imagine
₆ ₇
that many butterflies!" Delia said.

We visited the rock <u>collections; then</u> we gaped at a model
₈
of a huge blue whale. We ended our day at the planets exhibit.
Some of <u>Jupiters</u> moons have their own atmospheres. <u>Io
₉
Europa and Callisto</u> are three of that planet's moons. We
₁₀
learned a lot during our museum visit.

1.
   A   museum.
   B   museum!
   C   museum?
   D   correct as is

2.
   A   family—we
   B   family, we
   C   family; we
   D   correct as is

3.
   A   "Look at those
        dinosaurs!
   B   "Look at those
        dinosaurs!"
   C   "Look at those
        dinosaurs"!
   D   correct as is

4.
   A   dinosaurs, we
   B   dinosaurs. We
   C   dinosaurs' we
   D   correct as is

5.
   A   18,000
   B   18.000
   C   180,00
   D   correct as is

6.
   A   sister's
   B   "sisters"
   C   sisters'
   D   correct as is

7.
   A   c'ant
   B   can't
   C   cant'
   D   correct as is

8.
   A   collections then
   B   collection's then
   C   collections Then
   D   correct as is

9.
   A   Jupiters'
   B   Jupiters's
   C   Jupiter's
   D   correct as is

10.
   A   Io, Europa, and
        Callisto
   B   Io, Europa and,
        Callisto
   C   Io, Europa and
        Callisto
   D   correct as is

Editing for Mechanics

Capitalization

508.1
Proper Nouns and Adjectives

Capitalize all proper nouns and proper adjectives. A proper noun names a specific person, place, thing, or idea. A proper adjective is formed from a proper noun.

Proper Nouns:

Beverly Cleary	Golden Gate Bridge
Utah Jazz	Thanksgiving Day

Proper Adjectives:

American citizen	Chicago skyline
New Jersey shore	Belgian waffle

508.2
Names of People

Capitalize the names of people as well as the initials or abbreviations that stand for those names.

John Steptoe	Harriet Tubman
C. S. Lewis	Sacagawea

508.3
Titles Used with Names

Capitalize titles used with names of persons.

President Carter   Dr. Li Tam   Mayor Rita Gonzales

TIP: Do not capitalize titles when they are used alone: *the president, the doctor, the mayor.*

508.4
Abbreviations

Capitalize abbreviations of titles and organizations.

M.D. (doctor of medicine)   **Mr. Martin Lopez**
ADA (American Dental Association)

508.5
Organizations

Capitalize the name of an organization, an association, or a team, as well as its members.

Girl Scouts	the Democratic Party
Chicago Bulls	Republicans

Capitalization 1

■ Proper Nouns and Adjectives
■ Organizations

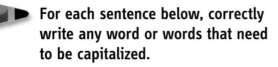

For each sentence below, correctly write any word or words that need to be capitalized.

Example: Our boy scout troop went on a bus trip to Washington, D.C.

Boy Scout

1. Mr. rodriguez, our troop leader, went with us.

2. We rode on a bridge over the chesapeake bay.

3. The bus driver took us right to the white house.

4. A guide from capital tour company met us there.

5. She had just finished taking a canadian group on a tour.

6. She led us through the jefferson memorial.

7. We had american cheese sandwiches for lunch.

8. The troop leader said, "I would love to come back here on independence day."

Next Step: Write a brief paragraph about a trip you've taken or would like to take. Use at least one proper noun, one proper adjective, and one name of an organization.

Capitalization . . .

Words Used as Names

Capitalize words such as *mother, father, aunt,* and *uncle,* when these words are used as names.

Ask Mother what we're having for lunch.
(*Mother* is used as a name; you could use her first name in its place.)

Words such as *dad, uncle, mother,* and *grandma* are not usually capitalized if they come after a possessive pronoun (*my, his, our*).

Ask my mother what we're having for lunch.
(In this sentence, *mother* refers to someone but is not used as a name.)

Days, Months, and Holidays

Capitalize the names of days of the week, months of the year, and holidays.

Wednesday	**March**	**Easter**
Arbor Day	**Passover**	**Juneteenth Day**

TIP: Do not capitalize the seasons.

winter   spring   summer   fall (or **autumn**)

Names of Religions, Nationalities, and Languages

Capitalize the names of religions, nationalities, and languages.

Christianity, Hinduism, Islam (religions)

Australian, Somalian, Chinese (nationalities)

English, Spanish, Hebrew (languages)

Official Names

Capitalize the names of businesses and official product names. (These are called trade names.)

Budget Mart   Crispy Crunch cereal   Smile toothpaste

TIP: Do not capitalize a general word like *toothpaste* when it follows the product name.

Capitalization 2

■ Days, Months, and Holidays
■ Words Used as Names

For each sentence below, correctly write any word that is not properly capitalized.

Example: Last month, auntie came over for thanksgiving.

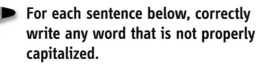
Auntie, Thanksgiving

1. She stayed from tuesday to saturday.

2. My sister and I won't have school for the last two weeks of december.

3. We're going to spend some time with grandma.

4. We will go skiing after christmas.

5. We asked mom and dad if they wanted to join us.

6. Dad said that he has to work until new year's day.

7. Mom said that she could join us on thursday.

8. Grandma will take care of us until january 2.

Next Step: Write a sentence or two about your favorite holiday. Tell what month and day it is on.

Capitalization . . .

512.1 Names of Places

Capitalize the names of places that are either proper nouns or proper adjectives.

Planets and heavenly bodies . . . . **Earth, Jupiter, Milky Way**

Continents . . . . **Europe, Asia, South America, Australia**

Countries . . . . **Chad, Haiti, Greece, Chile, Jordan**

States . . . . **New Mexico, West Virginia, Delaware**

Provinces . . . **Alberta, British Columbia, Quebec, Ontario**

Cities . . . . **Montreal, Portland**

Counties . . . . **Wayne County, Dade County**

Bodies of water . . . . **Hudson Bay, North Sea, Lake Geneva, Saskatchewan River, Gulf of Mexico**

Landforms . . . . . **Appalachian Mountains, Bitterroot Range**

Public areas . . . . **Vietnam Memorial**

Roads and highways . . . . **New Jersey Turnpike, Interstate 80, Central Avenue**

Buildings . . . . **Pentagon, Oriental Theater, Empire State Building**

Monuments . . . . **Eiffel Tower, Statue of Liberty**

512.2 Sections of the Country

Capitalize words that name particular sections of the country. (Also capitalize proper adjectives formed from these words.)

A large part of the United States population lives on the East Coast. (*East Coast* is a section of the country.)

Southern cooking   out West

Do *not* capitalize words that simply show direction.

If you keep driving west, you will end up in the Pacific Ocean. (direction)

western Brazil   northeasterly wind

Capitalization 3

■ Names of Places

For each sentence, write the word or words that should be capitalized.

Example: My family took a trip around one of the great lakes.

Great Lakes

1. We started at our home in Traverse City, michigan.

2. Mom and Dad drove us south along the lakeshore all the way to chicago.

3. We saw the sears tower as we went through the city.

4. The road followed the shore of lake michigan into wisconsin.

5. If we had kept going north, we would have ended up in canada.

6. Instead, we drove east through hiawatha national forest.

7. We loved going over the mackinac bridge.

8. We took interstate 75, which intersected with the road back to our house.

Next Step: Write a few sentences about a trip you would like to take. Tell where you would start and where you would end up.

Capitalization . . .

514.1
Historical Events

Capitalize the names of historical events, documents, and periods of time.

> **Boston Tea Party**
> **Emancipation Proclamation**
> **Stone Age**

514.2
Titles

Capitalize the first word of a title, the last word, and every word in between except short prepositions, coordinating conjunctions, and articles *(a, an, the)*.

> *National Geographic World* (magazine)
> **"The Star-Spangled Banner"** (song)
> *Beauty and the Beast* (movie)
> *In My Pocket* (book)

514.3
First Words

Capitalize the first word of every sentence.

> **We play our first basketball game tomorrow.**

Capitalize the first word of a direct quotation.

> **Jamir shouted, "Keep that ball moving!"**

Capitalize	Do Not Capitalize
January, March	winter, spring
Grandpa (as a name)	my grandpa
Mayor Sayles-Belton	the mayor
President Washington	our first president
Ida B. Wells Elementary School	the local elementary school
Lake Ontario	the lake area
the South (section of the country)	south (a direction)
planet Earth	a mound of earth (dirt)

Capitalization 4

■ Titles
■ First Words

For each sentence, write the word or words that should be capitalized.

Example: Jeanne and Joe Pacific wrote a book called *Big blue planet*.
Blue Planet

1. they were famous for working under the sea.

2. They wrote articles about the ocean for *wide seas* magazine.

3. The publisher said, "our readers love their articles!"

4. Jeanne and Joe also made films about fish for the TV show *undersea Animals*.

5. People around the world saw their movie *Watching the whales.*

6. would you like to sail the seas with Joe and Jeanne Pacific?

Next Step: Have you seen a movie, a TV show, or an article about animals or nature lately? Write a sentence about it that includes its title.

Plurals

516.1

Most Nouns

Form the **plurals** of most nouns by adding -*s*.

    balloon—balloons   **shoe—shoes**

516.2

Nouns Ending in *sh*, *ch*, *x*, *s*, and *z*

Form the plurals of nouns ending in *sh*, *ch*, *x*, *s*, and *z* by adding -*es* to the singular.

    brush—brushes   **bunch—bunches**   **box—boxes**
    dress—dresses   **buzz—buzzes**

516.3

Nouns Ending in *o*

Form the plurals of most words that end in *o* by adding -*s*.

    patio—patios   **rodeo—rodeos**

For most nouns ending in *o* with a consonant letter just before the *o*, add -*es*.

    echo—echoes   **hero—heroes**

However, musical terms and words of Spanish origin form plurals by adding -*s*; check your dictionary for other words of this type.

    piano—pianos   **solo—solos**
    taco—tacos   **burrito—burritos**

516.4

Nouns Ending in -*ful*

Form the plurals of nouns that end with -*ful* by adding an -*s* at the end of the word.

    two spoonfuls   **three tankfuls**
    four bowlfuls   **five cupfuls**

516.5

Nouns Ending in *f* or *fe*

Form the plurals of nouns that end in *f* or *fe* in one of two ways.

1. If the final *f* is still heard in the plural form of the word, simply add -*s*.

    goof—goofs   **chief—chiefs**   **safe—safes**

2. If the final *f* has the sound of *v* in the plural form, change the *f* to *v* and add -*es*.

    calf—calves   **loaf—loaves**   **knife—knives**

Plurals 1

- Nouns Ending in *o*
- Nouns Ending in *f* or *fe*

▶ **Write the plural form of each of the following words.**

Example: taco
        tacos

1. wife
2. radio
3. leaf
4. tomato
5. life
6. roof
7. banjo
8. brief
9. studio
10. half

11. reef
12. duo
13. proof
14. soprano
15. hoof
16. alto
17. wolf
18. potato
19. cafe
20. portfolio

Next Step: Select two words from the list above. Write a sentence for each, using the plural form of the word.

Plurals . . .

Nouns Ending in y

When a common noun ends in a consonant + *y*, form its plural by changing the *y* to *i* and adding *-es*.

    sky—skies   **bunny**—bunnies
    story—stories   **musky**—muskies

For proper nouns, do *not* change the letters—just add *-s.*

    area Bargain Citys   **the Berrys**   **two Timmys**

For nouns that end in a vowel + *y*, add only *-s.*

    donkey—donkeys   **monkey**—monkeys   **day**—days

Compound Nouns

Form the plurals of most compound nouns by changing the most important word in the compound to its plural form.

    sisters-in-law   **maids of honor**
    secretaries of state   **life jackets**

Irregular Nouns

Some nouns form plurals using an irregular spelling.

    child—children   **goose**—geese   **foot**—feet
    man—men   **woman**—women **tooth**—teeth
    ox—oxen   **mouse**—mice
    cactus—cacti or **cactuses**

A few words have the same singular and plural forms.

Singular:	**Plural:**
That sheep wanders away.	The other sheep follow it.
I caught one trout.	Dad caught three trout.

Others: deer, moose, buffalo, fish, aircraft

Adding an 's

The plurals of symbols, letters, numerals, and words discussed as words are formed by adding an apostrophe and *-s.*

    two ?'s and two !'s   **five 7's**   *x*'**s and** *y*'**s**

TIP: For more information on forming plurals and plural possessives, see page 492.

Plurals 2

■ Nouns Ending in *y*
■ Irregular Nouns

For each of the following sentences, write the correct plural form of the underlined word.

Example: Many <u>city</u> have youth centers.

cities

1. My friends and I go to our city youth center on <u>Monday</u>.

2. Lots of the other <u>child</u> from my neighborhood go, too.

3. The two <u>Tommy</u> from down the street go.

4. They have some new <u>toy</u> to show us next time.

5. On one Monday field trip, some neighborhood <u>man</u> volunteered to take us out in boats.

6. A bunch of <u>fish</u> started flying into one boat!

7. They were probably <u>trout</u>.

8. Maybe they were trying to escape some <u>osprey</u>, which are fish-eating hawks.

9. Last week on a field trip, we got to ride <u>pony</u>.

10. We have some great <u>story</u> to tell about the center.

Next Step: Write one or two sentences using the correct plural forms of *woman* and *puppy*.

Abbreviations

An **abbreviation** is the shortened form of a word or phrase.

520.1
Common Abbreviations

Most abbreviations begin with a capital letter and end with a period. In formal writing, do *not* abbreviate the names of states, countries, months, days, or units of measure. Also do *not* use symbols (%, &) in place of words.

TIP: The following abbreviations are always acceptable in both formal and informal writing:

Mr.	Mrs.	Ms.	Dr.	Jr., Sr.
M.D.	B.C.E.	C.E.	a.m., p.m. (A.M., P.M.)	

520.2
Acronyms

An **acronym** is made up of the first letter or letters of words in a phrase. An acronym is pronounced as a word, and it does not have any periods.

SADD (**S**tudents **A**gainst **D**estructive **D**ecisions)

PIN (**p**ersonal **i**dentification **n**umber)

520.3
Initialisms

An **initialism** is like an acronym except the letters that form the abbreviation are pronounced individually (not as a word).

TV (**t**ele**v**ision)	DA (**d**istrict **a**ttorney)
CD (**c**ompact **d**isc)	PO (**p**ost **o**ffice)

Common Abbreviations

a.m.	ante meridiem (before noon)	**Inc.**	incorporated	**oz.**	ounce
ATM	automatic teller machine	**kg**	kilogram	**pd.**	paid
B.C.E.	before the Common Era	**km**	kilometer	**p.**	page
C.E.	the Common Era	**lb.**	pound	**p.m.**	post meridiem (after noon)
etc.	and so forth	**M.D.**	doctor of medicine	**qt.**	quart
FYI	for your information	**mpg**	miles per gallon		
		mph	miles per hour		

Abbreviations 1

■ Common Abbreviations, Acronyms, and Initialisms

For each sentence, write the word or words that each underlined abbreviation stands for.

Example: <u>Dr.</u> Bertha Byrd was a member of the Baby Bird Defense League.

Doctor

1. She took time off from her job as a <u>M.D.</u> to help little birds.

2. "Birds that weigh less than an <u>oz.</u> should stay out of the sun," she noted.

3. Today, just before noon, she went to the <u>ATM</u>.

4. She used her <u>PIN</u>, took out some money, and bought an umbrella.

5. She held the umbrella over the nest and played a <u>CD</u> of bird whistles to calm the babies.

6. "My husband, <u>Mr.</u> Byrd, will defend your nest tomorrow," she told them.

7. "He's one of the best bird-watchers in the <u>U.S.A.</u>"

Next Step: Make up an acronym or initialism of your own. Then write what that abbreviation stands for.

Abbreviations . . .

522.1
State and Address Abbreviations

You may use a state or an address abbreviation when it is part of an address at the top of a letter or on an envelope. (Also see pages 476–477.) Remember, do not use these abbreviations in sentences.

On a letter:

2323 N. Kipp St.
Cleveland, OH 52133

On an envelope:

7828 E FIRST AVE
ORONO ME 04403

In sentences:

Jasper lives at 2323 North Kipp Street, Cleveland, Ohio.

His old address was 7828 East First Avenue, Orono, Maine 04403.

State Postal Abbreviations

Alabama	AL	Idaho	ID	Missouri	MO	Pennsylvania	PA
Alaska	AK	Illinois	IL	Montana	MT	Rhode Island	RI
Arizona	AZ	Indiana	IN	Nebraska	NE	South Carolina	SC
Arkansas	AR	Iowa	IA	Nevada	NV	South Dakota	SD
California	CA	Kansas	KS	New Hampshire	NH	Tennessee	TN
Colorado	CO	Kentucky	KY	New Jersey	NJ	Texas	TX
Connecticut	CT	Louisiana	LA	New Mexico	NM	Utah	UT
Delaware	DE	Maine	ME	New York	NY	Vermont	VT
District of		Maryland	MD	North Carolina	NC	Virginia	VA
Columbia	DC	Massachusetts	MA	North Dakota	ND	Washington	WA
Florida	FL	Michigan	MI	Ohio	OH	West Virginia	WV
Georgia	GA	Minnesota	MN	Oklahoma	OK	Wisconsin	WI
Hawaii	HI	Mississippi	MS	Oregon	OR	Wyoming	WY

Address Abbreviations

Apartment	Apt.	Expressway	Expy.	Parkway	Pkwy.	Square	Sq.
Avenue	Ave.	Heights	Hts.	Place	Pl.	Station	Sta.
Boulevard	Blvd.	Highway	Hwy.	Road	Rd.	Street	St.
Court	Ct.	Lane	Ln.	Route	Rte.	Terrace	Terr.
Drive	Dr.	North	N.	Rural	R.	Turnpike	Tpke.
East	E.	Park	Pk.	South	S.	West	W.

Abbreviations 2

■ **State and Address Abbreviations**

▶ **Write each of the following addresses using abbreviations.**

Example: 101 Duck Pond Road
St. Ann, Missouri 63070
101 Duck Pond Rd.
St. Ann, MO 63070

1. 2001 West Lunar Highway
Houston, Texas 77001

2. 500 Sunshine Boulevard
Hollywood, California 90028

3. 1623 Pilgrim Founders Street
Plymouth, Massachusetts 02360

4. 1 South Parthenon Way
Nashville, Tennessee 37201

5. 1337 East Tundra Terrace
Juneau, Alaska 99801

6. 1963 West Route 66
Lake Havasu City, Arizona 86403

Next Step: Write your own address as if you were writing it
at the top of a letter.

Numbers

524.1
Numbers from 1 to 9

Numbers from one to nine are usually written as words. (Most of the time, numbers 10 and higher are written as numerals.)

one   three   nine   10   115   2,000

Keep any numbers that are being compared in the same style, either words or numerals.

Students from 8 to 11 years old are invited.

Students from eight to eleven years old are invited.

524.2
Very Large Numbers

You may use a combination of numbers and words for very large numbers.

15 million   1.2 billion

You may spell out large numbers that can be written as two words, but if you need more than two words to spell out a number, write it as a numeral.

three million   fifteen thousand   3,275,100   7,418

524.3
Sentence Beginnings

Use words, not numerals, to begin a sentence.

Fourteen new students joined the jazz band.

Fifty-two cards make up a deck.

524.4
Numerals Only

Use numerals for numbers in the following forms:

decimals	**25.5**
with dollar signs	**$3.97**
percentages	**6 percent**
chapters	**chapter 8**
pages	**pages 17–20**
addresses	**445 E. Acorn Dr.**
dates	**June 19, 2005**
times with a.m. or p.m.	**1:30 p.m.**
statistics	**a vote of 5 to 2**

Numbers

- Numbers from 1 to 9
- Very Large Numbers

For each sentence, write the numbers correctly. If the number is already correct, write "C."

Example: I went on a field trip with
twenty-eight classmates.

28

1. We rode a school bus to an apple farm 3 miles out of town.

2. "Wow! There must be thirty-nine million apples here!" Evan said as we drove up.

3. "I've never counted them all," the farmer told us, "but we do sell thirty-four varieties."

4. He handed us each an apple and said, "We sell about three hundred sixty apples in an hour."

5. "That means you sell two thousand eight hundred eighty apples a day!" Judy exclaimed.

6. "We sell even more when we keep the store open longer than 8 hours," the farmer replied.

7. Someone said farmers in the United States sell more than one hundred fifty million apples in one year.

Next Step: Write two sentences about something you like to eat. Tell how much you might eat in a day and in a year. Use numbers in their correct forms.

Test Prep

> **Number your paper from 1 to 10. For each underlined part in the following paragraph, write the letter of the reason it is incorrect. Your choices are listed below and on the next page.**

$\underset{1}{\underline{2}}$ ways to rank the states are by size and by population.

$\underset{2}{\underline{\text{for}}}$ example, $\underset{3}{\underline{\text{alaska}}}$ is the largest state in size, but it is

number $\underset{4}{\underline{\text{forty-seven}}}$ in population. The state with the most

people (over $\underset{5}{\underline{\text{thirty-five million}}}$) is California. $\underset{6}{\underline{498{,}703}}$ people

live in $\underset{7}{\underline{\text{wyoming}}}$. It has the fewest residents. Rhode $\underset{8}{\underline{\text{island}}}$

has $\underset{9}{\underline{\text{one thousand forty-five}}}$ square miles. $\underset{10}{\underline{\text{it}}}$ is the tiniest state.

---

1. The numeral *2* should be written as a word because . . .
- **A** it is a large number.
- **B** it begins a sentence.
- **C** it is being compared to another number in the sentence.

2. *For* should be capitalized because . . .
- **A** it is part of a title.
- **B** it is a proper adjective.
- **C** it is the first word in a sentence.

3. *Alaska* should be capitalized because . . .
- **A** it is a geographic name that is a proper noun.
- **B** it is the first word in a sentence.
- **C** it is the name of a language.

4. The number *47* should be written as a numeral because . . .
   A it is between one and nine.
   B it is a number larger than nine.
   C it is part of an address.

5. The number *35 million* can be written as a combination of numbers and words because . . .
   A it is a very large number.
   B it is between one and nine.
   C it begins a sentence.

6. The beginning of this sentence should be rewritten using words because . . .
   A words, not numerals, begin a sentence.
   B the number is less than nine.
   C the number is a decimal.

7. *Wyoming* should be capitalized because . . .
   A it names a religion.
   B it is the first word in a sentence.
   C it is a proper noun.

8. *Island* should be capitalized because . . .
   A it names a religion.
   B it is part of a geographic name that is a proper noun.
   C it is a historical event.

9. The number *1,045* should be a numeral because . . .
   A it is between one and nine.
   B it is a large number that requires more than two words.
   C it is part of a date.

10. *It* should be capitalized because . . .
    A it is a proper noun.
    B it is an abbreviation.
    C it is the first word in a sentence.

Improving Spelling

528.1
i* before *e

Write *i* before *e*—except after *c* or when the word rhymes with *say* as in *neighbor* and *weigh*.

believe	**chief**	**receive**	**freight**

Exceptions to the *i* before *e* rule include the following:

either	**neither**	**heir**	**leisure**	**species**
foreign	**height**	**seize**	**weird**	

528.2
Silent *e*

If a word ends with a silent *e*, drop the *e* before adding a suffix (ending) that begins with a vowel.

judge—judging   **continue**—continual

create—creative—creation   **relate**—relating—relative

528.3
Words Ending in *y*

When a word ends in a consonant + *y*, change the *y* to *i* before adding a suffix. Do not, however, change the *y* when adding the *-ing* suffix.

happy—happiness   **try**—tries—trying

lady—ladies   **cry**—cried—crying

When forming the plural of a word that ends in *y* with a vowel just before it, add *-s*.

holiday—holidays   **key**—keys   **boy**—boys

528.4
Words Ending in a Consonant

When a one-syllable word ends in a consonant that has a single vowel before it, double the final consonant before adding a suffix that begins with a vowel.

beg—begging   **hop**—hopped   **sit**—sitting

When a word with more than one syllable ends with a vowel + consonant, double the final consonant only if the accent is on the last syllable and the suffix begins with a vowel.

admit—admitting   **occur**—occurrence

Spelling 1

- *i* before *e*
- Silent *e*

▶ **For each sentence, write any misspelled words correctly. Follow the rules on page 528.**

Example: Fred recieved a letter from Fran.

received

1. Fran and Fred have been good freinds since they met.

2. Aren't they a loveable pair?

3. Fran is saveing some money to buy Fred a gift.

4. They like jogging through parks and feilds.

5. They go skateing together sometimes.

6. Today they are bikeing in the state park.

7. Although Fred looks a bit tired, Fran seems tirless!

8. Fred needs a breif break.

9. Fred's dad was bakeing yesterday, so Fred brought some homemade granola bars with him.

10. In a quiet moment, Fran says, "I'd love a granola bar."

Next Step: Write a sentence describing what Fred and Fran did next. Make sure you spell all words correctly.

Spelling 2

■ Words Ending in *y*
■ Words Ending in a Consonant

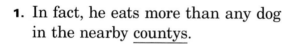

For each sentence, write the correct spelling of the underlined word or words.

Example: Harley is the <u>hungryest</u> dog in the neighborhood.

hungriest

1. In fact, he eats more than any dog in the nearby <u>countys</u>.

2. His owner <u>grined</u> and said, "He eats people food."

3. He eats pizza with lots of <u>topings</u>.

4. He doesn't just like people food; he also likes children's <u>toyes</u>.

5. He likes human music, too. The <u>Flieing Donkies</u> seems to be his favorite group.

6. He <u>buryed</u> some of their CD's so he could listen to them later, I guess.

7. I suppose he'll be <u>diging</u> them up again.

8. He put them in the two <u>allies</u> next to his favorite bones.

Next Step: Write a list of three words that end in *y*. Then add a suffix and write the correct spelling of the word.

Spelling Review

For each of the following sentences, write the correct spelling of the underlined word.

Example: This kite is not behaveing!
        behaving

1. I have trouble geting it up in the air.

2. I wonder if the kite wieghs too much.

3. The wind keeps changeing direction.

4. The kite flys, but then it crashes to the ground.

5. Maybe the wind is too feirce.

6. It keeps tuging at the kite.

7. Does the cloudyness cause a problem?

8. Does my kite need batterys?

9. This really annoyes me.

10. I am leaveing.

11. Next time I'll be tieing a long tail on my kite.

12. Then my only worrys will be trees and houses.

Next Step: From the spelling words list, select three words that give you trouble. Write a sentence for each.

Proofreader's Guide to Improved Spelling

Be patient. Becoming a good speller takes time and practice. Learn the basic spelling rules.

Check your spelling by using a dictionary or a list of commonly misspelled words.

Check a dictionary for the correct pronunciation of each word you are trying to spell. Knowing how to pronounce a word will help you remember how to spell it.

Look up the meaning of each word. Knowing its meaning will help you to use it and spell it correctly.

Study the word in the dictionary. Then look away from the dictionary page and picture the word in your mind's eye. Next, write the word on a piece of paper. Finally, check its spelling in the dictionary. Repeat these steps until you can spell the word correctly.

Make a spelling dictionary. Include any words you frequently misspell in a special notebook.

A

	addition	almost	another	arrange
	address	alone	answer	arrival
ability	adjust	along	antarctic	article
able	admire	a lot	anxious	asleep
aboard	adventure	already	anybody	assign
about	advise	although	anyone	assist
above	afraid	altogether	anything	athlete
absence	afternoon	aluminum	anyway	athletic
absent	again	always	anywhere	attach
accept	against	American	apartment	attack
accident	agreeable	among	apologize	attention
according	agreement	amount	appointment	attitude
account	aisle	ancient	April	attractive
ache	alarm	angel	architect	audience
achieve	alert	anger	arctic	August
acre	alley	angle	aren't	aunt
across	allow	angry	argument	author
action	allowance	animal	arithmetic	automobile
actual	all right	announce	around	autumn

avenue
average
award
awareness
awful
awhile

B

baggage
baking
balance
balloon
banana
bandage
barber
bargain
basement
beautiful
beauty
because
becoming
been
before
beginning
behave
behind
believe
belong
between
bicycle
blizzard
borrow
bother
bottom
bought
bounce
breakfast
breath
breathe
breeze
bridge
brief

bright
brother
brought
buckle
budget
build
built
burglar
bury
business
busy

C

cafeteria
calendar
cancel
candidate
candle
canoe
canyon
captain
cardboard
care
career
carpenter
catalog
catcher
caught
ceiling
celebration
century
certain
challenge
champion
change
chapter
character
chief
children
chocolate
choice
choir

choose
chorus
chose
church
circle
citizen
city
clear
climate
climb
close
closet
clothes
coach
cocoa
cocoon
college
color
column
comedy
coming
commercial
committee
common
communicate
community
company
comparison
complain
complete
concern
concert
concrete
condition
conference
confidence
confuse
congratulate
connect
continue
convince
cooperate
correction
cough

could
country
county
courage
cousin
cozy
crawl
cried
crowd
cruel
crumb
curiosity
curious
current
customer
cycle

D

daily
damage
danger
dangerous
dare
daughter
December
decide
decision
decorate
definition
delicious
describe
description
design
develop
dictionary
difference
different
disappear
discover
discuss
discussion
disease

distance
divide
division
doctor
does
doesn't
dollar
done
doubt
during

E

eager
early
earn
easily
easy
edge
eight
eighth
either
electricity
elephant
eleven
else
embarrass
emergency
encourage
enormous
enough
entertain
entrance
environment
equal
equipment
escape
especially
every
everybody
exactly
excellent
except

excited
exercise
exhausted
expensive
experience
experiment
explain
extinct
extreme
eyes

F

face
familiar
family
famous
fashion
favorite
February
field
fierce
fifty
finally
first
foreign
forty
forward
fountain
fourth
fragile
Friday
friend
frighten
from
fuel

G

gadget
general
generous

genius
gentle
geography
giant
ghost
goes
gone
government
governor
graduation
grammar
grateful
great
grocery
group
guarantee
guard
guess
guilty
gymnasium

H

half
handsome
happen
happiness
have
headache
health
heard
heavy
height
history
holiday
honest
honor
horrible
hospital
however
hundreds
hygiene

I

icicle
ideal
illustrate
imaginary
imagine
imitate
imitation
immigrant
important
impossible
incredible
independent
individual
initial
innocent
instead
intelligent
interest
interrupt
invitation
island

J

January
jealous
jewelry
join
journal
journey
judgment
July
June

K

knew
knife
knives
knowledge

L

label
language
laugh
lawyer
league
learn
least
leave
length
library
lightning
liquid
listen
loose
lovable

M

machine
magazine
many
March
marriage
material
mathematics
May
mayor
meant
measure
medicine
message
might
millions
miniature
minute
mirror
mischief
misspell
Monday
morning

mountain
multiplication
muscle
music
musician
mysterious

N

nation
national
natural
nature
necessary
neighborhood
neither
nephew
nervous
newspaper
nickel
niece
nineteen
ninth
nobody
noisy
no one
nothing
notice
November

O

obey
occasion
o'clock
October
of
off
office
often
once
only

operate
opinion
opposite
ordinary
original
over

P

package
paid
paragraph
parallel
patience
people
perfect
perhaps
personal
persuade
photo
picture
pleasant
please
point
popular
possess
possible
practical
practice
preparation
president
pretty
privilege
probably
problem
produce
protein

Q

quarter
quickly

quiet
quit
quite
quotient

R

raise
ready
really
reason
receive
recipe
recognize
recommend
relatives
relief
remember
responsibility
reply
restaurant
review
revolves
rhyme
rhythm
right
rough
route

S

safety
salary
Saturday
says
scared
scene
schedule
science
scissors
search
secretary

separate
September
serious
several
similar
simple
sign
since
sincerely
skiing
soldier
something
sometimes
spaghetti
special
south
statement
statue
stomach
stood
straight
strength
stretch
studying
subtraction
succeed
success
suddenly
sugar
Sunday
suppose
sure
surprise
surround
system

T

table
teacher
tear
temperature
terrible

Thanksgiving
theater
themselves
thief
though
thought
thousand
through
Thursday
tired
together
tomorrow
tongue
touch
toward
treasure
tried
trouble
truly
Tuesday
type

U

uncle
unique
universe
unknown
until
unusual
upon
upstairs
use
usually

V

vacation
vacuum
valuable
vegetable
vehicle

view
visitor
voice
volume
volunteer

W

wander
was
watch
weather
Wednesday
weigh
weight
weird
welcome
went
what
whenever
where
which
while
who
whole
women
wonderful
worse
world
write
written
wrong
wrote

Y

yellow
yesterday
young
yourself

Using the Right Word

You need to use "the right words" in your writing and speaking, and this section will help you do that. First, look over the commonly misused words on the next 21 pages. Then, whenever you have a question about which word is the right word, come back to this section for help. (Remember to look for your word in a dictionary if you don't find it here.)

536.1
a, an

We took a ride to look for wildlife.
(Use *a* before words beginning with a consonant sound.)
José saw an eagle and an antelope.
(Use *an* before words beginning with a vowel sound.)

536.2
accept, except

Zachary walked up to accept his award.
(*Accept* means "to receive" or "to approve of.")
Except for his sister, the whole family was there.
(*Except* means "other than.")

536.3
allowed, aloud

We are allowed to read to partners in class.
(*Allowed* means "permitted.")
We may not read aloud in the library, however.
(*Aloud* is an adverb meaning "out loud" or "clearly heard.")

536.4
a lot

A lot of my friends like chips and salsa.
(*A lot* is always two words.)

536.5
already,
all ready

I already finished my homework.
(*Already* is an adverb telling when.)
Now I'm all ready to shoot some buckets.
(*All ready* is a phrase meaning "completely ready.")

536.6
ant, aunt

A large black ant crawled across the picnic blanket.
Aunt Lucinda, my mom's sister, got out of its way.

Using the Right Word 1

■ a, an; **accept, except;** allowed, aloud; **a lot;** ant, aunt

For each sentence, write the correct word or words from the choices in parentheses.

Example: Over the summer I received
an *(ant, aunt)* farm
as a gift.
ant

1. *(Ant, Aunt)* Jo gave it to me.

2. I like the ant farm *(a lot, alot)*.

3. Auntie Jo always brings my sister and me *(a, an)* present.

4. She reads *(allowed, aloud)* to us, too.

5. I like all her stories *(except, accept)* the one about the fairy princess.

6. We're *(allowed, aloud)* to stay up until nine o'clock.

7. Dad says I have to *(except, accept)* this bedtime until I get older.

8. Then I can have *(a, an)* later bedtime.

Next Step: Write two more sentences using the words *ant* and *aunt* correctly.

538.1
ate, eight

I ate a bowl of popcorn.

He had eight pieces of candy.

538.2
bare, bear

She put her bare feet into the cool stream.

She didn't see the bear fishing on the other side.

538.3
blew, blue

I blew on my cold hands.

The tips of my fingers looked almost blue.

538.4
board, bored

One board in the wooden floor was loose.

With nothing to do, I felt bored.

538.5
borrow, lend

It's so cold—could I borrow a sweater?
(*Borrow* means "receive.")

It's so cold—could you lend me a sweater?
(*Lend* means "give.")

538.6
brake, break

Pump the brake to slow down.

You could break a bone if you skateboard without pads and a helmet.

538.7
breath, breathe

Take a deep breath and calm down. (*Breath* is a noun.)

My nose is so stuffed up that it's hard to breathe.
(*Breathe* is a verb.)

538.8
bring, take

Please bring me my glasses.
(*Bring* means "to move toward the speaker.")

Take your dishes to the kitchen.
(*Take* means "to carry away.")

538.9
by, buy

Chuck stopped by the store window.

He wanted to buy a new baseball glove.

Using the Right Word 2

■ ate, eight; **bare, bear;** blew, blue; **brake, break;**
breath, breathe; **by, buy**

▶ **Write the correct word from
each pair in parentheses.**

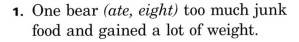

Example: A *(bare, bear)* will eat all
summer long to get ready
for a long winter.
bear

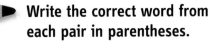

1. One bear *(ate, eight)* too much junk
food and gained a lot of weight.

2. He couldn't *(by, buy)* his own food, so he looked for
scraps all the time.

3. Once he gulped down *(ate, eight)* picnic baskets from a
campground *(by, buy)* the lake.

4. A camper got so mad that she turned *(blew, blue)* in
the face.

5. The bear would *(brake, break)* anything he sat on.

6. If he sat on me, I would not be able to *(breath, breathe)*!

7. To scare the bear away, the park ranger took a deep
(breath, breathe) and *(blew, blue)* her whistle.

8. Unfortunately, that bear had no *(brake, break)* on his
appetite.

Next Step: Write an ending to this story. Use two or more of
the words from the list at the top of the page.

540.1
can, may

Do you think I can go off the high dive?
(I am asking if I have the *ability* to do it.)
May I go off the high dive?
(I am asking for *permission* to do something.)

540.2
capital, capitol

The capital city of Texas is Austin.
Be sure to begin Austin with a capital letter.
My uncle works in the capitol building.
(*Capitol*, with an *ol*, refers to a government building.)

540.3
cent, scent, sent

Each rose cost one cent less than a dollar.
The scent of the flowers is sweet.
Dad sent Mom a dozen roses.

540.4
choose, chose

David must choose a different instrument this year.
Last year he chose to take drum lessons.
(*Chose* [chōz] is the past tense of the verb
choose [chōōz].)

540.5
close, clothes

Please close the window.
Do you have all your clothes packed for your trip?

540.6
coarse, course

A cat's tongue feels coarse, like sandpaper.
I took a course called "Caring for Cats."

540.7
creak, creek

Old houses creak when the wind blows hard.
The water in the nearby creek is clear and cold.

540.8
dear, deer

Amber is my dear friend.
The deer enjoyed the sweet corn in her garden.

Using the Right Word 3

■ can, may; **cent, scent, sent;** choose, chose;
close, clothes; creak, creek; **dear, deer**

Look at the underlined word in each of the following sentences. Write a "C" if it is used correctly. If it is not, write the correct word.

Please pass the salt, Dear.

Example: Last night, Mr. Elk and his wife <u>choose</u> a nice restaurant for dinner.

chose

1. They dressed in their best <u>close</u> and went downtown.

2. "<u>May</u> we sit here?" Ms. Elk asked the waiter.

3. "I like the view of the <u>creak</u>," she said.

4. "Yes," he agreed, as he went to <u>clothes</u> the kitchen door.

5. "We might see some <u>dear</u> there," she said.

6. When they were seated, Mr. Elk said, "There is so much to <u>choose</u> from on the menu."

7. "I don't think I <u>may</u> decide!" he continued.

8. Ms. Elk <u>cent</u> the waiter to the kitchen for a bowl of soup.

9. After his meal, Mr. Elk noticed a <u>creak</u> in his chair.

10. "Oh, <u>dear</u>," he said, "I think I ate too much."

542

542.1 desert, dessert	Cactuses grow in the desert near our house. My favorite dessert is strawberry pie.
542.2 dew, do, due	The dew on the grass got my new shoes wet. I will do my research after school since the report is due on Wednesday.
542.3 die, dye	The plant will die if it isn't watered. The red dye in the sweatshirt turned everything in the wash pink.
542.4 doesn't, don't	She doesn't like green bananas. (*Doesn't* is the contraction of *does not*.) I don't either. (*Don't* is the contraction of *do not*.)
542.5 fewer, less	We had fewer snow days this winter than we did last year. (*Fewer* refers to something you can count.) That meant less time for ice-skating. (*Less* refers to an amount that you cannot count.)
542.6 flower, flour	A tulip is a spring flower. Flour is the main ingredient in bread.
542.7 for, four	The friends looked for a snack. They found four apples on the table.
542.8 forth, fourth	We set forth on our journey through the forest. Reggie was the fourth player to get hurt during the game.
542.9 good, well	Ling looks good in that outfit. (*Good* is an adjective. Adjectives modify nouns or pronouns.) It fits her well. (*Well* is an adverb modifying *fits*.)

Using the Right Word 4

■ desert, dessert; **die, dye;** doesn't, don't; **flower, flour;** for, four; **good, well**

▶ **For each sentence, write the correct word from each pair in parentheses.**

Example: I *(doesn't, don't)* like my
cowboy job very much.

don't

1. My horse *(doesn't, don't)* like it,
either.

2. This sandy, old *(desert, dessert)* is very hot.

3. Sand always gets into the *(flower, flour)* I use
(for, four) cooking.

4. A person could *(die, dye)* from thirst out here.

5. Nothing much grows here, so we hardly ever see a
(flower, flour).

6. The *(die, dye)* from my kerchief has stained all
(for, four) of my work shirts.

7. My horse's saddle doesn't fit very *(good, well)*, either.

8. I'd rather be eating a nice *(desert, dessert)*, like some
(good, well) old-fashioned apple pie.

Next Step: Imagine that this cowboy weren't so grouchy.
Write two sentences about his experiences from
a happier point of view.

544.1
hair, hare

Celia's hair is short and curly.

A hare looks like a large rabbit.

544.2
heal, heel

Most scrapes and cuts heal quickly.

Gracie has a blister on her heel.

544.3
hear, here

I couldn't hear your directions.

I was over here, and you were way over there.

544.4
heard, herd

We heard the noise, all right!

It sounded like a herd of charging elephants.

544.5
hi, high

Say hi to the pilot for me.

How high is this plane flying?

544.6
hole, whole

A donut has a hole in the middle of it.

Montel ate a whole donut.

544.7
hour, our

It takes one hour to ride to the beach.

Let's pack our lunches and go.

544.8
its, it's

This backpack is no good; its zipper is stuck.
(*Its* shows possession and never has an apostrophe.)

It's also ripped. (*It's* is the contraction of *it is.*)

544.9
knew, new

I knew it was going to rain.

I still wanted to wear my new shoes.

544.10
knot, not

I have a knot in my shoelaces.

I am not able to untie the tangled mess.

544.11
knows, nose

Mr. Beck knows at least a billion historical facts.

His nose is always in a book.

Using the Right Word 5

■ hair, hare; **hear, here;** heard, herd; **hi, high;**
hole, whole; **hour, our;** its, it's; **knows, nose**

**For each pair of words in parentheses
below, write the line number and the
correct choice.**

Example: 1 Before their famous race,
          2 the turtle and the
          3 *(hare, hair)* were chatting.

3. hare

1   "*(Hi, High)*, Turtle. *(Its, It's)* a nice day for the race,
2 isn't it?" Rabbit said.

3   "Yes," Turtle replied. "I *(heard, herd)* that everyone
4 expects you to win."

5   Rabbit said, "You *(hear, here)* a lot, even without big
6 ears." He stroked the fine *(hare, hair)* on his long ears.

7   "I like your ears," Turtle said, "but who *(knows, nose)*
8 how the race will turn out? I have been training for a
9 *(hole, whole)* month. I may win by a *(knows, nose)*."

10   "I'll stop by my rabbit *(hole, whole)* for a nap," Rabbit
11 laughed. "There's one *(hour, our)* before the race."

12   "Be sure you're back *(hear, here)* by then," said Turtle.

13   Rabbit grinned at the turtle. "I think *(hour, our)* little
14 race will be over almost before it begins," he said. "I can
15 already see my victory flag waving *(hi, high)* on *(its, it's)*
16 pole at the finish line."

546.1
lay, lie

Just lay the sleeping bags on the floor.
(*Lay* means "to place.")

After the hike, we'll lie down and rest.
(*Lie* means "to recline.")

546.2
lead, led

Today I will lead (lēd) the ponies around the show ring.
Yesterday I led (lĕd) them, too.
(*Led* is the past tense of the verb *lead*.)

Some old paint contains the metal lead (lĕd).

546.3
learn, teach

I need to learn these facts about the moon.
(*Learn* means "to get information.")

Tomorrow I have to teach the science lesson.
(*Teach* means "to give information.")

546.4
loose, lose

Lee's pet tarantula is loose!
(*Loose* [lōōs] means "free or untied.")

No one but Lee could lose a big, fat spider.
(*Lose* [lōōz] means "to misplace" or "to fail to win.")

546.5
made, maid

Yes, I have made a big mess.

I need a maid to help me clean it up!

546.6
mail, male

Many people get more mail on their computers than in their mailboxes.

Men are male; women are female.

546.7
meat, meet

I think meat can be a part of a healthful diet.

We were so excited to finally meet the senator.

546.8
metal, medal

Gold is a precious metal.

Is the Olympic first-place medal actually made of gold?

Using the Right Word 6

■ learn, teach; **loose, lose;** made, maid; **mail, male;** meat, meet

▶ **For the following sentences, write the correct word from each pair in parentheses.**

Example: A letter about a cooking contest arrived in the (mail, male).

mail

1. I asked Dad to (learn, teach) me how to make egg rolls.

2. When he was young, he (made, maid) a lot of egg rolls in my grandma's restaurant.

3. He said that he was the only (mail, male) baker there.

4. "I'm sure you'll (learn, teach) this in no time," he said, "as long as you don't (loose, lose) the recipe!"

5. The recipe called for (loose, lose) flour, so I started by sifting the flour into a fine powder.

6. We used cabbage and (meet, meat) to fill the egg rolls.

7. When we finished cooking, I wished we had a (made, maid) to clean up the mess!

8. I called Grandma to see if she could (meat, meet) us at the contest and taste our egg rolls.

Next Step: Write two sentences about something you'd like to cook. Use the words *learn* and *teach* correctly.

548.1
miner, minor

A coal miner may one day get black lung disease.

A minor is a young person who is not legally an adult.

A minor problem is one of no great importance.

548.2
oar, or, ore

Row the boat with an oar in each hand.

Either Kim or Mike will give a report on the iron ore mines near Lake Superior.

548.3
one, won

Markus bought one raffle ticket.

He won the bike with that single ticket.

548.4
pain, pane

Injuries like cuts and scrapes cause pain.

After cleaning the dirty window, we could see through the pane of glass.

548.5
pair, pare, pear

A pair (two) of pigeons roosted on our windowsill.

To pare an apple means to peel it.

A ripe pear is sweet and juicy.

548.6
passed, past

The school bus passed a stalled truck.

In the past, most children walked to school.

548.7
peace, piece

Ms. Brown likes peace and quiet in her room.

Would you like a piece of pizza, Jake?

548.8
peak, peek

The whipped topping formed a peak on my pudding.

Alex stood on a footstool to peek inside the jar.

548.9
pedal, petal

Even though one pedal on the bike was broken, I was still able to pedal to school.

Chantal plucked one petal after another from the daisy.

Using the Right Word 7

■ one, won; **pair, pare, pear;** passed, past; **peace, piece;** peak, peek; **pedal, petal**

▶ **For the following sentences, write the correct word from the choices in parentheses.**

Example: My egg rolls *(passed, past)* the first round of tasting in the cooking contest.

passed

1. I took a *(pair, pare, pear)* of the egg rolls to the school for judging.

2. I almost didn't make it in time because a *(pedal, petal)* on my bike jammed.

3. When I arrived, I took a *(peak, peek)* at the other entries.

4. *(One, Won)* entry was a whole cooked salmon.

5. Another looked like a *(pair, pare, pear)* cobbler, and I could smell the sweet fruit.

6. A *(peace, piece)* of cinnamon stick stood in a dish of applesauce; I'm glad I didn't have to *(pair, pare, pear)* all those apples!

7. The judges were *(passed, past)* winners.

8. The judging took time, but my egg rolls *(one, won)* first place!

Next Step: Use the words *petal, peak,* and *peace* correctly in three sentences.

550.1
plain, plane

Toni wanted a plain (basic) white top.

The coyote ran across the flat plain.

A stunt plane can fly upside down.

550.2
poor, pore, pour

The poor man had no money at all.

Every pore on my nose is clogged with oil.

Please pour the lemonade.

550.3
principal, principle

Our principal visits the classrooms often.
(The noun *principal* is a school administrator.)

Her principal job is to be sure we are learning.
(The adjective *principal* means "most important.")

She asks students to follow this principle: Respect each other, and I'll respect you.
(*Principle* means "idea" or "belief.")

550.4
quiet, quit, quite

Libraries should be quiet places.

Quit talking, please.

I hear quite a bit of whispering going on.

550.5
raise, rays

Please don't raise (lift) the shades.

The sun's rays are very bright this afternoon.

550.6
read, red

Have you read any books by Betsy Byars?

Why are most barns painted red?

550.7
real, really

Mom gave me a stuffed animal, but I wanted a real dog.
(Use *real* as an adjective.)

I was really disappointed.
(*Really* is an adverb.)

550.8
right, write

Is this the right (correct) place to turn right?

I'll write the directions on a note card.

Using the Right Word 8

■ poor, pore, pour; **quiet**, **quit**, **quite**; read, red; **real**, **really**; right, write

Look at each underlined word in the following sentences. Write a "C" if it is used correctly. If it is not, write the correct word.

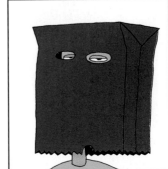

Example: The teacher asked Peter
to <u>poor</u> the juice.
pour

1. Peter was a <u>quite</u> boy.

2. Those who talked to him knew that he was <u>quiet</u> nice.

3. Peter would often <u>write</u> letters to his uncle.

4. "Our class did a <u>real</u> fun experiment," Pete wrote.

5. When Pete's uncle wrote back, Pete <u>red</u>, "I'd like to hear about it, Peter."

6. For the experiment, Mr. Baxter asked Roberto and Matt to wear big <u>red</u> paper bags over their heads.

7. Mr. Baxter told those <u>pore</u> kids to go left, <u>right</u>, backward, and forward until they were all mixed up.

8. Then he asked the rest of the class, "Who is the <u>real</u> Roberto?"

Next Step: Write two sentences about the end of the experiment. Use two words from the list at the top of the page.

552.1
road, rode, rowed

My house is one block from the main road.

I rode my bike to the pond.

Then I rowed the boat to my favorite fishing spot.

552.2
scene, seen

The movie has a great chase scene.

Have you seen it yet?

552.3
sea, see

A sea is a body of salty water.

I see a tall ship on the horizon.

552.4
seam, seem

The seam in my jacket is ripped.

I seem to always catch my sleeve on the door handle.

552.5
sew, so, sow

Shauna loves to sew her own clothes.

She saves her allowance so she can buy fabric.

I'd rather sow seeds and watch my garden grow.

552.6
sit, set

May I sit on one of those folding chairs?

Yes, if you help me set them up first.

552.7
some, sum

I have some math problems to do.

What is the sum of 58 + 17?

552.8
son, sun

Joe Jackson is the son of Kate Jackson.

The sun is the source of the earth's energy.

552.9
sore, soar

Our feet and legs were sore after the long hike.

We watched hawks soar above us.

552.10
stationary, stationery

A stationary bike stays in place while you pedal it.

Wu designs his own stationery (paper) on the computer.

Using the Right Word 9

■ sea, see; **seam, seem;** sew, so, sow;
sit, set; some, sum; **son, sun**

▶ **Look at each underlined word in the
following sentences. Write a "C" if
it is used correctly. If it is not, write
the correct word.**

Example: It's not hard for the postal
carrier to <u>sea</u> me every day.

see

1. Most often, the postal carrier will just <u>set</u> the
   mail by the gate.

2. I have never bitten the carrier, but once she tore a
   <u>seam</u> in her pants while she ran away.

3. My people offered to <u>sow</u> it for her.

4. Mostly I just <u>set</u> around my people's house by the <u>see</u>
   all day.

5. Their <u>son</u> plays with me, <u>sew</u> I get some exercise.

6. Sometimes I lie in the <u>son</u> to warm up.

7. <u>Some</u> days I crawl into the shade of my house to cool
   down.

8. I may <u>seam</u> scary, but I don't look for trouble.

Next Step: Write two sentences using the words *sow* and
sum correctly.

554.1 steal, steel
Our cat tries to steal our dog's food.
The food bowl is made of stainless steel.

554.2 tail, tale
A snake uses its tail to move its body.
"Sammy the Spotted Snake" is my favorite tall tale.

554.3 than, then
Jana's card collection is bigger than Erica's.
(*Than* is used in a comparison.)
When Jana is finished, then we can play.
(*Then* tells when.)

554.4 their, there, they're
What should we do with their cards?
(*Their* shows ownership.)
Put them over there for now.
They're going to pick them up later.
(*They're* is the contraction of *they are*.)

554.5 threw, through
He threw the ball at the basket.
It swished through the net.

554.6 to, too, two
Josie passed the ball to Maria.
Lea was too tired to guard her. (*Too* means "very.")
Maria made a jump shot and scored two points.
The fans jumped and cheered, too. (*Too* can mean "also.")

554.7 waist, waste
My little sister's waist is tiny.
Do not waste your time trying to fix that bike chain.

554.8 wait, weight
I can't wait for the field trip.
Many students complain about the weight of their bookbags.

554.9 way, weigh
What is the best way to get to the park?
Birds weigh very little because of their hollow bones.

Using the Right Word 10

■ tail, tale; **than, then;** their, there, they're; **threw, through;** to, too, two; **waist, waste;** wait, weight; **way, weigh**

▶ **For each of the following sentences, write the correct word from the choices in parentheses.**

Example: Herbert was listed in *Dragons of the World* for *(to, too, two)* years.

two

1. He was proud of getting *(threw, through)* the judging.

2. "*(Their, There, They're)* very picky about who they let in," he told his friends.

3. He sniffed, "It would be a *(waist, waste)* of time *(to, too, two)* put dragons like Nokum and Wally in *(their, there, they're)*."

4. "This magnificent *(tail, tale)* surely helped me."

5. "I'm sure my *(wait, weight)* impressed the judges, *(to, too, two)*," he added.

6. He fetched his mirror, sucked in his *(waist, waste)*, admired himself, and *(than, then)* smiled.

7. "I'm so much greater *(than, then)* other dragons in every *(way, weigh)*," Herbert said.

Next Step: Write a paragraph telling what you think about Herbert. Use words from the top of this page.

556.1
weak, week

The opposite of strong is weak.

There are seven days in a week.

556.2
wear, where

Finally, it's warm enough to wear shorts.

Where is the sunscreen?

556.3
weather,
whether

I like rainy weather.

My dad goes golfing whether it's nice out or not.

556.4
which, witch

Which book should I read?

You'll like *The Lion, the Witch, and the Wardrobe.*

556.5
who, that,
which

The man who answered the phone had a loud voice.
(*Who* refers to people.)

The puppy that I really wanted was sold already. Its brother, which had not been sold yet, came home with me. (*That* and *which* refer to animals and things. Use commas around a clause that begins with *which*.)

556.6
who, whom

Who ordered this pizza?

And for whom did you order it?

556.7
who's, whose

Who's that knocking at the door?
(*Who's* is a contraction of *who is.*)

Mrs. Lang, whose dog ran into our yard, came to get him.

556.8
wood, would

Some baseball bats are made of wood.

Would you like to play baseball after school?

556.9
your, you're

You'll get your ice cream; be patient.

You're talking to the right person!
(*You're* is the contraction of *you are.*)

Using the Right Word 11

■ weak, week; **wear, where;** which, witch;
who's, whose; wood, would; **your, you're**

▶ **For the following sentences, write the correct word from each pair in parentheses.**

Example: Just as a *(witch, which)* has
a certain hat, so do I.
witch

1. You can see by the hat I
(wear, where) that I'm a park ranger.

2. *(Who's, Whose)* job is it to manage a national park?
It's mine.

3. Rangers work every *(weak, week)* of the year.

4. If *(you're, your)* wondering *(wear, where)* to pitch
(your, you're) tent, I'll be happy to show you.

5. I know *(which, witch)* locations in the park are best.

6. I keep track of *(who's, whose)* visiting the park.

7. I might cut the *(wood, would)* of a fallen tree into
logs—so this is not a job for a *(weak, week)* person!

8. *(Wood, Would)* you like to have a job like mine?

Next Step: Write a sentence or two about a job you'd like to
do. Use at least one of the words from the list at
the top of the page.

Test Prep

> For each sentence below, write the letter of the line in which the underlined word is used incorrectly. If there is no mistake, choose "D."

1. A Aunt Josephine
   B scent me a bunch
   C of blue flowers.
   D no mistakes

2. A Down by the see,
   B we sit and smile
   C because we feel so good.
   D no mistakes

3. A If you pour juice
   B over your computer,
   C it will brake.
   D no mistakes

4. A We hired a maid
   B to clean sum rooms
   C and two hallways.
   D no mistakes

5. A The floorboards creak
   B in our family cabin;
   C they seem weak.
   D no mistakes

6. A I through the ball
   B so high in the sky that
   C it got lost in the sun.
   D no mistakes

7. A The hare and the turtle
   B meet once a year
   C down buy the forest.
   D no mistakes

8. A Sometimes they sit
   B near the rabbit's whole
   C and learn bunny songs.
   D no mistakes

9. A The silly grizzly bear
   B threw away his clock
   C just to sea time fly.
   D no mistakes

10. A That dragon don't
   B breathe fire and smoke
   C out of his nose.
   D no mistakes

11. A   Try not to <u>loose</u>
    B   any of my <u>mail</u> as
    C   you <u>pedal</u> downtown.
    D   no mistakes

12. A   <u>Set</u> your boots by the door
    B   <u>sow</u> you don't get mud
    C   on our <u>wood</u> floor.
    D   no mistakes

13. A   One <u>peace</u> of pear
    B   for <u>dessert</u> will
    C   not add to my <u>waist</u>.
    D   no mistakes

14. A   We are not <u>aloud</u> to
    B   leave the cabinets open <u>here</u>;
    C   we must <u>close</u> them.
    D   no mistakes

15. A   We climbed a mountain <u>peak</u>
    B   one day last <u>week</u>;
    C   after that we were <u>real</u> tired.
    D   no mistakes

16. A   I think <u>their</u> dog
    B   is meaner <u>then</u> any dog
    C   <u>except</u> my cousin's dog.
    D   no mistakes

17. A   <u>Its</u> a perfect day
    B   to <u>sit</u> by the fire
    C   and <u>read</u> a book.
    D   no mistakes

18. A   I will <u>write</u> a
    B   note to <u>except</u>
    C   <u>your</u> invitation.
    D   no mistakes

19. A   Mom wants to <u>learn</u>
    B   me how to <u>sew</u>
    C   my own <u>clothes</u>.
    D   no mistakes

20. A   We could not <u>weight</u>
    B   to taste the
    C   <u>meat</u> we grilled.
    D   no mistakes

Understanding Sentences

A **sentence** expresses a complete thought. Usually it has a subject and a predicate. A sentence begins with a capital letter and ends with a period, a question mark, or an exclamation point.

Parts of a Sentence

560.1 **Subjects**	A **subject** is the part of a sentence—a noun or pronoun—that names who or what is doing something. Marisha **baked a pan of lasagna.** A subject can also be the part that is talked about. She **is a marvelous cook.**
560.2 **Simple Subjects**	A simple subject is the subject without the words that describe or modify it. Marisha's little **sister** likes to help.
560.3 **Complete Subjects**	The complete subject is the simple subject along with all the words that describe it. **Marisha's little sister** likes to help.
560.4 **Compound Subjects**	A compound subject has two or more simple subjects joined by a conjunction *(and, or)*. **Marisha and her sister** worked on the puzzle.

Parts of a Sentence 1

■ Subjects

▶ **Write the complete subject of each sentence.**

Example: Mark Twain was born in Missouri in 1835.
Mark Twain

1. His real name was Samuel L. Clemens.

2. His job for about five years was Mississippi riverboat pilot.

3. Mark Twain's first story was published in 1865.

4. "The Celebrated Jumping Frog of Calaveras County" is a funny story.

5. Twain and his wife moved to Hartford, Connecticut, in 1870.

6. People enjoy Mark Twain's tall tales.

7. His most famous book is *The Adventures of Huckleberry Finn*.

8. Many pictures of Twain show him dressed in a white suit.

Next Step: Which sentence above has a compound subject? Write the two simple subjects in the compound subject.

Parts of a Sentence . . .

562.1
Predicates

A **predicate** is the part of the sentence that contains the verb. The predicate can show action by telling what the subject is doing.

> **Marisha baked the cake for my birthday.**

A predicate can also say something about the subject.

> **She is a good cook.**

562.2
Simple Predicates

A simple predicate is the verb without any of the other words that modify it.

> **Marisha baked the cake yesterday.**

562.3
Complete Predicates

The complete predicate is the verb along with all the words that modify or complete it.

> **Marisha baked the cake yesterday.**
>
> **She had made cupcakes, too.**

562.4
Compound Predicates

A compound predicate has two or more verbs.

> **She decorated the cake and hid it in a box in the cupboard.**

562.5
Modifiers

A modifier is a word (an adjective or an adverb) or a group of words that describes another word.

> **My family planned a surprise party.** (*My* modifies *family*; *a* and *surprise* modify *party*.)
>
> **They hid behind the door and waited quietly.** (*Behind the door* modifies *hid*; *quietly* modifies *waited*.)

Parts of a Sentence 2

■ Predicates

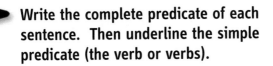

Write the complete predicate of each sentence. Then underline the simple predicate (the verb or verbs).

Example: A dog named Junkyard
lives in the city.

<u>lives</u> in the city

1. Junkyard likes to eat a lot.

2. He will gulp down almost anything.

3. He looks for food scraps behind garbage cans.

4. Some people drop food on the sidewalk or in the park.

5. Junkyard can find it like a detective.

6. Some of these people chase Junkyard.

7. Junkyard escapes every time.

8. His favorite food is sub sandwiches.

9. He loves old sandwiches with stale bread and cheese.

10. Junkyard has little taste!

Next Step: Write two sentences about a dog. Underline the
simple predicate in each sentence.

Parts of a Sentence . . .

564.1
Clauses

A **clause** is a group of words that has a subject and a predicate. A clause can be independent or dependent.

564.2
Independent Clauses

An independent clause expresses a complete thought and can stand alone as a sentence.

> **I ride my bike to school.**

> **Bryan gets a ride from his dad.**

564.3
Dependent Clauses

A dependent clause does not express a complete thought, so it cannot stand alone as a sentence. Dependent clauses often begin with subordinating conjunctions like *when* or *because*. (See **600.2**.)

> **when the weather is nice**

Some dependent clauses begin with relative pronouns like *who* or *which*. (See **580.1**.)

> **who works near our school**

A dependent clause must be joined to an independent clause. The result is a complex sentence.

> **I ride my bike to school when the weather is nice. Bryan gets a ride from his dad, who works near our school.**

Parts of a Sentence 3

■ Clauses

For each clause below, write an "I" for independent clause or a "D" for dependent clause.

Example: the tired knight didn't see the owl on his shoulder

I

1. since he was asleep

2. Sir Gordon often stayed up too late

3. when he worked on guard duty

4. which made him doze off

5. the owl didn't like to be alone

6. Sir Gordon's armor was cold

7. before the sun came up

8. because the owl kept quiet

9. the knight never noticed his new friend

Next Step: Choose a dependent clause and an independent clause from the list above. Combine them to make one complex sentence.

Parts of a Sentence . . .

566.1
Phrases

A **phrase** is a group of related words. Phrases cannot stand alone as sentences since they do *not* have both a subject and a predicate.

566.2
Noun Phrases

A noun phrase doesn't have a predicate. A noun and the adjectives that describe it make up a noun phrase.

the new student

566.3
Verb Phrases

A verb phrase doesn't have a subject. It includes a main verb and one or more helping verbs.

could have written

566.4
Prepositional Phrases

A prepositional phrase begins with a preposition. It doesn't have a subject or a predicate. However, it can add important information to a sentence. (See page 598.)

about George Washington

566.5
Appositive Phrases

An appositive phrase is another way of saying or renaming the noun or pronoun before it.

George Washington, our first president

NOTE: When you put these phrases together, they become a sentence.

The new student could have written about George Washington, our first president.

Parts of a Sentence 4

■ Phrases

Identify the underlined phrases. Write "N" for a noun phrase, "V" for a verb phrase, "P" for a prepositional phrase, or "A" for an appositive phrase.

Example: Cecil called his two best friends, <u>Mary and Andy</u>.

A

1. "What can we do <u>for fun</u>?" asked Cecil.

2. "We <u>could set up</u> a lemonade stand," Mary suggested.

3. "I'll get <u>the old wooden table</u> we used last year," Cecil said.

4. "I'll get the can Cecil keeps <u>under his bed</u>," Andy said.

5. The can, <u>Cecil's money bank</u>, had a big "five cent" sign on it.

6. The three friends made two big batches <u>of lemonade</u>.

7. "We <u>will need</u> to sell lots of lemonade to fill that can," Andy said.

8. Cecil said, "All we need is <u>a few good customers</u>."

Next Step: Write a sentence about two good friends. Include an appositive phrase and a prepositional phrase in your sentence.

Test Prep

Number your paper from 1 to 10. Read the paragraphs below. Then identify each underlined sentence part. Choose from the answers on the next page.

<u>A grocery store in our town</u> held a cooking contest for
      1

kids. I <u>wanted to enter the contest</u>. My dad and I <u>read</u> food
        2   **3**

magazines together. Then my two <u>sisters</u> got interested, too.
                      4

We <u>found good recipes and made them</u>. We <u>must have made</u>
        5   **6**

nearly a hundred kinds of food!

<u>My favorite recipe</u> turned out to be the one for tamales.
     7

My sisters <u>liked</u> the meat loaf best. The <u>three</u> of us entered
      8   **9**

our creations in the contest. Our dinners <u>didn't win</u> the prize.
                                    10

But it was a fun family project—and we got to eat our entries!

1. **A** simple subject
   B complete subject
   C simple predicate
   D complete predicate

2. **A** simple subject
   B complete subject
   C simple predicate
   D complete predicate

3. **A** simple subject
   B complete subject
   C simple predicate
   D complete predicate

4. **A** simple subject
   B complete subject
   C simple predicate
   D complete predicate

5. **A** simple subject
   B complete subject
   C simple predicate
   D complete predicate

6. **A** verb phrase
   B noun phrase
   C prepositional phrase
   D appositive phrase

7. **A** simple subject
   B complete subject
   C simple predicate
   D complete predicate

8. **A** simple subject
   B complete subject
   C simple predicate
   D complete predicate

9. **A** simple subject
   B complete subject
   C simple predicate
   D complete predicate

10. **A** simple subject
    B complete subject
    C simple predicate
    D complete predicate

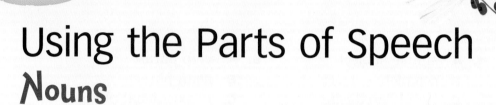

Using the Parts of Speech
Nouns

A **noun** is a word that names a person, a place, a thing, or an idea.

Kinds of Nouns

570.1 **Proper Nouns**	A proper noun names a specific person, place, thing, or idea. Proper nouns are capitalized. **Roberta Fischer Millennium Park *Shrek* Labor Day**
570.2 **Common Nouns**	A common noun does *not* name a specific person, place, thing, or idea. Common nouns are not capitalized. **woman park movie holiday**
570.3 **Concrete Nouns**	A concrete noun names a thing that you can experience through one or more of your five senses. Concrete nouns are either common or proper. **magazine rose Washington Monument chocolate**
570.4 **Abstract Nouns**	An abstract noun names a thing that you can think about but cannot see, hear, or touch. Abstract nouns are either common or proper. **love democracy Judaism Wednesday**
570.5 **Compound Nouns**	A compound noun is made up of two or more words. **busboy** (spelled as one word) **blue jeans** (spelled as two words) **two-wheeler sister-in-law** (spelled with hyphens)
570.6 **Collective Nouns**	A collective noun names a certain kind of group. Persons: **class team clan family** Animals: **herd flock litter pack** Things: **bunch batch collection**

Nouns 1

■ Common and Proper Nouns
■ Compound Nouns

For each sentence, write whether the underlined noun is common or proper. If the word is a compound noun, add a "C" after your answer.

Example: Kayla worked on her seashell collection last summer.
common, C

1. <u>Kayla</u> had a great time playing in the sand with her brother, Sam.

2. They found a <u>starfish</u> hiding behind a bunch of rocks.

3. A pair of old <u>sunglasses</u> had fallen on top of the starfish.

4. "This starfish looks like it's wearing the sunglasses!" <u>Sam</u> exclaimed.

5. Before going <u>home</u>, Sam and Kayla fed a flock of seagulls.

6. "I really love coming to <u>Swift's Beach</u>," Kayla said.

Next Step: Write down three more nouns from the sentences above. Tell whether each is proper or common. Also write a "C" if it's a compound noun.

Nouns . . .

Number of Nouns

Singular Nouns

A singular noun names just one person, place, thing, or idea.

| room | paper | pen pal | hope |

Plural Nouns

A plural noun names more than one person, place, thing, or idea.

| rooms | papers | pen pals | hopes |

Gender of Nouns

Noun Gender

The gender of a noun refers to its being *feminine* (female), *masculine* (male), *neuter* (neither male nor female), or *indefinite* (male or female).

Feminine (female): mother, sister, women, cow, hen

Masculine (male): father, brother, men, bull, rooster

Neuter (neither male nor female):
tree, closet, cobweb

Indefinite (male or female):
child, pilot, parent, dentist

Nouns 2

■ Number of Nouns
■ Ged Number of Nouns
■ Gender of Nouns

Identify the underlined noun in each sentence as "F" for feminine, "M" for masculine, "N" for neuter, or "I" for indefinite.

Example:　My <u>sister</u> Kitty likes to
　　　　　　climb a lot.
　　　　　　F

1. Kitty climbs on the monkey bars at the <u>playground</u>.

2. <u>Dad</u> always tells her to be careful.

3. One day, she spotted a <u>bluebird</u> in a tall tree.

4. She climbed into the tree's top <u>branches</u> to get a better look.

5. Unfortunately, <u>Kitty</u> got stuck.

6. She called out to some <u>kids</u> playing nearby.

7. Two kids told their <u>mothers</u>, who called the fire department.

8. The rescue unit came in a big red fire <u>truck</u>.

9. One <u>firefighter</u> put up a big ladder and got Kitty down.

Next Step:　Look at the underlined nouns above again and add either "S" for singular or "P" for plural to your answer.

Nouns . . .

Uses of Nouns

574.1

Subject Nouns

A noun may be the subject of a sentence. (The subject is the part of the sentence that does something or is being talked about.)

Joe ran away from the bee.

574.2

Predicate Nouns

A predicate noun follows a form of the verb *be* (*is, are, was, were*) and renames the subject.

The book is a mystery.

574.3

Possessive Nouns

A possessive noun shows ownership. (See **490.2** and **492.1** for information on forming possessives.)

The book's ending is a big surprise. (one book)

The books' bindings are torn and weak. (more than one book)

574.4

Object Nouns

Direct Object: A direct object is the word that tells *what* or *who* receives the action of the verb. The direct object completes the meaning of the verb.

Nadia spent all her money. (*What* did Nadia spend? The verb *spent* would be unclear without the direct object, *money.*)

Indirect Object: An indirect object names the person *to whom* or *for whom* something is done.

Joe gave Nadia the book. (The book is given *to whom*? The book is given to *Nadia*, the indirect object.)

Object of a Preposition: An object of a preposition is part of a prepositional phrase. (See page **598**.)

Nadia put the book on the shelf. (The noun *shelf* is the object of the preposition *on*.)

Nouns 3

■ Uses of Nouns

▶ **Identify the underlined nouns in the sentences as subject nouns or predicate nouns.**

Example: One day, a <u>penguin</u> named
Paulie went out for a walk
all by himself.
subject noun

1. Paulie was an <u>adventurer</u>.

2. A <u>snowstorm</u> blew in while he walked, and Paulie got lost.

3. The nearby <u>mountains</u> disappeared into the blizzard.

4. The blowing snow was a <u>sheet</u> of white.

5. <u>Paulie</u> couldn't see his flippers in front of his face!

6. "I am a very lost <u>bird</u>," he moaned.

7. "My <u>binoculars</u> are fogging up, too."

8. Paulie's <u>toes</u> started to feel very cold.

9. Just then, the little penguin's <u>mother</u> and <u>father</u> appeared.

10. They were two relieved <u>parents</u>!

Next Step: First find the two possessive nouns in the sentences above. Then write a sentence using a possessive noun to finish Paulie's story.

Pronouns

A **pronoun** is a word used in place of a noun.

576.1
Antecedents

An antecedent is the noun that a pronoun refers to or replaces. All pronouns have antecedents.

> **Anju's brother has his own skateboard now.**
> (*Brother* is the antecedent of the pronoun *his*.)

Number of Pronouns

576.2
Singular and Plural Pronouns

Pronouns can be either singular or plural.

> **I grabbed my skateboard and joined LeRon.**
> **We were going to the skate park.**

Person of Pronouns

The *person* of a pronoun tells whether the antecedent of the pronoun is speaking, being spoken to, or being spoken about.

576.3
First-Person Pronouns

A first-person pronoun is used in place of the name of the speaker.

> **Petra said, "I like raspberry ice cream."** (*I* replaces the name *Petra*, the person who is speaking.)

576.4
Second-Person Pronouns

A second-person pronoun names the person spoken to.

> **Su, have you decided on a flavor?** (*You* replaces the name *Su*, the person being spoken to.)

576.5
Third-Person Pronouns

A third-person pronoun is used to name the person or thing spoken about.

> **Jon said that he wants pumpkin ice cream because it is so good.** (*He* refers to *Jon*, the person being spoken about, and *it* refers to *ice cream*, the thing being spoken about.)

Pronouns 1

■ Antecedents
■ Number of Pronouns

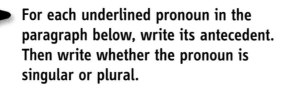

For each underlined pronoun in the paragraph below, write its antecedent. Then write whether the pronoun is singular or plural.

Example: The baseball park was
hosting <u>its</u> home team.
park, singular

(1) Wendy grabbed <u>her</u> bat. (2) <u>She</u> was the best hitter on the Fairweather baseball team. (3) Carrie and Phyllis cheered when <u>they</u> saw her. (4) Wendy was focusing and didn't notice <u>them</u>. (5) Wendy thought, "<u>I</u> must try to get a home run so we'll win the game." (6) As Wendy's home run cleared the wall, the fans cried, "<u>Our</u> team wins!"

Next Step: Pretend you were at the celebration in the ballpark. Write a sentence using a pronoun with an antecedent. Then underline the pronoun and circle the antecedent.

Pronouns . . .

Uses of Pronouns

578.1 Subject Pronouns

A subject pronoun is used as the subject of a sentence.

I can tell jokes well.

They really make people laugh.

578.2 Object Pronouns

An object pronoun is used as a direct object, an indirect object, or the object of a preposition.

Mr. Otto encourages me. (direct object)

Mr. Otto gives us help with math. (indirect object)

I made a funny card for him. (object of the preposition)

578.3 Possessive Pronouns

A possessive pronoun shows ownership. It can be used before a noun, or it can stand alone.

Gloria finished writing her story.

(*Her* comes before the noun *story*.)

The idea for the plot was mine. (*Mine* can stand alone.)

Before a noun: *my, your, his, her, its, our, their*

Stand alone: *mine, yours, his, hers, ours, theirs*

Uses of Personal Pronouns

	Singular Pronouns			Plural Pronouns		
	Subject Pronouns	Possessive Pronouns	Object Pronouns	Subject Pronouns	Possessive Pronouns	Object Pronouns
First Person	I	my, mine	me	we	our, ours	us
Second Person	you	your, yours	you	you	your, yours	you
Third Person	he	his	him	they	their, theirs	them
	she	her, hers	her			
	it	its	it			

Pronouns 2

■ Uses of Pronouns

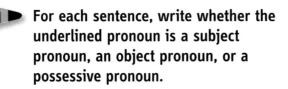

For each sentence, write whether the underlined pronoun is a subject pronoun, an object pronoun, or a possessive pronoun.

Example: My sister and I like going
outside during the winter.
subject pronoun

1. We put on our coats, hats, and scarves.

2. Then we go outside and wait for the snow to fall.

3. When we see the first snowflakes, we try to catch them.

4. I always try to catch snowflakes in my hand.

5. My sister likes catching them on her tongue.

6. She gets one every time!

7. After a while, the cold gives her a red nose.

8. Sometimes Dad fixes hot orange drink for us.

Next Step: Write two sentences about going to the movies. Use at least one subject pronoun, one object pronoun, and one possessive pronoun.

Pronouns . . .

Types of Pronouns

580.1 Relative Pronouns

A relative pronoun connects a dependent clause to a word in another part of the sentence.

> Students **who want to join band should see Carlos.**

Relative pronouns: *who, whose, whom, which, what, that, whoever, whomever, whichever, whatever*

580.2 Interrogative Pronouns

An interrogative pronoun asks a question.

> Who **is going to play the keyboard?**

Interrogative pronouns: *who, whose, whom, which, what*

580.3 Demonstrative Pronouns

A demonstrative pronoun points out a noun without naming it. Demonstrative pronouns: *this, that, these, those*

> That **sounds like a great idea!**

TIP: When *this, that, these,* and *those* are used before nouns, they are adjectives, not pronouns. *That* hat is red.

580.4 Intensive and Reflexive Pronouns

An intensive pronoun stresses the word it refers to. A reflexive pronoun refers back to the subject. These pronouns have *-self* or *-selves* added at the end.

> Carlos **himself taught the group.** (intensive)

> Carlos enjoyed **himself.** (reflexive)

580.5 Indefinite Pronouns

An indefinite pronoun refers to people or things that are not named or known.

> Nobody **is here to videotape the practice.**

Singular	Plural	Singular or Plural
another, something, nobody, neither, either, everybody, everyone, anybody, anyone, no one, somebody, anything, someone, one, each, everything, nothing	both few many several	all, any most none some

Pronouns 3

■ Interrogative Pronouns
■ Demonstrative Pronouns

▶ **Identify the underlined pronouns in the paragraphs below. Write the line number and then write "I" for interrogative or "D" for demonstrative.**

Example: 1 <u>This</u> was supposed to be
2 a lovely day.

1. D

1   <u>What</u> is going on here? The sun is out, but it's raining.
2 The rain starts, and stops, and starts again. What could
3 make <u>that</u> happen? I don't think <u>these</u> are normal rain
4 showers.
5   I'm glad I brought umbrellas. <u>Which</u> of <u>these</u> should I
6 use? <u>Whose</u> is this red one with yellow daisies, I wonder.
7   I just noticed that the island I'm perched on is
8 moving. <u>What</u> could be causing <u>this</u>? Should I ask the
9 whales I see nearby? Their spouts shoot into the sky like
10 fountains, and <u>those</u> look very much like the rain that's
11 been bothering me.
12   Hey, wait a minute . . . maybe I should be asking <u>who</u>
13 is causing the rain!

Next Step: Write another question the bird might have
asked. Use an interrogative pronoun.

Verbs

A **verb** shows action or links the subject to another word in the sentence. The verb is the main word in the predicate.

Types of Verbs

582.1
Action Verbs

An action verb tells what the subject is doing.

The wind blows.   I pull my sweater on.

582.2
Linking Verbs

A linking verb links a subject to a noun or an adjective in the predicate part of the sentence. (See chart below.)

That car is a convertible. (The verb *is* links the subject *car* to the noun *convertible*.)

A new car looks shiny. (The verb *looks* links the subject *car* to the adjective *shiny*.)

582.3
Helping Verbs

Helping verbs (also called auxiliary verbs) come before the main verb and give it a more specific meaning.

Lee will write in his journal. (The verb *will* helps state a future action.)

Lee has been writing in his journal. (The verbs *has* and *been* help state a continuing action.)

Linking Verbs

am, is, are, was, were, being, been, smell, look, taste, remain, feel, appear, sound, seem, become, grow

Helping Verbs

shall, will, should, would, could, must, can, may, have, had, has, do, did, does

The forms of the verb *be (am, is, are, was, were, being, been)* may also be helping verbs.

Verbs 1

■ Action, Linking, and Helping Verbs

For each sentence, write whether the underlined verb is an action verb, a linking verb, or a helping verb.

Example: Mightyman <u>flies</u> through
the air high above the city.
action verb

1. He <u>is</u> the most powerful superhero in the area.

2. To hunt down criminals, Mightyman <u>uses</u> his mega-vision.

3. "They <u>will</u> not escape!" he shouts.

4. "We <u>must</u> do everything we can to stamp out crime," Mightyman declares.

5. When criminals see Mightyman, they <u>shake</u> in their boots.

6. They <u>look</u> frightened of him.

7. They know they <u>do</u> not have a chance against him.

8. We <u>are</u> lucky Mightyman is around.

Next Step: Write a sentence about a superhero. Underline a verb in the sentence and exchange papers with a classmate. Tell whether each other's verb is an action verb, a linking verb, or a helping verb.

Verbs . . .

Simple Verb Tenses

The tense of a verb tells when the action takes place. The simple tenses are *present, past,* and *future.* (See page 418.)

584.1
Present Tense Verbs

The present tense of a verb states an action (or state of being) that is *happening now* or that *happens regularly.*

I like soccer.   We practice every day.

584.2
Past Tense Verbs

The past tense of a verb states an action or (state of being) that *happened at a specific time in the past.*

Anne kicked the soccer ball.   She was the goalie.

584.3
Future Tense Verbs

The future tense of a verb states an action (or state of being) that *will take place.*

I will like soccer forever.   We will practice every day.

Perfect Verb Tenses

Perfect tense is expressed with certain helping verbs.

584.4
Present Perfect Tense Verbs

The present perfect tense states an action that is *still going on.* Add *has* or *have* before the past participle form of the main verb.

Alexis has <u>slept</u> for two hours so far.

TIP: The past participle (underlined) is the same as the past tense of most verbs.

584.5
Past Perfect Tense Verbs

The past perfect tense states an action that *began and ended in the past.* Add *had* before the past participle.

Jondra had slept for eight hours before the alarm rang.

584.6
Future Perfect Tense Verbs

The future perfect tense states an action that *will begin in the future and end at a specific time.* Add *will have* before the past participle form of the main verb.

Riley will have slept for 12 hours by 9:00 a.m. tomorrow.

Verbs 2

■ Present, Past, and Future Tenses

▶ **Write the tense–past, present, or future–of the underlined verbs in the following sentences.**

Example: The chicken <u>wants</u> to cross the road.

present

1. She <u>crossed</u> the road this morning.

2. She <u>will cross</u> the road again soon.

3. The grass on the other side of the road always <u>looks</u> greener than it does on the side she is on.

4. She <u>stands</u> at the side of the road to think.

5. "Yesterday, I <u>came</u> over to this side," she says.

6. "If I go back to the other side today," she wonders, "<u>will</u> I <u>want</u> to come back to this side tomorrow?"

7. She <u>knows</u> she must decide before long.

8. Otherwise, she <u>will waste</u> her whole day by the side of the road!

Next Step: Write a sentence telling what the chicken decided to do. Underline your verb and tell what tense it is.

Verbs . . .

Forms of Verbs

Transitive and Intransitive Verbs

An action verb is called a transitive verb if it is followed by a direct object (noun or pronoun). The object makes the meaning of the verb complete.

Direct Object: **Ann Cameron writes books about Julian.**

A transitive verb may also be followed by an indirect object. An indirect object names the person *to whom* or *for whom* something is done.

Indirect Object: **Books give children enjoyment.**
(*Children* is the indirect object. *Give* is a transitive verb, and *enjoyment* is the direct object.)

A verb that is not followed by a direct object is intransitive.

Ann Cameron writes about Julian in her books. (The verb is followed by two prepositional phrases.)

Active and Passive Verbs

A verb is active if the subject is doing the action.

Tia threw a ball. (The subject *Tia* is doing the action.)

A verb is passive if the subject does not do the action.

A ball was thrown by Tia. (The subject *ball* is not doing the action.)

Singular and Plural Verbs

A singular verb is used with a singular subject.
Ben likes cream cheese and olive sandwiches.

A plural verb is used when the subject is plural. (A plural verb usually does not have an *s* at the end, which is just the opposite of a plural subject.)
Black olives taste like wax.

Irregular Verbs

Some verbs in the English language are irregular. Instead of adding *-ed*, the spelling of the word changes in different tenses. (See page 588 for a chart of irregular verbs.)

I speak.   Yesterday I spoke.   I have spoken.

Verbs 3

■ Singular and Plural Verbs

For each sentence below, tell whether the underlined verb is singular or plural.

Example: The players <u>meet</u> at the field.

plural

1. They <u>pick</u> sides to make teams.

2. One player <u>volunteers</u> to be the team captain.

3. Another <u>chooses</u> a name for the team.

4. The Herd, the Grazers, and the Cheeseheads <u>are</u> some of the names.

5. I <u>think</u> these are funny names.

6. To these players, though, they <u>seem</u> normal.

7. The best hitter <u>is</u> named Babe Moooth.

8. The pitcher <u>throws</u> the first ball of the game.

9. The ball <u>zooms</u> over home plate and into the catcher's glove.

10. The fans <u>cheer</u> wildly.

Next Step: Write two sentences about this baseball game. Use a singular verb in one and a plural verb in the other.

Verbs . . .
Forms of Verbs

Common Irregular Verbs

The principal parts of some common irregular verbs are listed below. The past participle is used with the helping verbs *has, have,* or *had.*

Present Tense	I hide.	She hides.
Past Tense	Yesterday I hid.	Yesterday she hid.
Past Participle	I have hidden.	She has hidden.

Present Tense	Past Tense	Past Participle	Present Tense	Past Tense	Past Participle	Present Tense	Past Tense	Past Participle
am, is, are	was, were	been	give	gave	given	shrink	shrank	shrunk
begin	began	begun	go	went	gone	sing	sang, sung	sung
bite	bit	bitten	grow	grew	grown	sink	sank, sunk	sunk
blow	blew	blown	hang	hung	hung	sit	sat	sat
break	broke	broken	hide	hid	hidden, hid	sleep	slept	slept
bring	brought	brought	hold	held	held	speak	spoke	spoken
buy	bought	bought	keep	kept	kept	spring	sprang, sprung	sprung
catch	caught	caught	know	knew	known	stand	stood	stood
come	came	come	lay (place)	laid	laid	steal	stole	stolen
dive	dived, dove	dived	lead	led	led	swear	swore	sworn
do	did	done	leave	left	left	swim	swam	swum
draw	drew	drawn	lie (recline)	lay	lain	swing	swung	swung
drink	drank	drunk	make	made	made	take	took	taken
drive	drove	driven	ride	rode	ridden	teach	taught	taught
eat	ate	eaten	ring	rang	rung	tear	tore	torn
fall	fell	fallen	rise	rose	risen	throw	threw	thrown
fight	fought	fought	run	ran	run	wake	woke	woken
fly	flew	flown	see	saw	seen	wear	wore	worn
freeze	froze	frozen	shake	shook	shaken	weave	wove	woven
get	got	gotten	shine (light)	shone	shone	write	wrote	written

* The following verbs are the same in each of the principal parts: *burst, cost, cut, hurt, let, put, set,* and *spread.*

Verbs 4

■ Irregular Verbs

For each sentence, write the correct past tense form of the verb or verbs in parentheses.

Example: Aunt Tamika and her friend *(take)* me to the park yesterday.
took

1. We *(ride)* our bikes down Martin Luther King, Jr., Drive to get there.

2. First, I *(swing)* on the swings.

3. Then we all *(throw)* a baseball to each other until we *(get)* hungry.

4. Aunt Tamika *(bring)* bagged lunches for all of us.

5. We *(sit)* down on the grass and *(eat)* our sandwiches.

6. After lunch, we *(run)* around on the soccer field.

7. I *(give)* Aunt Tamika a daisy I found near the goalpost.

Next Step: Use the past tense of the words *spring, teach,* and *break* in sentences.

Adjectives

Adjectives are words that modify (describe) nouns or pronouns. Adjectives tell *what kind, how many,* or *which one.* (Also see pages 423–425.)

590.1 Articles

The adjectives *a, an,* and *the* are called articles.

"Owlet" is the name for a baby owl.

The article *a* comes before singular words that begin with consonant sounds. Also use *a* before singular words that begin with the long *u* sound.

a shooting star   a unique constellation

The article *an* comes before singular words that begin with any vowel sounds except for long *u.*

an astronaut   an inquiring mind   an unusual outfit

590.2 Proper and Common Adjectives

Proper adjectives are formed from proper nouns. They are always capitalized.

On a cold Minnesota day, a Hawaiian trip sounds great.

Common adjectives are any that are *not* proper.

I'll pack my big blue suitcase for a weeklong trip.

590.3 Predicate Adjectives

Predicate adjectives follow linking verbs and describe subjects. (See page 470.)

The apples are juicy. They taste sweet.

590.4 Compound Adjectives

Compound adjectives are made up of more than one word. Some are spelled as one word; others are hyphenated.

evergreen tree   white-throated sparrows

590.5 Demonstrative Adjectives

Demonstrative adjectives point out specific nouns.

This nest has four eggs, and that nest has two.

These eggs will hatch before those eggs will.

TIP: When *this, that, these,* and *those* are not used before nouns, they are pronouns, not adjectives.

Adjectives 1

■ Common and Proper Adjectives
■ Demonstrative Adjectives

For the sentences below, tell whether each underlined adjective is common or proper. Add a "DA" if it is a demonstrative adjective.

Example: <u>Those</u> muffins look delicious!

common, DA

1. Tami brought <u>banana</u> muffins to school.

2. They were our <u>Friday</u> treats.

3. Some of them had <u>roasted</u> nuts on top.

4. Some had <u>cream-cheese</u> frosting.

5. Tami did not use <u>Swiss</u> chocolate in them.

6. <u>This</u> muffin has raisins on top.

7. Nick is going to bring spumoni <u>next</u> week.

8. It's his <u>Italian</u> grandmother's recipe.

9. Mmmm . . . I can't wait to taste <u>that</u> treat!

Next Step: Write a sentence or two about a yummy treat. Use adjectives that help the reader see, smell, and taste the treat.

Adjectives . . .

592.1
Indefinite Adjectives

Indefinite adjectives tell approximately (not exactly) *how many* or *how much.*

> **Most students love summer.**
>
> **Some days are rainy, but few days are boring.**

Forms of Adjectives

592.2
Positive Adjectives

The positive (base) form of an adjective describes a noun without comparing it to another noun. (See page **424**.)

> **A hummingbird is small.**

592.3
Comparative Adjectives

The comparative form of an adjective compares two people, places, things, or ideas. The comparison is formed by adding *-er* to one-syllable adjectives or the word *more* or *less* before longer adjectives.

> **A hummingbird is smaller than a sparrow.**
>
> **Hummingbirds are more colorful than sparrows.**

592.4
Superlative Adjectives

The superlative form of an adjective compares three or more people, places, things, or ideas. The superlative is formed by adding *-est* to one-syllable adjectives or the word *most* or *least* before longer adjectives.

> **The hummingbird is the smallest bird I've seen.**
>
> **The parrot is the most colorful bird in the zoo.**

592.5
Irregular Forms of Adjectives

The comparative and superlative forms of some adjectives are different words. *More* or *most* is not needed with these words.

Positive	Comparative	Superlative
good	better	best
bad	worse	worst
many	more	most
little	less	least

Adjectives 2

■ Positive, Comparative, and Superlative Adjectives

For each sentence, write whether the underlined adjective is positive, comparative, or superlative.

Example: <u>Many</u> competitors arrived for the pond track meet.
positive

1. There was a <u>bigger</u> crowd than Franklin expected.

2. "I will show everyone that I'm the <u>best</u> jumper," he said.

3. Hilo was a <u>good</u> runner.

4. Hilo said, "Ellie is a <u>faster</u> runner than I am."

5. She added, "Frederick is the <u>fastest</u> runner of all."

6. "I just want to have a <u>better</u> finish than I did last time," Hilo said.

7. When the contest ended, Franklin had the <u>highest</u> jump of all.

8. Everyone who took part did a <u>fine</u> job.

Next Step: Write three sentences about an activity you and your friends enjoy. Use a different form of adjective in each sentence.

Adverbs

Adverbs are words that modify (describe) verbs, adjectives, or other adverbs. (Also see pages 426–427.)

The softball team practices faithfully.
(*Faithfully* modifies the verb *practices*.)

Yesterday's practice was extra **long.**
(*Extra* modifies the adjective *long*.)

Last night the players slept quite **soundly.**
(*Quite* modifies the adverb *soundly*.)

Types of Adverbs

594.1
Adverbs of Time

Adverbs of time tell *when*, *how often*, or *how long*.

Max batted first. (when)

Katie's team plays weekly. (how often)

Her team was in first place briefly. (how long)

594.2
Adverbs of Place

Adverbs of place tell *where*.

When the first pitch curved outside, **the batter leaned** forward.

"Hit it there!**" urged the coach, pointing to right field.**

594.3
Adverbs of Manner

Adverbs of manner tell *how* something is done.

Max waited eagerly **for the next pitch.**

He swung powerfully **but missed the ball.**

594.4
Adverbs of Degree

Adverbs of degree tell *how much* or *how little*.

The catcher was totally **surprised.** (how much)

He scarcely **saw the fastball coming.** (how little)

TIP: Adverbs often end in *-ly*, but not always. Words like *not*, *never*, *very*, and *always* are common adverbs.

Adverbs 1

■ To Modify Verbs, Adjectives, and Other Adverbs

For each sentence, write the word that the underlined adverb modifies. Tell whether the word is a verb, an adjective, or an adverb.

Example: I'll <u>always</u> remember my trip to the circus.

remember — verb

1. My Uncle Tito <u>never</u> missed the circus when it came to town.

2. He promised to take me if I was <u>extra</u> good.

3. We <u>eagerly</u> drove out to the fairgrounds to see the show.

4. The elephants performed <u>first</u>.

5. The audience cheered <u>wildly</u>.

6. Lions and tigers growled <u>fiercely</u> in their cages.

7. An acrobat walked <u>very</u> slowly on a tightrope above a big net.

8. A <u>brightly</u> painted clown smiled happily at us.

Next Step: Write a sentence about a circus. Use an adverb in your sentence. Circle the adverb and draw an arrow to the word it modifies.

Adverbs . . .

Forms of Adverbs

596.1
Positive Adverbs

The positive (base) form of an adverb does not make a comparison. (See page **426**.)

Max plays hard from the first pitch to the last out.

596.2
Comparative Adverbs

The comparative form of an adverb compares how two things are done. The comparison is formed by adding *-er* to one-syllable adverbs or the word *more* or *less* before longer adverbs.

Max plays harder than his cousin plays, and he plays more often than his cousin does.

596.3
Superlative Adverbs

The superlative form of an adverb compares how three or more things are done. The superlative is formed by adding *-est* to one-syllable adverbs or the word *most* or *least* before longer adverbs.

Max plays hardest in close games. He plays most often in center field.

596.4
Irregular Forms of Adverbs

The comparative and superlative forms of some adverbs are different words. *More* or *most* is not needed with these words.

Positive	Comparative	Superlative
well	**better**	**best**
badly	**worse**	**worst**

TIP: Do not confuse *well* and *good*. Good is an adjective and *well* is usually an adverb. (See **592.5**.)

Adverbs 2

■ **Comparative and Superlative Adverbs**

▶ **For each sentence, write the correct comparative or superlative form of the adverb from the choices given in parentheses.**

Example: My dog Bosco learns the
(most quickly, quicker) of
any other dog in his class.
most quickly

1. He behaves *(better, weller)* than the other dogs do, too.

2. During Bosco's lessons, he sits *(most quiet, more quietly)* than my friend's dog sits.

3. The obedience-school teacher says that Bosco works the *(most hard, hardest)* of any pet in the school.

4. Of all his obedience-school "classmates," Bosco gets treats *(most often, oftenest)*.

5. He can run *(faster, fastest)* than any kid on our block.

6. Of all the kids who love Bosco, it is my neighbor Kendra who *(clearliest, most clearly)* adores him.

Next Step: For each answer you wrote, write a "C" for a comparative adverb or an "S" for a superlative adverb.

Prepositions

Prepositions are words that introduce prepositional phrases. They can show position or direction, or they can show some other relationship between the words in a sentence. (Also see pages 428 and 430.)

Our cats do what they please in our house.

<table>
<tr><td>

598.1

Prepositional Phrases

</td><td>

Prepositional phrases include a preposition, the object of the preposition (a noun or pronoun that comes after the preposition), and any words that modify the object.

Jo-Jo sneaks toward the gerbil cage. (*Toward* is the preposition, and *cage* is the object of the preposition. *The* and *gerbil* modify *cage*.)

Smacker watches from the desk drawer and then ducks inside it. (The noun *drawer* is the object of the preposition *from*, and the pronoun *it* is the object of the preposition *inside*.)

NOTE: If a word found in the list of prepositions has no object in a sentence, then it is not a preposition in that sentence. It could be an adverb or a conjunction.

</td></tr>
</table>

Common Prepositions

aboard	around	but	into	over	until
about	at	by	like	past	up
above	before	down	near	since	up to
across	behind	during	of	through	upon
across from	below	except	off	throughout	with
after	beneath	except for	on	till	within
against	beside	for	on top of	to	without
along	besides	from	onto	toward	
along with	between	in	out	under	
among	beyond	inside	outside	underneath	

Prepositions

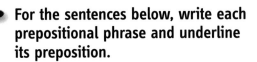

For the sentences below, write each prepositional phrase and underline its preposition.

Example: The Roman Empire started long ago in Italy.
<u>in</u> Italy

1. The empire soon spread across much of Europe.

2. Romans lived without modern tools.

3. Sundials and water clocks measured time for them.

4. Water clocks had a set amount of water that flowed from one part to another.

5. Most Romans did not have horses, so they walked to nearby towns.

6. Wealthy Romans with two homes rode horses between them.

7. People who lived near the sea often traveled in boats.

8. People of the Roman Empire valued art, reading, and writing.

Next Step: Write two sentences about what you think it would be like to live during the Roman Empire. Underline any prepositional phrases you use.

Conjunctions

Conjunctions connect individual words or groups of words.

Coordinating Conjunctions

A coordinating conjunction connects equal parts: two or more words, phrases, or clauses.

> The river is wide **and** deep. (words)
>
> We can fish in the morning **or** in the evening. (phrases)
>
> The river rushes down the valley, **and** then it winds through the prairie. (clauses)

Subordinating Conjunctions

A subordinating conjunction is often used to introduce the dependent clause in a complex sentence.

> Our trip was delayed **when** the snowstorm hit.
>
> **Until** the snow stopped, we had to stay in town.

> **TIP:** Relative pronouns can also be used to connect clauses. (See **564.3**.)

Correlative Conjunctions

Correlative conjunctions are used in pairs.

> **Either** snow **or** wind can make the trip dangerous.

Common Conjunctions

Coordinating Conjunctions
and, but, or, nor, for, so, yet

Subordinating Conjunctions
after, although, as, as if, as long as, as though, because,
before, if, in order that, since, so, so that, that,
though, unless, until, when, where, whereas, while

Correlative Conjunctions
either/or, neither/nor, not only/but also, both/and, whether/or, as/so

Conjunctions

■ Coordinating Conjunctions
■ Subordinating Conjunctions

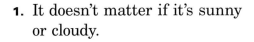 **Write the conjunction or conjunctions from each sentence below.**

Example: Our cat likes to run and play outside.
and

1. It doesn't matter if it's sunny or cloudy.

2. The cat sits by the door and meows until we let him out.

3. When I let him out earlier today, he quickly climbed a tree.

4. He has climbed very high, and now he can't get down.

5. He looks scared because all of his fur is standing up.

6. Should we get a ladder, or should we call someone for help?

7. We could call the fire department, but rescuing cats is really not their job.

8. While we were wondering what to do, that cat came down on his own.

Next Step: Now write "C" for coordinating conjunction or "S" for subordinating conjunction next to each conjunction you wrote.

Interjections

Interjections are words or phrases that express strong emotion. Commas or exclamation points are used to separate interjections from the rest of the sentence.

Wow, **look at those mountains!**

Hey! **Keep your eyes on the road!**

Quick Guide: Parts of Speech

Nouns   Words that name a person, a place, a thing, or an idea (**Bill, office, billboard, confusion**)

Pronouns   Words used in place of nouns (**I, me, her, them, who, which, those, myself, some**)

Verbs   Words that express action or state of being (**run, jump, is, are**)

Adjectives   Words that describe a noun or pronoun (**tall, quiet, three, the, neat**)

Adverbs   Words that describe a verb, an adjective, or another adverb (**gently, easily, fast, very**)

Prepositions   Words that show relationship and introduce prepositional phrases (**on, near, from, until**)

Conjunctions   Words that connect words or groups of words (**and, or, because**)

Interjections   Words (set off by commas or exclamation points) that show emotion or surprise (**Wow, Oh, Yikes!**)

Parts of Speech Review

Write down the part of speech that is underlined in each sentence below.

noun   preposition   adjective
pronoun   conjunction   adverb
verb   interjection

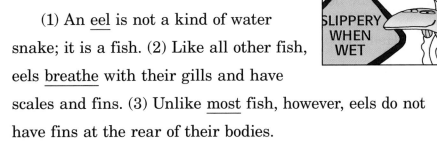

(1) An <u>eel</u> is not a kind of water snake; it is a fish. (2) Like all other fish, eels <u>breathe</u> with their gills and have scales and fins. (3) Unlike <u>most</u> fish, however, eels do not have fins at the rear of their bodies.

(4) Baby eels <u>are called</u> "elvers." (5) All <u>they</u> want to do is eat, eat, eat! (6) They do not see very well, <u>but</u> they have a good sense of smell. (7) They eat at night, <u>and</u> they rest during the day.

(8) The <u>largest</u> eel is the moray eel. (9) Some <u>of</u> these eels can grow to be 11 feet long! (10) They have sharp <u>teeth</u>, which they use to eat other fish. (11) A moray eel could <u>possibly</u> reach 30 years of age.

(12) Eels are <u>flavorful</u> fish with lots of protein. (13) People in Japan and Europe especially like to eat them. (14) American colonists used to eat them <u>often</u>. (15) People like me may say "<u>Ugh!</u>" if eel is on the menu.

Test Prep

Tell the part of speech for each underlined word below by writing the correct letter from the answer choices on the next page.

Late in the <u>afternoon</u>, Elgin the eel arrived at his
1

aunt's home near the city. Aunt Eeloise lived <u>in</u> a drainpipe.
2

"Hello, Elgin," Eeloise <u>said</u>. "It's nice to see you again."
3

<u>They</u> decided to visit the <u>new</u> art exhibit. "We should see
4   **5**

it soon," Eeloise said.

They swam <u>swiftly</u> upstream to a lagoon near a parking
6

lot. There they saw dozens <u>of</u> brightly colored street signs
7

lying in the water.

"That one is new," Elgin said. He <u>swam</u> circles around a
8

red <u>and</u> white stop sign.
9

"I like it," Eeloise said, "<u>but</u> I prefer <u>this</u> 'One Way' sign."
10   **11**

"It's too bad <u>we</u> cannot take these pieces of art home with
12

us," Elgin said with a sigh.

1. **A** noun
    B verb
    C pronoun
    D adjective

2. **A** preposition
    B adverb
    C adjective
    D conjunction

3. **A** noun
    B interjection
    C adverb
    D verb

4. **A** verb
    B pronoun
    C noun
    D adverb

5. **A** conjunction
    B preposition
    C adjective
    D verb

6. **A** conjunction
    B preposition
    C adverb
    D verb

7. **A** adverb
    B verb
    C adjective
    D preposition

8. **A** noun
    B verb
    C pronoun
    D adjective

9. **A** interjection
    B noun
    C adverb
    D conjunction

10. **A** conjunction
    B verb
    C preposition
    D adverb

11. **A** adjective
    B adverb
    C verb
    D noun

12. **A** verb
    B noun
    C pronoun
    D adjective

Credits

Photos:

www.jupiterimages.com: page 475

Acknowledgements

We're grateful to many people who helped bring *Write Source* to life. First, we must thank all the teachers and students from across the country who contributed writing models and ideas.

In addition, we want to thank our Write Source/Great Source team for all their help:

Steven J. Augustyn, Laura Bachman, Ron Bachman, William Baughn, Heather Bazata, Colleen Belmont, Evelyn Curley, Sandra Easton, Chris Erickson, Mark Fairweather, Jean Fischer, Hillary Gammons, Mariellen Hanrahan, Tammy Hintz, Mary Anne Hoff, Rob King, Lois Krenzke, Mark Lalumondier, Joe Lee, Joyce Becker Lee, Ellen Leitheusser, Dian Lynch, Sheryl Mendicino, Kevin Nelson, Douglas Niles, Sue Paro, Pamela Reigel, Pat Reigel, Jason C. Reynolds, Christine Rieker, Susan Rogalski, Chip Rosenthal, Janae Sebranek, Lester Smith, Richard Spencer, Julie Spicuzza, Thomas Spicuzza, Stephen D. Sullivan, Jean Varley, and Claire Ziffer.

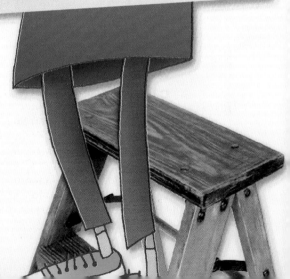

Index

The **index** will help you find specific information in this book. Words that are in italics are from the "Using the Right Word" section.

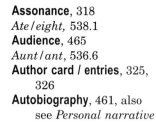

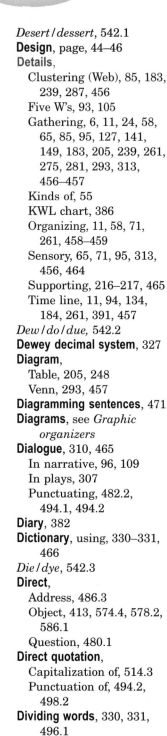